Our Only Hope

Distinguished Dissertations in Christian Theology

Series Foreword

We are living in a vibrant season for academic Christian theology. After a hiatus of some decades, a real flowering of excellent systematic and moral theology has emerged. This situation calls for a series that showcases the contributions of newcomers to this ongoing and lively conversation. The journal *Word & World: Theology for Christian Ministry* and the academic society Christian Theological Research Fellowship (CTRF) are happy to cosponsor this series together with our publisher Pickwick Publications (an imprint of Wipf and Stock Publishers). Both the CTRF and *Word & World* are interested in excellence in academics but also in scholarship oriented toward Christ and the Church. The volumes in this series are distinguished for their combination of academic excellence with sensitivity to the primary context of Christian learning. We are happy to present the work of these young scholars to the wider world and are grateful to Luther Seminary for the support that helped make it possible.

Alan G. Padgett
Professor of Systematic Theology
Luther Seminary

Beth Felker Jones
Assistant Professor of Theology
Wheaton College

www.ctrf.info
www.luthersem.edu/word&world

Our Only Hope

More than We Can Ask or Imagine

Margaret B. Adam

PICKWICK *Publications* · Eugene, Oregon

OUR ONLY HOPE
More than We Can Ask or Imagine

Distinguished Dissertations in Christian Theology 12

Copyright © 2013 Margaret B. Adam. All rights reserved. Except for brief quotations in critical publications or reviews, no part of this book may be reproduced in any manner without prior written permission from the publisher. Write: Permissions, Wipf and Stock Publishers, 199 W. 8th Ave., Suite 3, Eugene, OR 97401.

Pickwick Publications
An Imprint of Wipf and Stock Publishers
199 W. 8th Ave., Suite 3
Eugene, OR 97401

www.wipfandstock.com

ISBN 13: 978-1-61097-759-3

Cataloguing-in-Publication data:

Adam, Margaret B.

    Our only hope : more than we can ask or imagine / Margaret B. Adam.

    Distinguished Dissertations in Christian Theology 12

    x + 246 pp. ; 23 cm. Includes bibliographical references and indexes.

    ISBN 13: 978-1-61097-759-3

    1. Hope—Religious aspects—Christianity. 2. Moltmann, Jürgen. 3. Eschatology. I. Series. II. Title.

BV4638 .A33 2013

Manufactured in the U.S.A.

To

AKMA

Contents

Acknowledgments ix

Introduction 1

1 Moltmann's Hope and Moltmannian Theological Hope 7

2 The Costs of a Moltmannian Hope 77

3 A Thomistic Grammar of Hope 112

4 Provocative Hope 167

5 Our Only Hope 215

Bibliography 225

Scripture Index 237

Subject and Name Index 239

Acknowledgments

I AM GRATEFUL FOR my friends.

My respect, admiration, and appreciation go to Professors Mary McClintock Fulkerson, Stephen Fowl, Stanley Hauerwas, and Kenneth Surin who guided me through my dissertation and have shared their wisdom, guidance, inspiration, and friendship over the course of many years.

Jon Walters and Helen Silverstein have been my close friends since we all began at Bowdoin College, and they still help me find humor in all the ups and downs. Melinda Fowl and Hilary Winter have walked with me through darker and brighter times, parenting, transitions, and treasured companionship. Leanne Rodgers helped me find the wherewithall to heal and thrive, when prospects seemed dim. John Utz is the best writing companion, cook, crisis-handler ever, a true ally and a constant friend. David Cunningham, Stephen Fowl, and Phil Kenneson graciously included me in their theological conversations long before I knew I was a theologian. David walked me in the academy door and showed me the systematic theology room; Steve helped me start teaching and finish my dissertation. Phil taught me to write and to keep writing. In steadfast friendship, they have encouraged, challenged, and sustained me in more ways than I will probably ever know.

The strong women of God whose lives and scholarship overlapped with mine at Duke continue to provide a community of mutual support, witness, prayer, and delight: Thank you Jana Bennet, Jenny Copeland, Holly Taylor Coolman, Dana Dillon, Beth Felker Jones, In-Yong Lee, Rachel Maxson, Sarah Musser, Sarah Sours, and Laura Yordy. Thanks also to Amy Laura Hall who has shared her home, family, friendship, and unflagging confidence in me.

In two panicky moments of writing and revision, I reached out for urgent help from Rob MacSwain and from Sam Tongue, both of whom dropped everything, read the whole manuscript, and offered last minute suggestions and gracious reassurance. Thank you both. Thanks also to Fiona Macdonald, for magnificent help with the index.

Thanks to the Theology Department of Loyola University of Maryland for trusting me to teach their students and for their gifts of guidance,

Acknowledgments

wisdom, collegiality. Thanks to the Theology and Religious Studies Department of the University of Glasgow for including me as a colleague in study and teaching.

Thank you Rich King, Meg MacDonald, and Madhavi Nevader for providing the right mix of provocation, commiseration, and chocolate at the more trying moments of writing and revision, and the gift of sturdy friendship before, during, and after.

When I started my studies at Duke, Sarah Musser shared with me an academic alliance through classes, exams, and the nurturing of ideas. Along the way, she became a dear and precious friend, whose constancy in faith, hope, and love inspires and sustains me daily. Sarah helps me order my hope toward God, and she has—quite literally—led me to stop and smell the flowers when I had forgotten they were there. She and Clay, Luke, and Adam are a steady supply of abundant generosity to our whole family.

Thank you to the coffee shops and their employees, who have provided tea, kindness, and a place to write in comfort and good company: Small World, Princeton; Peets, Evanston; Mad Hatter, Durham; Open Eye, Carrboro; One World, Baltimore; and S'mug, Glasgow. I am grateful for the congregations which have shaped me in the body of Christ: St. Mary's, Rockport; St. Paul's, Brunswick; Calvary, Pittsburgh; St. Andrew's, Pittsburgh; Christ Church, New Haven; St. Philips's, Durham; St. James, St. Petersburg; DaySpring, Palmetto; Trinity, Princeton; St. Luke's, Evanston; Holy Family, Durham; the Cathedral of the Incarnation, Baltimore; the Cathedral of St. Mary, Glasgow; and now, St. Bride's, Glasgow. I am blessed by the ongoing guidance and fellowship of old and new friends of The Ekklesia Project.

Many thanks to my parents, my sister, my sister-in-law, and my mother-in-law, for their loving support, and I give thanks for the life of my father-in-law who died four years ago. Thank you, Jeanne, for breathing and seeing and sharing with your sister, your whole life. I am still learning about the depths of God's love from our children, their spouses, and the extended family members who have shared their lives with ours. Thank you Pippa, Si and Laura, Nate and Laura, Jennifer, and Juliet. I love you so.

At seventeen, I began a conversation with the man who, although he did not know it at the time, would become my lifelong conversation partner and the love of my life. Ever since then, we have shared joys, challenges, more joy, and hope. I trust he knows that there are not enough pixels in creation for me to express my undying gratitude and love.

Soli Deo gloria

Introduction

Glory to God whose power working in us can do infinitely more than we can ask or imagine: Glory to him from generation to generation in the church, and in Christ Jesus forever and ever. Amen.[1]

YEARS AGO, I HEARD a sermon about hope as I sat with my baby girl near the back of our Episcopal church. The preacher urged the congregation to face life's challenges with hope. He gently criticized the parishioners for their tendency to sit back and let life go by, and he championed instead more active, responsible, and upbeat engagements with the world. He proclaimed the virtue of making a difference in one's own life and in the world by adopting an attitude of hopefulness. I listened to this sermon from within the depths of an overwhelming bout of depression. I have suffered from chronic depression all my life, and when I heard this sermon I was just beginning the long-term treatment and therapy that now help me function and thrive. At the time though, I had yet to reap any of the benefits of treatment and therapy. I felt most powerfully a need for hope to make it through the morning, then the afternoon, then the night. The sermon was incomprehensible to me. I could not imagine any way I could participate in the hope described. I could not pull myself up by my bootstraps and take on a life of active hope any more than I could imagine ever feeling anything other than despair. I could not imagine mustering the strength to find and act on a upbeat hope, when all of my strength was devoted to trying to hold myself together in some semblance of a person who could reasonably care for her child. Instead I felt criticized for my insufficient hopefulness.

As I sat feeling miserable, inadequate, and utterly alienated, I began to notice who else was sitting at the back of the church. Charlotte was a regular at worship, and her life was shaped by far more suffering than mine. She had been a successful ballet dancer, wife, and mother, before she

---

1. Eph 3:20–21; 1979 *Book of Common Prayer*, 102.

was consumed by schizophrenia. She had lost her vocation, her home, and her family. She had great difficulty establishing and sustaining relationships, and she was frequently not able to receive the occasional gestures of welcome and offers of help from church members and the available community resources. She seemed to find some slight continuity of identity and community on the edges of Sunday eucharist and weekday evening prayer, participating silently or sometimes with contributions the rest of us could not understand. I doubted that Charlotte heard words of accessible hope that day. If she could make a difference in her life and the world by rallying some hopeful enthusiasm, she would have done so years ago.

A dozen years later, the baby in my lap at the back of the church was a teenager being confirmed. Confirmands and their families from several other nearby congregations had joined the congregation of our parish church (in a different state from the one above) for this annual Confirmation service. The confirmands were chiefly upper-class, suburban youths. The families carried cameras and jockeyed for pew positions with a good view of their sons in blue blazers and ties and their daughters in lovely dresses.

The preacher for the confirmation, priest of one of the visiting parishes, spoke of his experience with a particular social ministry event in Chicago, which involved counting homeless people throughout the city one night a year. He shared statistics about the demographics of Chicago's homeless people (noting especially the large number of homeless children), and he described how moved he was to make some connections with the homeless people he was counting. He explained to the confirmands that their mission of ministry was to address the needs of the homeless. He noted ways that the young people, as they stepped into adult positions of employment, could use their talents and positions to make a difference in the lives of the needy. In his conclusion, he told the confirmands that hope for the homeless now rested in their hands. While I was and still am eager for my daughter to continue to develop as a disciple of Christ through ministry to the needy, I did wonder what differentiated this sermon from any number of high school graduation speeches that proclaim the new graduates as the hope of the future. I worried that if we were investing our hope in these upstanding and promising youths, we might be missing out on hope for ends beyond the challenges of juggling successful careers with serving the homeless.

As a life-long Episcopalian who has spent many years in seminary communities, I have heard hundreds of sermons. The two sermons I mention here represent much of what I have heard from the pulpit about hope, and I have often wondered about the emphasis on hope for present and near future improvements in life as we know it, brought about by human determination and effort. Surely there must be more to theological hope. Surely those who cannot themselves muster upbeat, life-changing hope should have access to a hope not limited by the circumstances of a broken and limited world. Isn't there something more possible in the hope of the Gospel?

I now understand that these preachers were responding at least in part to a problematic presentation of hope they perceived in the church. They were countering an incomplete version of hope that dreams of a heavenly end and ignores participation in hope through active work for God's justice here and now. They were keenly aware of the well-intentioned Christians who believe that "the poor will always be with us" means that we are not called to improve the conditions of the poor. They had seen church funds spent on new pews rather than on soup kitchens, and they knew well that comfortable visions of eternal life with God can distract Christians from attending to those systemically deprived of comfort in this life. They found support and guidance from secular and theological resources that emphasize a responsible, social action narrative and performance of hope.

The theological movement that counters a heavenly hope with a more earthly-oriented hope swings on a pendulum to the opposite side of the hope it opposes. On-the-ground hope rescues theological hope from one extreme but risks settling on another extreme. At points of extremity, alternate accounts of hope fade from view, and an integrated, less-dualistic account of hope seems less possible. In the process, reconciliation among those who are divided falls from the realms of current and eschatological hope.

The Anglican Communion currently struggles with painful conflicts within its international body. While it has historically aimed for unity in the midst of differences and strife, present issues and present members seem particularly resistant to compromise. Hope for reconciliation is in short supply. Agreements and arguments alike reveal few explicit references to any uniquely Christian accounts of hope. The Anglican Communion resembles more a couple who has decided on divorce than a couple who has begun counseling in order to restore a broken marriage. Whether or not these are the only outcomes remains to be seen.

Our Only Hope

My experience, albeit limited, suggests that hope focused on improvements people might accomplish in the foreseeable future is most appealing and accessible to people already in a position to accomplish improvements in the foreseable future. Hope in that which cannot be readily attained is much more difficult to establish and sustain, whether it is hope in healing, justice, and reconciliation now (or soon), or hope in healing and justice in resurrected life in Christ. My interest is in building vocabulary and fluency in a rich and sound theological hope that can stand up in the midst of crisis for those who are plagued by division, depression, disability, and disaster. I am looking for accessible, theological hope resources to help the families of the church work toward health and relationships that reflect hope in eschatological healing and reconciliation.

I am not here offering strategies of hope to the Anglican Communion, to the Episcopal Church in the United States, or to any other specific community looking to Christian theology for guidance about hope. Instead, I am encouraging theologians to continue critical and creative examinations of the hope they teach, promote, and presuppose; I am recommending that those examinations include a reconsideration of dismissed traditional doctrine and a readiness to consider current discourses not traditionally consulted for input on theological hope.

The length and breadth of Christian teaching might be pictured as a wide and deep river. Within this river flows Christian tradition. Christians throughout the ages discuss, debate, and teach collective wisdoms of Christianity, and they mark specifics with buoys: "Don't stray too far toward these rocks"; "Watch out for those eddies." On some points of faith and practice, many Christians share the same assessments of the markers within which Christian doctrine thrives most faithfully. On other points, differing communities of Christians disagree greatly about which route through the rapids is wisest. And, at still other points, Christians may mark certain rough waters as sites where differing currents of Christian tradition meet in passionate and as-yet-unresolved conflict; and yet, this conflict persists within the breadth of the wide streams of Christian thought. Despite some shifts over time and some conflicts within time about how to mark the river, for the most part, a bird's-eye view of Christianity's theological nautical map reveals a recognizable route. Some of the edges vary, and some streams branch off in radically distinct directions, but there is a route on this map that almost all Christians identify as the territory in the river within which Christian theology lives. Streams that lie entirely outside the buoys are more difficult to recognize as Christian

Introduction

tradition. Geological features outside the river and weather may contribute to the flow and vitality of the river.[2]

Jürgen Moltmann introduced a theology of hope, almost half a century ago, that captured the imaginations of many theologians looking to respond to atheist dismissals of God after the Holocaust while developing an up-to-date theological hope for modern Christians. As Moltmann continued (and continues today) to write about theological topics, his theology of hope has developed and shifted along with his own developing positions and wider, ongoing cultural shifts. Currently, Moltmann's theology of hope shares presuppositions and sensibilities with a large body of American Christians who might describe themselves as generally liberal, ecclesially and politically. I am not attempting here to establish which came first, Moltmann's theology of hope or the ideological climate in which it flourishes. In either case, the theology of hope that can be described as a reflection of Moltmann's work resonates with some contemporary Christian assumptions about doctrines of God, eschatology, and anthropology to the extent that sharp distinctions are difficult to discern. I call this shared theological hope "Moltmannian hope," because he has articulated some of the basis for and applications of this now-familiar hope.

Moltmannian hope, the stream of theological hope that approximately reflects the work of Jürgen Moltmann, currently functions as normative for many theologians and those whom they influence. Moltmannian hope veers away from some of the older streams of tradition and toward some of the boundary buoys. An exclusive reliance on a Moltmannian theology of hope deprives the church of crucial resources for a robust eschatological hope and its practices. Critical attention to additional streams of theological hope, and to applicable discourses within and without Christian theology, provides the church with strength and resilience to sustain a distinctly Christian theological hope through and beyond disaster, despair, suffering, and death. Jesus Christ, the perfect hope, embodies the life—earthly and eternal—of humanity and its eschatological end, a life in which humans can participate, through grace and discipleship.

To make this argument, I will first sketch a rough picture of Moltmannian hope. Then I will propose some challenges and additions to that

---

2. As Richard King helpfully observed in a personal conversation, the image of the river of Christian tradition has a number of limitations. It does not, for example, illustrate the extent to which Christianity interacts and overlaps with, and separates from, other bodies of water (and the rest of the landscape). I wholeheartedly agree that this image has only a narrow range of applicability, and I am eager to receive recommendations—geographical or otherwise—for alternative metaphors.

discourse, in order to clarify and enrich resources of hope for the church and its mission. For the purposes of this project, I will direct my arguments and observations toward Christian theologians in the United States, especially those who are invested in the theology of hope.

Chapter 1 reviews some aspects of the theological hope offered by Moltmann, followed by examples of Moltmannian hope, which reflect—but do not necessarily accurately represent—the scope of Moltmann's theology of hope. I highlight the doctrine of God that determines the hope and the anthropology of hope in Moltmannian theology. I describe a 2007 conference about eschatology that celebrated and presented a Moltmannian theology of hope; and I present a book about hope written by a theologian strongly influenced by Moltmann. Chapter 2 identifies some of the features of theological hope that are lost when Moltmannian hope becomes the dominant ideology of hope. The costs of exclusive reliance on Moltmannian hope include a lack of critical engagement with the doctrines Moltmann rejected when constructing his theological hope. The apparent appropriateness of Moltmannian hope hinders considerations of new contributions to hope. Chapter 3 considers Thomas Aquinas's presentation of theological hope and twenty-first century treatments of hope from theologians appreciative of his systematic theology. I provide an overview of Aquinas's theology of hope as presented in the *Summa Theologica,* and I correct some Moltmannian misunderstandings of Thomistic hope. I add relevant contributions from Pope Benedict XVI, Daniel Castelo, Paul Gavrilyuk, D. Stephen Long, Kathryn Tanner, and Thomas Weinandy. Each section begins with the lyrics of a song from the distinctly non-Thomistic canon of old-timey gospel/blues/bluegrass music about hope and heaven, as evidence of faithful discourses of hope that persevere outside the realm of Moltmannian hope. Chapter 4 briefly addresses five contemporary discourses not conventionally considered as resources for theological hope and suggests how they might contribute to a more intentionally cohesive narrative and performance of theological hope. I look at nihilism, lament, disability theology, feminist theory, and feminist theology to explore the wisdom and clarity they might offer to Christian theological hope. The conclusion proposes a small exercise to help imagine on-the-ground lives in eschatological hope.

1

Moltmann's Hope and Moltmannian Hope

THE PATRON OF THEOLOGICAL hope in the United States for the past fifty years has been Jürgen Moltmann. His celebrated book of 1964, *Theology of Hope: On the Ground and the Implications of a Christian Eschatology*, reinvigorated theological scholarship about hope and still inspires academic and congregational engagements with hope. His account of hope emphasizes God's experience of crucified godforsakenness, Jesus Christ's promise of resurrection, the future coming of God's new creation, and the work of hope in this life, now. Moltmann's theology inspires a body of writing and belief—Moltmannian hope—that approximately reflects his work and functions as normative for a significant number of Christian theologians, church leaders, and lay people. Moltmannian hope tries to resist, on the one hand, the resigned escapism that gives up on this world and dreams of an otherworldy kingdom, and on the other, the superficial hopes of a commodified world. Moltmannian hope instead looks for future possibilities for a compassionate God's new creation of this world.

OUR ONLY HOPE?

In this age of unsatiable desire, hopes and accompanying proclamations of hope fill news stories, advertisements, and commentaries. Christians wanting to make sense of theological hope and theologians wanting to convey a message of specifically Christian hope must clear their ways through a flood of distinctly non-theological hope. A casual scan of

Our Only Hope

assorted media reveals a plethora of claims about the identity of *our only hope*, from a rock/metalcore/pop band,[1] to spray tanning,[2] to the Gospel. Medical candidates for *our only hope* include stem cells,[3] charity hospitals in India,[4] IVF treatments,[5] and genetic research.[6] Those concerned about the environment argue that *our only hope* rests in organic food,[7] carbon capture,[8] desalination of sea water,[9] the sea itself,[10] or geoengineering.[11] *Our only hope* for appropriate health care is regulation[12]—or deregulation.[13] In American politics, *our only hope* might be President Obama's audacious hope,[14] the hope of his campaign's slogans: "Hope + Belief =

1. Our Only Hope. Band. Online: http://www.reverbnation.com/ouronlyhope.

2. Thomas describes how spray tanning is the only way she can get a tan without burning her fair skin, in "Spray-Tanning, The Only Hope for People Like Me."

3. Burns proposes that the metaphor for research and use of stem cells shift to "superheroes," in "You are our only hope."

4. A hospital outside Kalkata provides inexpensive care for the needy. Dhar, "Are charity hospitals the only hope for India's poor?"

5. Parents of triplets tell their story: "Cherelle and Thomas Southerland wanted a baby so badly that they couldn't think of a future without one. . . . Four ectopic pregnancies ended in miscarriage. She suffered hemorrhages and had to have both fallopian tubes removed. With each loss, she wanted a baby more. So in 1999, the Southerlands decided to try in vitro fertilization (IVF).

"'It was a little scary because it was our only hope of getting pregnant,' says Cherelle, who also works at Cincinnati Children's Hospital Medical Center. 'We didn't really have the funds, but God made a way.'" CincinnatiChildrens, "Worth the Wait: Triplets Mom Counts Her Blessings." Online: http://www.youtube.com/watch?v=KfRS4ls9xFU.

6. "Hope—It's In Our Genes," is a rare disease campaign slogan translated into multiple international languages and Braille. Global Genes Project.

7. Beauley, "Organically Grown Foods: Our Only Hope."

8. Blunt, "Carbon Capture and Storage: Our Only Hope to Avoid Global Warming?"

9. Jervey, Contributing Editor and Planet Ambassador to the Pepsi Refresh Project, explains that "The tough reality of the world's increasingly dire water crisis means that desalination isn't merely an option, but a necessity. The only sensible way to power these processes—without further contributing to one of the main causes of the freshwater shortages—is to do it without greenhouse gas emissions. Without exception, desalination needs to be coupled with clean energy" ("Seawater: Our Only Hope for a Drink").

10. Cousteau, "Ocean."

11. Blunt, "Stop Emitting Co2 or Geoengineering Could Be Our Only Hope."

12. Helms, "Health Cost Problem: Is Regulation Our Only Hope?"

13. Ralston, "Universal Freedom: The Only Hope For Health Care."

14. Barack Obama, *The Audacity of Hope: Thoughts on Reclaiming the American Dream*.

Change,"[15] "Hope, Action, Change,"[16] or an opposing campaign slogan: "Overrated: No Hope, Just Hype."[17] Some argue that *our only* national *hope* combines American values and Christianity: *our only hope* is the radicalization of fellowship preached by Martin Luther King Jr.,[18] or the distinctive "Jesus Our Only HOPE Hoodie," which shows an illustration of Jesus in the format of the famous Obama poster.[19] During the 2012 presidential election campaign, President Obama, the leading Republican candidates (Mitt Romney, Rick Santorum, Newt Gingrich, Michele Bachmann, Ron Paul), and the Occupy Movement have all been named "our only hope" by their various constituencies.

Each declaration of *our only hope* names or assumes the desired end of that hope; few people are likely to confuse an online gaming quest in World of Warcraft called "Our Only Hope"[20] with a wildlife sanctuary's mission for protecting injured animals through educating potential protectors.[21] Few Christians are likely to confuse IVF treatment with the *only hope* in Jesus Christ that Christian scripture, teaching, and tradition have consistently proclaimed. However, when news reports, political propaganda, product advertising, social advocacy, and medical research use the *only hope* trope to express multiple degrees of importance and multiple sorts of hope, Christians may well find it difficult to determine precisely how Christian hope in Jesus Christ is different from all other hopes.

Initial inquiries about a specifically Christian hope today frequently meet with two sorts of Christian hope: on the one hand, there is the

---

15. Zazzle Hope+Belief=Change! Customised T-Shirt. Online: http://www.zazzle.co.uk/hope_belief_change_obama_08_customised_tshirt-235476764300328824.

16. VICTORYSTORE.COM. Barack Obama Hope Action Change Banner. Online: http://victorystore00.stores.yahoo.net/noname19.html.

17. American Elephant. T-Shirt. Online: http://americanelephant.com/latest-designs/anti-obama-t-shirt-of-the-day-overrated-no-hope-just-hype.

18. "Our only hope today lies in our ability to recapture the revolutionary spirit and go out into a sometimes hostile world declaring eternal hostility to poverty, racism, and militarism." King, "Why."

19. SpreadShirt Hoodie. Online: http://www.spreadshirt.com/white-jesus-our-only-hope-hooded-sweatsh-C3376A3384731.

20. World of Warcraft, "Our Only Hope" quest. *Game Atlas Guide and Data Base*. Online: http://wow.gamepressure.com/quest.asp?ID=5088.

21. Genesis Wildlife Sanctuary: "We are a haven for injured, orphaned and abused animals, dedicated to rescue, rehabilitation, release, and education. We believe that our only hope for the survival of the wildlife is the teaching of its importance to those who will be their protectors. It is in this spirit that we offer our experience to groups of all ages, but, in particular, the children."

mistaken hope that looks to an idyllic heaven in a land far away; on the other hand, there is the more responsible hope that looks to the efforts of good people to make a better world today. The older and outdated sort of hope pertains to the less-immediate and somewhat awkward topic of eternal salvation with God. "In the old days," the story goes, "the church used to care chiefly about hopes for heavenly rest; and in the process it dismissed and denigrated the urgent suffering of people living on this earth. Now we should know better."[22] The newer and more appropriate hope is practical and calls engaged church members to help the needy improve their material conditions and social positions, through personal aid and through public policy. The primary proponents of practical hope remember (or would like to remember) the sixties, when the church was socially active and cared about issues that really mattered, thereby correcting the previous detached, overly-spiritual, approach of the church. Now, they argue, the church has lost much of that enthusiastic activism.[23] Even though the church did not fully live up to this nostalgic vision of hope-filled activism for civil rights and peace fifty years ago, and even though mainstream Christianity has not, on the whole, lapsed into a dreamy belief in a pie-in-the-sky fulfillment of hope, concern for correction remains. Theologians and clergy urge parishioners toward an appropriate commitment to on-the-ground activities of Christian hope instead of succumbing to the distracting influence of fluffy-cloud idyllism or of Rapture-focused apocalypticism.[24]

Practical-hope theology shares many goals and aims that can be addressed within the sphere of United States political action. Federally funded programs and those who champion private sphere incentives both aim to benefit the less fortunate with an on-the-ground focus and a hope that supports theological priorities for the tangible needs of people, now. Thus, a theology of hope can encourage immediate, tangible care for those in the most vulnerable positions through, or in concert with, small- and large-scale political policies. With less energy spent in speculation about who will and won't end up in heaven, Christians can devote more of their efforts toward the social and political action that could make a difference in present day society; and yet, parishioners who already agree that these are the best expressions of hope still require frequent reminders to move from the pew to tasks in the real world. Theological books, essays, and

22. See Parker, "Holy."
23. See Borsch, *Outrage*.
24. Standaert, *Skipping*, 34.

lectures about practical hope offer resources to support the preaching and teaching of concerned church leaders.[25]

Meanwhile, Christians in America are finding it increasingly difficult to grasp and sustain hope in the face of unrelenting challenges. These challenges come in the form of natural disasters, human-caused disasters, economic downturns, high unemployment, housing crises, and the fact that things do not seem to be getting better every day, as previously expected. People are discouraged by tax hikes, the loss of programs through tax cuts, global terrorism, wars against terrorism, global warming, arguments about how to respond to global warming, and stalemated partisan politics. Victims of systemic oppression and inattention see little hope of relief; those benefiting from the goods of a capitalist democracy see diminished hope for retaining those goods; those who had felt that the American Dream of prosperity (or at least a somewhat more comfortable lifestyle) was almost in their grasp find their hopes dashed by a weakened economy and subsequent layoffs; those who had no hope of participating in the American Dream still have no hope of such participation. Those putting their trust in nationalism feel disappointed in the ways that the nation and its leaders do not not live up to their hopes. Those seeking reassurance from the church feel disappointed by institutional incompetence, the weakness of church leadership, irrelevance, trendy change, the closure of church buildings, and money spent on church buildings instead of the poor and needy. Those working to make a difference here and now feel frustrated that their efforts reap little visible change. Experts of science and reason argue against the bases of Christian hope, while medical research fails to eradicate suffering, death, and the common cold.

The need for hope seems greater than ever, as does the need for clear articulations and teachings of Christian theological hope. Since the 1960s, Moltmann has been the name most familiarly associated with theological hope. His work directly and indirectly influences a large body of theological hope resources today.[26]

---

25. See, for example: Osmer, *Teaching*.

26. A few of the theologians influenced by Moltmann include: Rubem Alves, Leonardo Boff, James Cone, Gustavo Gutierrez, Elizabeth Johnson, Catherine Keller, John Polkinghorne, Paul Ricoeur, Letty Russell, and Jon Sobrino.

Our Only Hope

Moltmann's Experience of Godforsakenness and Hope

Moltmann grew up in Hamburg, in a secular, academic family. His discovery of God, his vocation, and his theology of hope began near the end of World War II. He writes:

> In the last week of July 1943, Hamburg was destroyed in a firestorm as a result of the British Royal Air Force's "Operation Gomorrah." 40,000 people perished. With my school class I was in a flak battery in the inner city as an auxiliary. It was wiped out, but the bombs which tore away the school friend standing next to me spared me. In the night, for the first time I cried out to God. "My God, where are you?" was my question. "Why am I alive and not dead like the others?" During three years as a prisoner of war I looked for an answer, first in the Old Testament psalms of lamentation and then in the Gospel of Mark. When I came to Jesus' dying cry, I knew, "There is your divine brother and redeemer, who understands you in your godforsakenness."[27]

In prison, Moltmann experienced God's presence not only in divine understanding, but also in the graciousness of the local residents and in the community of prisoners: "The kindness which Scottish miners and English neighbours showed the German prisoners of war who were at that time their enemies shamed us profoundly. We were accepted as people, even though we were only numbers and wore the prisoner's patch on our backs. But that made it possible for us to live with the guilt of our own people, the catastrophes we had brought about and the long shadows of Auschwitz, without repressing them and without becoming callous."[28] Some of the prisoners were Protestant theologians, and they gathered Moltmann and other prisoners to read and study the Bible[29]; this experienced shaped the entire direction of Moltmann's life.

Hence, as a young man, Moltmann was transformed by the horrors of war, the revelation of God's presence in the midst of suffering, the solidarity with prisoners of war, the surprising hospitality of townspeople, and the practice of Bible study in community. He reports that "the experiences of the life of a prisoner have left a lasting mark on me: the suffering and the hope which reinforce each other. When one grasps the courage to

---

27. Moltmann, *How*, 13.
28. Moltmann, *End*, 35.
29. Moltmann, *How*, 13.

hope, the chains begin to hurt, but the pain is better than the resignation in which everything is a matter of indifference."[30]

In 1948, once released from prison, Moltmann went to seminary, where he was greatly influenced by Barth and the Confessing Church. After serving a rural church, he returned to scholarship and published *The Theology of Hope* in 1965. In this and in his many following books (on a variety of other theological topics), he describes an eschatological hope that is affirmed and yet unfinished in Christ until God's future fulfillment in the world's new creation. He counters the idea that Christ's resurrection happened in the past to establish our future. Rather, he argues, we live in the time of not yet, a present time determined by the future that will come to history. Throughout his life, he carries forward his powerful revelation of God suffering with him in godforsakenness as the future hope of God's presence in and with the new creation to come.

The God of Hope

God suffers. Moltmann's theology of hope relies on his characterization of God as passible and mutable: God suffers and God changes. God experiences suffering, regret, abandonment, and the effects of human history. This reversal of traditional doctrine about the nature of God so permeates Moltmann's work that it might be possible to argue that his is a theology of divine passibility, with a secondary account of hope. Ryan Neal observes that "any modern treatment of divine (im)passibility has to consider Moltmann, specifically in *The Crucified God* and *The Trinity and the Kingdom of God*. That many today speak of God's suffering without any conceptual or linguistic difficulty is due in large part to Moltmann and the favorable way he has been received by the academy along these lines."[31]

According to Moltmann, God's passibility determines the identity, actions, and relationships of God, Jesus Christ, and the Holy Spirit—separately and as the Trinity—and God's passibility allows for the possibility of

---

30. Ibid.

31. Neal, *Theology*, 70. Here, as elsewhere, it is impossible to declare with certainty whether a broader shift in doctrinal assumptions precedes Moltmann's claims. Either way, he articulates a change that many Christians are willing to accept. In 1986, Richard Goetz wrote "The Suffering God: The Rise of a New Orthodoxy," and his "new orthodoxy" label has been repeated countless times since. In 2003, Sturla Stålsett named passibilism "the dominant view, a theological commonplace," in *The Crucified and the Crucified*, 490, also 435.

hope. He recounts, in a 1997 essay, how his certainty that God is passible grew out of his experience of 1968:

> 1968 brought the climax and turning-point in the mood of a new awakening. Military intervention put an end to the Prague Spring. German and Polish troops also marched shamefully into Czechoslovakia. In Rome the encyclical *Humanae vitae* set a limit to the *aggiornamento* of the church; Catholic colleagues lost their posts. On 6 April Martin Luther King was shot. The black ghettoes burned. We were in America at that time. Rudi Dutschke was shot at a demonstration in Berlin. The student protest became more bitter. For me the political dream of a united Social Democratic Europe collapsed. The end in Prague paralysed me for weeks.[32]

These events raised questions that resonated with the questions Moltmann began considering in prison camp and with the persistent post-Holocaust questions about the possibility of hope after God's apparent abandonment of all those persecuted and murdered.

Moltmann's experiences framed his understanding of God from scripture. Israel's account of God throughout the Old Testament describes a God who creates the world and establishes order for God's people. God responds to God's people when they are needy and when they stray from God's order to disordered lives. God protects, corrects, and redirects the people toward righteousness, over and over. The stories of this relationship between God and Israel often present God in anthropomorphic terms, as a divine figure—the one God—who responds to Israel's ungodliness with frustration *and* with an unwavering faithfulness to the people with convenantal constancy. In these accounts, God sighs, acts out in anger, listens to and heeds the people's prayers, and delights in the people's righteousness. Moltmann endorses this representation of God, but he differs from much of Jewish and Christian theology which asserts that throughout, God remains almighty and impassible, steadfast and undiminished by lesser powers and human frailty.[33]

Moltmann finds the idea of an impassible God contradictory to the reality of God's love and compassion as described in scripture and in God's work on earth. He understands impassibility to conflict with eschatological hope based on God's suffering and death on the cross and on God's full presence in the new creation. As mentioned above, Moltmann's first

---

32. Moltmann, *How*, 17.
33. Chapters 2 and 3 cover impassibility in more depth.

revelation of God occurred in the coincidence of his powerful sense of abandonment—on the battlefield and as a prisoner of war—and his encounter with the Gospel account of Jesus' passion and death. Moltmann recognized his own abandonment in God's abandonment of Jesus Christ in the garden of Gethsemane and on the cross. Moltmann understood his experience as a reflection of Jesus' experience, and he felt consolation from the presence of God—newly discovered in the Bible he was given—who experienced his abandonment *with* him. A God who is not moved, changed, or wounded in the face of human suffering could not be the compassionate God revealed to Moltmann in the prison camp.

Moltmann cites Elie Wiesel's account from Auschwitz of the boy who is hanged, but dies very slowly, in the midst of great suffering. A man standing nearby with Wiesel asks, "Where is God?" and Wiesel answers, "He is here. He is hanging there on the gallows . . ."[34] Moltmann affirms Wiesel's answer and declares that "any other answer would be blasphemy. There cannot be any other Christian answer to the question of this torment. To speak here of a God who could not suffer would make God a demon. To speak here of an absolute God would make God an annihilating nothingness. To speak here of an indifferent God would condemn men to indifference."[35] Moltmann responds to those who cannot find God after Auschwitz by placing the suffering God in the midst of death at Auschwitz and therefore in the midst of all of humanity's suffering and death. He corrects those who claim an impassible God by separating divine absoluteness from divine compassion. The God of hope thus regains relevance in a world of horror and rejects divine power that would inhibit co-suffering with humanity.

Moltmann supports his account of God's passibility by noting how close early Christianity came to theological error before it was "in a position to identify God himself with the suffering and the death of Jesus."[36] Moltmann equates docetism, "according to which Jesus only appeared to suffer and only appeared to die abandoned by God: this did not happen in reality," with claims about God's impassibility.[37] Moltmann argues that this and Greek non-biblical philosophy separate divinity and humanity into distinct, separated, characters such that "God's being is incorruptible, unchangeable, indivisible, incapable of suffering and immortal; human

34. Moltmann, *Crucified*, 273–4.
35. Ibid., 274.
36. Ibid., 227.
37. Ibid.

nature, on the other hand, is transitory, changeable, divisible, capable of suffering and mortal."[38] Moltmann explains that the doctrine of Christ's two natures developed as a way to forge a connection between the impassible God and the human suffering Jesus endured, a connection that Christians hoped would bring them to a salvation of transcendence: "God became man that we men might participate in God (Athanasius)."[39] The problem with this hope, according to Moltmann, is that humans want to be immortal with an immortal God, and that hope "makes it impossible to regard Jesus as really being God and at the same time as being forsaken by God."[40]

Moltmann labels the doctrine of Christ's two natures a characteristic of theism, which he criticizes for prioritizing the oneness of God instead of the relatedness of the trinitarian persons and for maintaining an inviolable separation between the divine and the human: "The doctrine of two natures must understand the event of the cross statically as a reciprocal relationship between two qualitatively different natures, the divine nature which is incapable of suffering and the human nature which is capable of suffering."[41] Instead, Moltmann advocates a doctrine of God who is love and who loves always in relationships with the Son and the Holy Spirit, and whose love will be fulfilled eschatologically in the Trinity's open relationship with creation. Christ's suffering on the cross draws God into human suffering through God's love for creation. God's suffering love reflects the future new creation when God and creation will be wholly together in trinitarian perichoretic love.

God, the creator of eschatological relationships, provides hope through God's own suffering: "God is unconditional love, because he takes on himself grief at the contradiction in men and does not angrily suppress this contradiction. God allows himself to be forced out. God suffers, God allows himself to be crucified and is crucified, and in this consummates his unconditional love that is so full of hope."[42] God's embrace of human suffering demonstrates the victory of love over hate. "Thus [God's love's] suffering proves to be stronger than hate. Its might is powerful in weakness and gains power over its enemies in grief, because it gives life even to its enemies and opens up the future to change."[43] Moltmann argues that

38. Ibid., 228.
39. Ibid.
40. Ibid.
41. Ibid., 245.
42. Ibid., 248.
43. Ibid., 249.

the two-natured Christ doctrine freezes Jesus and God into a two-person, non-interactive relationship and leaves the Holy Spirit out all together. Moltmann's account of the Trinity focuses on the relationships of the persons of the Trinity more than on the oneness of the Trinity. Moltmann envisions the Trinity as three subjects in unity, instead of three persons in one.[44] Both God and creation hope for the inclusion of creation in the Trinity's perichoretic relationships of love, opened by the cross.

Moltmann's investigation of the early church Fathers leads him to identify Cyril of Alexandria as the most sympathetic to a single-natured Christ. Moltmann finds that the rest of the Fathers, as well as most of Christian doctrine that follows, fail to understand the limits of divine *apatheia* that Moltmann brings to light and that he sees in Cyril. In his narrative of the church's rejection of divine passibility, Moltmann describes how Cyril recognizes Jesus' forsakenness on the cross as the cry of the human *and* divine Christ, but then backtracks to cohere with the position of the church that God is impassible and only Christ's human nature was forsaken.[45]

> Even Cyril of Alexandria, who more than anyone else stressed the personal unity of Christ against those who pressed for the differentiation of the two natures, was not able to remedy the "error" which the whole of early Christian theology demonstrates at this point. As a consequence of his Christology of unity he really had to refer the cry of the forsaken Christ on the cross to the complete, divine and human person of the Son. But Cyril cannot manage that. Certainly it is Christ who says that, but it is not his own personal and human need that leads him to it. Anyone who claims that Christ is overcome with fear and weakness here, says Cyril, refuses to confess his God. Christ does not say this in his own name, but in the name of his total nature, because only this and not he himself fell prey to corruption. He is calling to the Father for us, and not for himself.[46]

Moltmann's understanding of Cyril contrasts with the early church councils that describe Jesus Christ as having two natures: in one nature,

---

44. Ibid.

45. Ibid., 229.

46. Ibid., 228–29. "This understanding of Christ's cry of desolation in Cyril is a last retreat before the axiom of *apatheia*. According to Thomas Aquinas, too, the suffering is only a *suppositum* of the divine nature in respect of the human nature which it assumed and which was capable of suffering; it did not relate to the divine nature itself, for this was incapable of suffering" (ibid., 299).

he is wholly divine; in the other, he is wholly human. He follows Chalcedon and Luther to claim that Christ's divine and human natures share properties, but he moves past the *communicatio idiomatum* and moves from the *communication* of distinct natures toward one shared nature. Thus, Jesus Christ's human suffering *is* God's divine suffering; what Jesus experiences, God experiences; at the crucifixion, God Godself experiences godforsakenness.

> When God becomes man in Jesus of Nazareth, he not only enters into the finitude of man, but in his death on the cross also enters into the situation of man's godforsakenness. In Jesus he does not die the natural death of a finite being, but the violent death of the criminal on the cross, the death of complete abandonment by God. The suffering in the passion of Jesus is abandonment, rejection by God, his Father. God does not become a religion, so that man participates in him by corresponding religious thoughts and feelings. God does not become a law, so that man participates in him through obedience to a law. God does not become an ideal, so that man achieves community with him through constant striving. He humbles himself and takes upon himself the eternal death of the godless and the godforsaken, so that all the godless and the godforsaken can experience communion with him.[47]

Although Moltmann rejects the two natures of Christ, he does present two aspects of Jesus; his account of the difference relies on a chronological and eschatological distinction rather than a divine and human distinction. From the perspective of the crucifixion and resurrection, Jesus functions as the temporary Lord, the one through whom God acts in the interim time, "the time from his exaltation until the consummation of his work of salvation."[48] Jesus as Lord stands in for God and offers access to God,[49] such that "God identifies himself with Jesus by receiving the crucified one into his future as mode of his being. If we start with the resurrection, we must say that God in his being does not become identical with Jesus, but identifies with Jesus through an act of his will. God has offered him up to a death at the cross of forsakenness. God has raised him from the dead and exalted him to be the Lord of his coming kingdom. In passion and

---

47. Ibid., 276.
48. Moltmann, "Theology as Eschatology," 24–5.
49. Ibid., 24.

resurrection God acts in Jesus."[50] Hope in Jesus as Lord rests not on what he has accomplished through his resurrection, but on what God will accomplish when all have been resurrected by God, eschatologically.

Moltmann recognizes that Jesus Christ might be described as mediator, but he finds the mediator role inadequate, arguing instead for a more direct connection between God and creation. A direct connection allows God to share in human suffering and pain as a promise of the release to come. Moltmann claims a single-natured Christ, such that whatever Jesus experiences, God experiences as well: "In the cross, Father and Son are most deeply separated in forsakenness and at the same time are most inwardly one in their surrender."[51] When Jesus prays to God in the garden of Gethsemane, and when Jesus cries out to God on the cross, God does not answer. Moltmann interprets Jesus' cry, "My God, why have you forsaken me?" to mean that Jesus not only feels forsaken by God but is, in fact, forsaken by God. Moltmann argues here that when Jesus feels that God is absent from him, God truly is absent, *and* God experiences the godforsakenness that Jesus experiences. While the two-natured Christology retains a real difference between humanity and divinity in Christ, Moltmann's single-natured Christ brings God's divinity closer to humanity. Jesus' humanity and divinity coinhere, and God shares unreservedly in Christ's adjoined humanity and divinity. God thus takes on two divinely intensified human-like experiences of suffering: God suffers as Father when God forsakes his Son and gives him up to death on the cross; God suffers as godforsaken when Christ is godforsaken.

Moltmann affirms the Nicaean critique of Arius that God is not changeable, adding that while God is not changeable the way creatures are, God is not unchangeable either. However he adds:

> That statement is not absolute; it is only a simile. God is not changeable as creatures are changeable. However, the conclusion should not be drawn from this that God is unchangeable in every respect, for this negative definition merely says that God is under constraint from that which is not of God. The negation of changeableness by which a general distinction is drawn between God and man must not lead to the conclusion that he is intrinsically unchangeable. If God is not passively changeable by other things like other creatures, this does not mean that he is not free to change himself, or even free to allow himself to be changed by

---

50. Ibid.
51. Moltmann, *Crucified*, 244.

> others of his own free will. True, God cannot be divided like his creation, but he can still communicate himself. Thus the relative definition of his unchangeableness does not lead to the assertion of his absolute and intrinsic unchangeableness.[52]

Moltmann sees a distinction between imposed suffering and voluntary suffering; God's suffering is voluntary and tied to God's love, which Moltmann marks as the essence of God's being.

Moltmann narrates the ultimate unity of the believer and the Trinity by charting a path of understanding, experience, and faith, from the crucifixion to human participation in the relations of the Trinity.

> If in the freedom given through experience of it the believer understands the crucifixion as an event of the love of the Son and the grief of the Father, that is, as an event between God and God, as an event within the Trinity, he perceives the liberating word of love which creates new life. By the death of the Son he is taken up into the grief of the Father and experiences a liberation which is a new element in this de-divinized and legalistic world, which is itself even a new element over against the original creation of the word. He is in fact taken up into the inner life of God, if in the cross of Christ he experiences the love of God for the godless, the enemies, in so far as the history of Christ is the inner life of God himself. In that, if he lives in this love, he lives in God and God in him. If he lives in this freedom, he lives in God and God in him. If one conceives of the Trinity as an event of love in the suffering and the death of Jesus—and that is something which faith must do—then the Trinity is no self-contained group in heaven, but an eschatological process open for men on earth, which stems from the cross of Christ. By the secular cross on Golgotha, understood as open vulnerability and as the love of God for loveless and unloved, dehumanized men, God's being and God's life is open to true man.[53]

In this way, Moltmann establishes that hope for the kingdom of God equals hope for participation within the accessible, receptive, and responsive trinitarian God.

To correct what he perceives to be the theological error of imagining a distant, detached God, Moltmann draws on an assessment of many twentieth-century biblical scholars that the true nature of God as revealed in Jesus Christ was corrupted by Greek metaphysical thought. Francis

---

52. Ibid., 237.
53. Ibid., 249.

Moltmann's Hope and Moltmannian Hope

Schüssler Fiorenza describes this claim that Hellenism and Christianity work with conflicting "symbolic systems": "Biblical categories understand the world as history, have space for God's act, and maintain an openness to the future. In contrast, Greek categories are said to be static, without genuine history, without space for God's historical acts, and closed to the future, viewing the cosmos as a cycle."[54] Moltmann argues that the God manifest in Jesus Christ is not the God of Hellenic philosophy prevalent during early Christianity, whose inaccesible and impersonal attributes usurped the passible God of love.

> Since the shaping of Christian dogmatics by Greek thought, it has been the general custom to approach the mystery of Jesus from the general idea of God in Greek metaphysics: the one God, for whom all men are seeking on the ground of their experience of reality, has appeared in Jesus of Nazareth—be it that the highest eternal idea of goodness and truth has found its most perfect teacher in him, or be it that in him eternal Being, the Source of all things, has become flesh and appeared in the multifarious world of transience and mortality. The mystery of Jesus is then the incarnation of the one, eternal, original, true and immutable divine Being.[55]

He adds that the Christian adoption of the Greek concept of a single deism wrongly identified God as immutable and impassible, thereby eliminating God's presence in the crucifixion, the resurrection, and the promised eschaton.[56]

The passibility of God supports Moltmann's theology of hope by holding together God's acts of creation, God's relationship with God's creatures and with Israel, God's godforsaken experience through Jesus Christ, and God's future coming into creation made new. In each case, God feels the negative results of limited and limiting created life, and can therefore most effectively bring about resurrection of all in the the final, perfect, new creation. Although Moltmann primarily underscores God's passibility, he extends his doctrinal correction of the transcendent God of Greek philosophy to address the other attributes of God previously assumed by Christian theology: immutability, perfection, simplicity, infinity, and goodness. Moltmann frees Christian hope from the constraints of an absolute ruler God, who surveys and judges creation from afar. Instead, he

---

54. Fiorenza, "Being," 351.
55. Moltmann, *Theology*, 140.
56. Ibid.

advocates a more relevant God whose passibility moves God to change—out of regret for God's initial incomplete act of creation—from creator to participant in creation.

Moltmann is certain that Greek-influenced Christianity and the Christian doctrinal traditions that followed cannot grasp "the eschatological future horizon of the Christian mission."[57] With his own experiences and his awareness of contemporary circumstances, Moltmann feels he has the perspective to clarify the true nature of God and to correct Christian teaching to fit hope in the coming God and God's new creation: "Every formulation of the Christian tradition according to the standard of classical tradition—and since the days of anti-revolutionary romanticism such formulations have often arisen in Catholicism and frequently in Protestantism—is wrong. Both the Christian *tradendum*, or object to be transmitted, and the process of tradition in the Christian proclamation break these grounds."[58] Moltmann's confidence that the new creation, which is no longer the end but the beginning, so transforms the past and present history of God with God's people, that the most prominent markers of Christian identity and teaching must be reconstructed. He claims that "Christian proclamation is not a tradition of wisdom and truth in doctrinal principles. Nor is it a tradition of ways and means of living according to the law. It is the announcing, revealing and publishing of an eschatological event. It reveals the risen Christ's lordship over the world, and sets men free for the coming salvation in faith and hope."[59] The gospel proclamation of Jesus thus takes the shape of eschatological anticipation, rather than fulfillment of past promises carried through Jewish law and taught in theological catechesis. Moltmann explains that the gospel "has a thoroughly proleptic thrust, for Jesus anticipates through his words, his deeds, and his life shared with other persons, what, according to the Old Testament expectancy, can only happen on the last day. He does already today what is supposed to come tomorrow. He lives entirely from the nearness of God's future. He can be properly understood, therefore, as the anticipator of the coming of God and the liberator of a bound humanity."[60]

According to Moltmann, Jesus himself displays the same relationship to tradition that Moltmann advocates, by leading his life on the terms of the kingdom yet to come:

57. Ibid., 299.
58. Ibid.
59. Ibid.
60. Moltmann, *Experiment*, 54.

He announced the kingdom, not as judgment but as joy. He celebrated its arrival in the "banquet for the just" with unjust sinners. He distributed the kingdom in the forgiveness of sins. This is what is so astonishingly new in the message of Jesus. Accordingly, he distanced himself from John the Baptist, from whom he had probably come to know the message of the near kingdom. The eschatology of Jesus is not the preaching of judgment, but the realization of pure grace and freedom. Therefore, his disciples did not fast and, to the continual indignation of many Christians also, he was known as a "glutton and wine-bibber."[61]

Moltmann extends his point even further to argue that Jesus detached himself completely from Judaism and Torah: "What right did Jesus have and what power did he use to introduce this astonishing and disarming message of the open and gracious future of God? Obviously, he renounced all the religious institutions of his people and did not call on the traditions of their holy history. He relied completely and exclusively on the future of God, whom he called 'my Father.'"[62] Moltmann consistently highlights the future and the need to break with the past.[63]

Moltmann works to free Christian theology from early Greek philosophical influences in order to show the passionate and compassionate God manifest in Jesus Christ. God does not stand apart from creation, waiting but unmoved by pain, suffering, and death. God's love for creation is so great that God suffers in God's own self the most desperate depths of human experience. When Jesus Christ lives the physical and emotional life of humanity, suffers the exquisite pain of God's abandonment in the Garden of Gethsemane and on the cross and then dies, God lives, suffers, and dies as well. God's passibility demonstrates God's limitless love that

61. Ibid.

62. Ibid. Moltmann continues: "With the claim 'But I say to you . . .' in the antitheses of the Sermon on the Mount, he placed himself above the authority of Moses as no prophet had done previously. By forgiving sins, he did what was reserved for God alone. We do not historically know who Jesus considered himself to be. But his total appearance shows that someone greater than Moses and the prophets was intended here, greater also than the figures of apocalyptic expectations, such as 'the Messiah' and the 'Son of man.' Otherwise, Jesus could not have identified the coming kingdom of God with his own person: 'And Blessed is he who takes no offense at me.' This means that his claim to power received no support from the past, but was totally directed toward confirmation by God in the future. His right to make such a claim hung, so to speak, 'in the air.' He based this claim on nothing, or rather on God himself" (ibid., 55).

63. For discussions of Moltmann's possible anti-Judaism, see Hofheinz, *Passionate*; Heschel, "Configuration"; and Bauckham, *Theology*.

embraces and takes on even the limited, finite life of humans. God's solidarity in suffering becomes God's promise of the new creation of salvation from suffering, when understood from the future perspective, looking back at the cross and resurrection. Through the promise of salvation for all, God's participation in human pain and suffering establishes eschatological hope.

God suffers at the crucifixion so powerfully that God's suffering encompasses all human suffering, and the meaning of God's suffering gives meaning to the suffering of humans. Paul Fiddes notes that Moltmann

> envisages God as an event of suffering in which human beings can take their place. He insists that what is visible at the cross is true of the being of God throughout history; there is an ever-present situation in which a divine Father suffers the loss of a Son, a Son suffers the loss of a Father, and a Spirit of self-giving love and hope flows between them. In his own Trinitarian history of suffering, God opens himself to include the uproar of all human history; oppressed and forsaken people can find themselves within the situation of a suffering God, and so can also share in his history of glorification.[64]

Jesus Christ brings God to share suffering with humanity so that humanity can hope for the new creation, when all will share in God's glory.

The Character of Hope

Moltmann's theology of hope connects the hopes of today with the future of God's coming kingdom through the extension of divine promise, and through the suffering shared by God and humanity. Moltmann's account of hope was formed not only by his war and postwar experiences and his new life as a Christian, but also by the work of his contemporary, and sometime neighbor, Ernst Bloch. Bloch's emphasis on the "future, the nature of God's being, and the question of hope's certainty"[65] sparked Moltmann's interest in the future's transformation of the historical present. This future of possibility reflects Bloch's philosophical development of Marxism, with its emphasis on history and human agency. Upon reading Bloch's *The Principle of Hope*,[66] Moltmann reported that his reaction was, "Why has Christian theology neglected this theme of hope, which is so

---

64. Fiddes, *Creative*, 151.
65. Neal, *Theology*, 24.
66. Bloch, *Principle*.

distinctively its own?" "What is left of the earliest Christian spirit of hope in present-day Christianity?"[67] Moltmann had not found in Christian theology or practice the enthusiasm and liveliness of the unconstrained hope he discovered in Bloch. Moltmann was also picking up on concurrent discussions within New Testament theology,[68] as well as the electrically charged air of potential political change in the Civil Rights actions in the United States. Moltmann appreciates Bloch's presentation of an "ontology of the not-yet-being," in which "the already real is surrounded by a sea of possibilities and again and again a new piece of reality arises out of this sea."[69] While recognizing that Bloch offers an atheistic philosophy,[70] Moltmann claims Bloch's philosophy as also "thoroughly religious," since it reaches beyond the life we know now to an open future, thereby aligning with Moltmann's account of religious experience.[71] Moltmann's Bloch-influenced hope embraces not only human hope in God's heaven, but also God's hope in humans, on earth. "In such [religious] experiences, man attains the unforgettable impression that he is, together with other people and this whole creation, the utopia of God."[72] "With the experiment 'man' and the experiment 'world' God has joined a hope. That gives man an unambiguous certainty of hope precisely at the place and time when he can no longer see any future ahead of him. It simultaneously places him in the open question of how he wants to fulfill, personally and together with society, that hope which God has placed in him and this world."[73] As Moltmann's theology develops, he increasingly transforms Bloch's future of possibilities—good or evil—into a more certain future hope in and of God's need of creation.

Moltmann draws on Bloch's future-philosophy to counter both protest atheism and escapist apocalypticism. He refutes the atheistic claim that the horrors of the World Wars and the Holocaust demonstrate the failure and death of God. Moltmann understands that the apparent absence of God can lead to the theodicy question, "If God cannot prevent or repair what happens in the world, then how can God be God?"[74]; he responds by pointing to the future, "which must be understood as 'mode

67. Moltmann, *History*, 169.
68. Moltmann, *Future*, 6.
69. Moltmann, *Experiment*, 24.
70. Ibid., 27.
71. Ibid.
72. Ibid.
73. Ibid.
74. Moltmann, "Theology as Eschatology," 4–5.

of God's being."⁷⁵ Life according to God's will, the kingdom of God, is coming still, in the future fulfillment of God's promises. Hope is not lost. "His deity will only be manifest with the coming of his kingdom. Only then will his glory be visible, and this revelation, this becoming visible, is the creation of new reality. God is not the ground of this world and not the ground of existence, but the God of the coming kingdom, which transforms this world and our existence radically."⁷⁶

Moltmann steps outside of a debate about whether God is or is not, by claiming an eschatological hope that says, "God's being is coming, that is, God is already present in the way in which his future masters the present because his future decides what becomes of the present."⁷⁷ In this way, Moltmann rebuts the atheist assumption that God is limited to that which happens in the world. The chaotic destruction, pain, and suffering of this world is not evidence against God, but that which God will transform in the fulfillment of promises in God's new creation. History matters, not as proof of God's weakness, but as that which God will renew when God indwells all of creation.⁷⁸

Before the promised transformation, God has not distanced Godself from the suffering and death of this world, as it may seem. Through Jesus' life, godforsakenness, and death God suffers pain, abandonment, and death *with* creation. In answer to the question, "Where was God in the Holocaust?", Moltmann replies that God was right there in the death camps, suffering alongside mothers holding their dead babies and children torn from their parents as they all faced certain death. God's future coming to creation names God's suffering presence on the cross and in history as the revelation of the coming resurrection of all.⁷⁹ "There is no suffering which in this history of God is not God's suffering; no death which has not been God's death in the history on Golgotha."⁸⁰ God's suffering presence with human suffering is a fundamental source of hope, when understood from the perspective of God's future indwelling with the transformed new creation. Moltmann posits that "with a trinitarian theology of the cross faith escapes the dispute between and the alternative of theism and atheism: God is not only other-worldly but also this-worldly; he is not only

75. Ibid., 9.
76. Ibid., 10.
77. Ibid.
78. Ibid.
79. Neal, *Theology*, 61
80. Ibid.; Moltmann, *Crucified*, 246.

Moltmann's Hope and Moltmannian Hope

God, but also man; he is not only rule, authority and law but the event of suffering, liberating love. Conversely, the death of the Son is not the 'death of God,' but the beginning of that God event in which the life-giving spirit of love emerges from the death of the Son and the grief of the Father."[81]

More recently, Moltmann reacts to apocalypticism with even less sympathy and more passion than his corrective to atheism. To those who claim that this world will end, Moltmann presents an eschatology of new creation and certain eternal life, which "rejects the traditional apocalyptic view of the coming of God."[82] He sees no place in Christian eschatology for end-time fatalism, which leads to human separation from creation; doomsday expectations distract Christians from responsible care for each other and the world. "The original and authentic Christian expectation of the future has nothing to do with the final destruction of the world God has created and loves."[83] Unlike contemporary escapist images of avenging angels laying waste to civilization and the natural world, Moltmann offers "the capacity to cherish this present life amidst death as a test of all eschatology, warning against any apocalypticism that sucks interest from this world by focusing on its 'end.'"[84] He sees no hope in the end of creation, nor any hope in the present defined by the imminent ruin of life as we know it. "Nothing is as fatal as the expectation of an unavoidable catastrophe."[85] Instead of fatalistic horror, the new beginnings promised by God and foreshadowed by Christ's resurrection constitute the hope determined by God's future new creation.

Moltmann's hope presents God's faithfulness and Christ's resurrection as future realities that shape the present. Resurrection hope extends the past into the future. "Christian hope is resurrection hope, and it proves its truth in the contradiction of the future prospects thereby offered and guaranteed for righteousness as opposed to sin, life as opposed to death, glory as opposed to suffering, peace as opposed to dissent."[86] Moltmann works to free eschatological hope from past, present, and future restraints. He criticizes the view that the Old Testament records a series of divine promises and their past fulfillment in the works of God. He affirms that divine promise marks God's relationship with Israel: the people of Israel

81. Moltmann, *Crucified*, 252.
82. Richardson, "Introduction."
83. Moltmann, "The Presence," 578.
84. Tanner, *Christ*, 383.
85. Moltmann, "Presence," 578.
86. Neal, *Theology*, 127.

began as nomadic people, dependent on the promise of new possibilities in new lands as they traveled, and they carried that promise with them into their new agrarian identity. Israel's faith, "which lives in forms of promise," a forward-looking faith that keeps them moving forward, helped them "to master the situations of the land settlement and later to master the situations of world history."[87] Moltmann extends those divine promises toward a future which is ever open, ever extending, and not yet fulfilled.

Some might argue that the Israelites may have understood God's action in their lives as the fulfillment of promises and the basis for hope; Moltmann critiques that understanding as relying on an abstract pattern of promise and premature, insufficient fulfillment. He corrects it with an anticipatory "not yet," which reads apparent fulfillment instead as a confirmation of greater things to come. The "not yet" of expectation describes the apparent fulfillment of promises in the past and present as the assurance of a greater hope to be completed in the resurrection of all. Moltmann reorients promise toward the future, which orients and establishes the present. Neal explains that, "in Moltmann's project, the future has priority over the present and the past to such an extent that the future, as it were, draws the present forward in a way that avoids any notion of the future being wholly determined by the present or the past."[88]

Thus, Moltmann dwells less on God's fulfilled promises to Israel and more on the eschatological divine fulfillment of all promises in the future. Moltmann claims that "the continuity with the Abrahamitic promise can therefore be taken neither as a product of historic development nor as a retrospective projection of faith. The continuity of the promise to Abraham exists according to Paul where the promise is eschatologically validated."[89] Accordingly, Moltmann argues, the gospel and the "event of Christ" do not fulfill God's promise to Abraham, but instead recast that promise in relation to God's future:[90]

> Paul discovers the promise to Abraham in the gospel of Christ and therefore recalls along with the gospel of Christ the promise to Abraham as well. This history of law and gospel takes its bearings from the theological problem of the past. The history of promise and gospel, however, takes its bearings from the eschatological problem of the future. Without the relation of the

---

87. Moltmann, *Theology*, 102.
88. Neal, *Theology*, 13.
89. Moltmann, *Theology*, 152.
90. Ibid.

gospel to what was promised in advance, it loses its own bearing on the eschatological future and threatens to transform itself into gnostic talk of revelation. Without relation to the promise in the gospel, faith loses the driving-power of hope and becomes credulity.[91]

Moltmann argues that *with* a promise-focused consideration of history, it is possible to understand God as opening up, rather than residing within, history through future abundance:

> If we would use this as a help towards understanding "the expanding and broadening history of promise," if we ask the reason for the abiding overplus of promise as compared with history, then we must again abandon every abstract schema of promise and fulfilment. We must then have recourse to the theological interpretation of this process: the reason for the overplus of promise and for the fact that it constantly overspills history lies in the inexhaustibility of the God of promise, who never exhausts himself in any historic reality but comes "to rest" only in a reality that wholly corresponds to him.[92]

God's openness to future possibilities reveals opportunities for change and hope otherwise obscured by the apparent constraints of the past and present. Moltmann explains that "it is the greatness of Ernst Bloch, whom we are basically following here, that he has developed not only a 'principle of hope' for man, but also an ontology of the not-yet-being and of possibility in the world process. Without real chances, the hope of man is meaningless."[93]

Moltmann's future-determined hope recasts the historical past of God's relationship with God's people: "the driving force behind thought and action is not prior condition but hope based on some sense of promise. Hope is a looking toward the future and an acting on the basis of that future."[94] He develops a theology of hope that resists cultural tendencies toward existential individualism; and he advocates a relational and community understanding and practice of hopeful action in the world,[95] arguing that the kingdom of God "does not mean merely salvation of the soul, individual rescue from the evil world, comfort for the troubled con-

---

91. Ibid.
92. Ibid., 106.
93. Moltmann, *Experiment*, 25.
94. Sturm, "Praxis," 740.
95. Ibid., 739.

science, but also the realization of the eschatological *hope of justice*, the *humanizing* of man, the *socializing* of humanity, *peace* for all creation."[96] Moltmann opens up possibilities by stretching out divine promises toward their future, eschatological, completion. When that time comes, God will fulfill the Old Testament promises, Christ will fulfill the law, Christ's resurrection will be effective for creation, and the Spirit will draw all together in new life. The Spirit is a downpayment, the sign that Christ's resurrection will be completed in the future resurrection of all creation.[97] Christ is a guarantor of previous promises still to be realized. Christ's resurrection does not so much accomplish salvation as it makes the future: "It is the inner necessity of the Christ event itself, the tendency of which is finally to bring out in all things the eternal life latent in him and the justice of God latent in him."[98] Moltmann understands Paul's declaration that, "In Christ all the promises of God are yea and Amen" (2 Cor 1:20), to indicate that, in Christ, God's promises are renewed rather than completed: "in him they are confirmed and validated, but not yet fulfilled."[99] Thus, Christ's resurrection from the dead stands as an offering, "a possible object of confident hope," or "an event which is understood only in the *modus* of promise."[100] Drawing on Paul (Rom 15:4), Moltmann argues that "what the scripture that was 'written before our time' offers must therefore contain possibilities and a future to which present hope can be directed."[101]

In the historical present, Moltmann calls for the work of Christians to be counter to the world that conflicts with Christ's future for Christ and the world. Moltmann directs Christians to a missional response to God's promises, a response that issues in a commitment to work and wait in hope for the coming fulfillment of those promises. He demonstrates his concern for those whose living conditions now are full of suffering and lack, by advocating an anti-establishmentarian Christan hope that "will therefore endeavour to lead our modern institutions away from their own immanent tendency towards stabilization, will make them uncertain, historify them and open them to that elasticity which is demanded by openness towards the future for which it hopes."[102] To share the good news in words

96. Moltmann, *Theology*, 329; cited in Sturm, "Praxis," 739–40.
97. Moltmann, *Experiences*, 100.
98. Moltmann, *Theology*, 216.
99. Ibid., 228.
100. Ibid., 190.
101. Ibid., 153; Rom 15:4.
102. Moltmann, *Theology*, 330.

and deeds now with Moltmannian hope means to point toward that which God has promised, which Christ has affirmed, and toward which the Spirit is drawing the universe. At the time of transformation, God will bring eternity into our time, God will dwell in creation, and God will establish God's kingdom for all of creation. Until then, we live in the transitional kingdom of the present that the future has made possible.

Moltmann grounds hope not in God's past promises and fulfillments, but in the eschatological future, which serves as the beginning for history, suffering and death, the cross, and Christ's resurrection which leads to the resurrection of all. Sometimes, Moltmann identifies the future as open, unconstrained by the past and the present, something new beyond the time and history we know, toward an open future of possibility that requires a resurrection not limited to experienced reality: "The real category of history is no longer the past and the transient, but the future."[103] This is the hope he appreciatively adopts from Bloch, although at other times, Moltmann's confidence about the resurrection of the world in God's new creation seems to close off the future. Bloch allows for all possibilites in the future. Richard Bauckham suggests: "For Bloch, hope negates the negative and transcends it by making every 'not' into a 'not yet.' But Moltmann responds that such hope can surmount only such *relative* negatives as have within them the possibility of becoming a 'not yet.'"[104] Moltmann's certainty about universal salvation and the ultimate good of God's new earth, as it is in heaven, stands in tension with an open future. Moltmann counters theological claims about what has already been accomplished in Christ's resurrection, pointing instead to the final resurrection. Future hope stands not on what God has done, but on what God will do in the future—a coming future that determines the present. "We do not look then from the present into the future, but from the future into the present. We do not *extrapolate* the future out of the present; rather we *anticipate* the future in the present."[105]

Moltmann does not dismiss history in favor of the future; he criticizes utopian views of a heaven that seem to cancel out or downplay creation and its trials in favor of a wholly other and unearthly eternal life: "we do not interpret past history. We do not emancipate ourselves from history altogether, but we enter into the history that is determined by the promised and guaranteed *eschaton,* and we expect from it not only the

---

103. Ibid., 260.
104. Ibid., 44.
105. Moltmann, *Experiment,* 52.

future of the present but also the future of the past."[106] He counters the idea that God adds the eschatological divine kingdom as a special bonus at the end of history. The influence of Greek philosphy, according to Moltmann, establishes the modern understanding of history as a cycle of the known, upset by the crisis of the new, which becomes the known which is upset by the next crisis of the new. God's new creation yet to come is not another crisis to upset or cancel out the familiar.[107] For Moltmann, the true historicity of history only comes when knowledge is filled with a forward moving sense of mission and growth for the world[108]; and God's future "is the mode of his being that is dominant in history."[109] Thus, Moltmann affirms Bloch's claim that "the nerve of the true historical concept is and remains the new,"[110] and he connects this history of the new with Paul's Christology: "If it is true that for Paul the lordship of Christ is limited and passing, and merely serves the purpose of giving way to the sole rule of God; if, for Paul, 'Christ is God's representative over against a world which is not yet fully subjected to God,' then the history of Christ and the presence of the Spirit must be understood in the light of this future and as moving towards it."[111]

Moltmann's emphasis on the hope of the future shapes the relation between his account of the cross and the resurrection. Christ's suffering and death on the cross serves as a revelation of hope, because Christ shares in human suffering and death, forging an intimate relationship between God and humans. "In surrendering himself to a God-forsaken death, Christ brought God to the God-forsaken."[112] By embracing all suffering and death in his own suffering and death, Christ both demonstrates God's love *and* brings God to those who suffer.[113] Now, no one need face suffering and death alone, since God's consoling presence reaches the depths of despair.[114]

In *Theology of Hope*, Moltmann describes the primary source of hope in Christ's resurrection and its promise of resurrection of all. He applies

---

106. Moltmann, *Theology*, 154.
107. Ibid., 230, 260.
108. Ibid., 262–63.
109. Moltmann, "Theology as Eschatology," 27.
110. Moltmann, *Theology*, 262.
111. Moltmann, "Theology as Eschatology," 27.
112. Moltmann, *End*, 70.
113. Ibid.
114. Moltmann, *Theology*, 203.

Bloch's open future focus to Christian hope determined by the resurrection life that Christ's resurrection anticipates. In the resurrection, God creates the world anew by joining God's own presence to and in the midst of creation forever. At the same time, the future of God's new world in the eschatological resurrection grounds Christ's resurrection. "The final resurrection is the basis of Jesus' resurrection. Rather than standing at the Open Tomb and looking forward, we are to project ourselves into the final resurrection. From there the resurrection of Jesus can be legitimatized."[115] Thus, Moltmann argues that the final resurrection of God amidst creation supplies the meaning for Christ's resurrection as the extension of the divine promises to Israel. He explains that "the resurrection of Christ was not understood merely as the first instance of a general resurrection of the dead and as a beginning of the revelation of the divinity of God in the non-existent, but also as the source of the risen life of all believers and as a confirmation of the promise which will be fulfilled in all and will show itself in the very deadliness of death to be irresistible."[116]

Moltmann tempers his early resurrection hope[117] with an emphasis on the hope of the crucifixion in *The Crucified God*.[118] He turns toward Christ's suffering and death as the source of hope through divine participation in the depths of humanity's unmitigated abandonment: "It is precisely here that the divine reason for the reconciliation of the universe is to be found. It is not the optimistic dream of a purified humanity, it is Christ's descent into hell that is the ground for the confidence that nothing will be lost but that everything will be brought back again and gathered into the eternal kingdom of God. The true Christian foundation for the hope of universal salvation is the theology of the cross, and the realistic consequence of the theology of the cross can only be the restoration of all things."[119] He asserts that God's primary identity is love, and there is no love without suffering.[120] Christ's suffering is the realization of hope[121] because it shows God's suffering in love and love in suffering: Christ reveals God who suffers and who takes suffering into God's own divine life. God is revealed precisely in the depths of the opposite of God—"in godless-

---

115. Scaer, "Moltmann," 73.
116. Moltmann, *Theology*, 197.
117. Ibid.
118. Moltmann, *Future of Creation*, 61.
119. Moltmann, *Crucified*, 251.
120. Ibid., 299.
121. Ibid., 222.

ness and God-forsakenness."[122] Crucifixion, the death of God on the cross, must be claimed in order for Christians to see and respond to the reality of the world. He writes that "it is only when Christian theology gives itself up unconditionally and without reserve to the primal event of faith that it will become a critical and liberating theology, and, becoming painfully conscious of the limitations of its economic, social and cultural conditioning, will go beyond these."[123]

Moltmann's turn to the cross affects his entire theology. In *The Crucified God* he writes: "The death of Jesus on the cross is the centre of all Christian theology. It is not the only theme of theology, but it is in effect the entry to its problems and answers on earth. All Christian statements about God, about creation, about sin and death have their focal point in the crucified Christ. All Christian statements about history, about the church, about faith and sanctification, about the future and about hope stem from the crucified Christ."[124] Later, in *The Experiment Hope*, he ties together hope constituted by the cross with eschatological hope in the coming of God in the fulfillment of resurrection. God's future kingdom establishes the meaning of the cross, as it does the resurrection, but crucifixion hope adds a present connection between those who suffer and God who suffers.[125] Neal explains that Moltmann connects Christ's passion with all of creation's suffering: Moltmann "identifies the cross as a source of hope for the outcasts of society, because the cross is a source of hope since it best exemplifies the suffering nature of God, who not only suffers in the event of the cross and also allows suffering to enter into the divine community, but is present in all suffering."[126] Moltmann argues that crucifixion hope keeps the focus of hope from straying toward utopian visions that obscure the site of suffering, the location of God's participation in this world, now. On his terms, the crucifixion releases humans from escapism and detachment, while providing hope for the hopeless:

> The cross of Christ is the sign of God's hope on earth for all those who live here in the shadow of the cross. Theology of hope is at its hard core theology of the cross. The cross of Christ is the presently given form of the kingdom of God on earth. In the crucified Christ we view the future of God. Everything else is

122. Moltmann, *Future of Creation*, 78.
123. Ibid., 61.
124. Moltmann, *Crucified*, 204.
125. Moltmann, *Experiment*, 64.
126. Neal, *Theology*, 158.

> dreams, fantasies, and mere wish images. Hope born out of the cross of Christ distinguishes Christian faith from superstition as well as from disbelief. The freedom generated by the cross distinguishes Christian faith from optimism as well as from terrorism.[127]

With that freedom, Christians are able to share with God in God's love. The experience of God's love now reflects and points toward the reality of the future that is coming with God. Moltmann continues: "The resurrection of the crucified Christ revealed the kingdom of the coming God as the power of anticipatory love. This love has no conditions placed on it and knows no boundaries. Through the love manifested in the resurrection that which is hateful is rendered lovable. Thus hope is disseminated for the hopeless. The future is inaugurated, not by way of examples and commands, but through the love, the patience, and the sacrifice of God."[128]

The hope that Bloch describes faces an open future, whose outcome is undetermined and unknowable, and this hope is necessarily disappointed: hope with too much certainty to be disappointed is not hope. It remains hope, even in the face of disappointment, because of the possibilities that openness provides.[129] Moltmann observes that the hope he proposes reflects Bloch's hope: "Like Bloch's hope, it is not certainty, for it is directed not to the visible, but to what is invisible. Nevertheless, it is not hope in an open possibility, and therefore it does not remain in the suspension of indecisiveness. Since it is hope in the power of God which calls nonbeing into being, it recognizes the beginning in the end. Its way is not the possibility of disappointment, but actual disappointment, for it is a hope which shines out of the denial of all possible hope through the crucifixion of Christ into the Easter appearances."[130] Moltmann's hope shares with Bloch's the anticipation of the future; however, Moltmann's hope rests not an openness but on what has been begun in the crucifixion. "The hope of which the Bible speaks, on the other hand, is 'hope for what we do not see' (Rom. 8:24–25), 'the conviction of things unseen' (Heb. 11.1)."[131] Despite the less-open and more determined hope in the coming of God, Christian hope includes inescapable disappointment, since it is

---

127. Moltmann, *Experiment*, 57–58.
128. Ibid., 57.
129. Ibid., 36.
130. Ibid.
131. Ibid., 37.

through the crucifixion, through the complete loss of hope, that hope can glimpse the future of hope in the kingdom of God.[132]

Moltmann holds the cross and the resurrection tightly together, since neither makes sense without the other. Resurrection hope contradicts present-day brokenness with God's faithfulness, manifest in God's suffering with those who suffer and in God's future fulfillment of promises.[133] God's compassionate suffering in unbearable human experiences supplies crucifixion hope in the ultimate indwelling of God throughout creation. The relationship between the cross and the resurrection remains in tension throughout Moltmann's work. His presentation of the cross as the revelation of God's full embrace of suffering and death supports his argument with the atheist objections: he claims that God is not absent in catastrophe but present and experiencing all human experience. God's companionship with humans in their suffering also helps support Moltmann's argument with Christian apocalypticists: he argues that the presence of God with humans in history deflates the belief that God will come to wipe out creation and history.

The consolation of God's suffering presence with humans sets up and points toward the future promised by the resurrection; but more importantly, the future fulfillment of the resurrection provides the meaning for the suffering and death that God shares with humans. Moltmann's understanding of the resurrection overlaps with the previous and ongoing Christian teaching that the hope of resurrection overcomes death "by proclaiming the victory of praise and therewith of life over death."[134] From that foundational point, Moltmann adds two claims distinctive to his theology of hope. First, he asserts that the resurrection victory over death is God's victory over the very absence of God. In Moltmann's account of Christ's suffering and death, Christ experiences the ontological absence of God. The suffering and death of human experience is not simply a matter of perception, in the context of the world's sin and brokenness; it is the actual absence of God. Christ's *experience* of being forsaken by God on the cross and in death is God's *actual* abandonment of Christ. Since God suffers when Christ suffers, God Godself is abandoned by God. The resurrection marks God's victory over God's own abandonment, so that humans will no longer be abandoned by God. In the eschatological fullness of resurrection the the kingdom of God, God will redress the abandonment of creation

---

132. Ibid., 36–37.
133. Neal, *Theology*, 127.
134. Moltmann, *Theology*, 210.

Moltmann's Hope and Moltmannian Hope

and of God, when God indwells this world made new. No longer will there be any separation from God: everything will be in God and God will be present in everything.[135] God embraces within Godself the brokenness and godforsakenness of creation through Christ's suffering and death on the cross. God consoles creation by sharing in the depths of total divine abandonment.

Second, Moltmann argues that Christ's resurrection does not so much accomplish God's victory over death as it promises victory that is to come.[136] Paul describes the kingdom of God effected by Christ's resurrection as both already and not-yet. Moltmann shares with Paul this characterization of Christ's resurrection: Moltmann directs hope toward Christ's coming (rather than toward Christ's second coming) and names Christ's arrival as "a future which is already present, yet without ceasing to be future."[137] Moltmann adds a heavy emphasis on the not-yet aspect of Christ's resurrection, the promissory note of universal resurrection to come.[138] The revelation of Christ's Easter resurrection does not proclaim the completion of the past or the fulfillment of divine promises, but the release of the unfinished future.[139] The freedom of the resurrection is found in openness to the future. Christ's resurrection affirms God's promises to Israel and opens history to a future unbound by what has happened, to a future that is truly new. Resurrection is therefore a process, rather than a completed event: "Resurrection doesn't mean a closed fact. It means a way: the transition from death to life."[140] And the crucifixion is God's connection through suffering with creation in suffering, rather than the death of a man or the death of God.[141] Moltmann identifies the crucifixion as an event that has happened and yet is still available for participation. Since the crucifixion, people can continue to experience God's suffering presence, brought to creation through Christ's suffering. Christ's resurrection also happened, but its primary accomplishment is the opening of the future toward the open end of God's new creation, at which point all of creation will experience the full existence of God interpenetrated with their own lives, and at which point Christ's resurrection will no longer be

135. Moltmann, *End*, 158.
136. Moltmann, *Theology*, 211–6.
137. Moltmann, *End*, 89.
138. Moltmann, *Theology*, 211.
139. Ibid., 88.
140. Neal, *Theology*, 163.
141. Moltmann, *Coming*, 274.

necessary as the promise of resurrection, since the resurrection of all will fulfill human and divine eschatological hope. Moltmann recasts Christ's crucifixion and the resurrection as the effects of God's not-yet-fulfilled powers and as the opened door to the future new creation that God brings.

As noted above, Moltmann began his theology of hope with the proclamation of the future, opened to God's new creation. Later, he turned to the hope accessible through God's suffering on the cross. Throughout the rest of his work, he develops both hopes as inseparable; and he negotiates a complicated relationship between the two. Resurrection hope declares an open future, full of possibilities and the confirmation that all of God's promises will be fulfilled in a glorious end-time. Therefore, according to Moltmann, "the resurrection of Christ was not understood merely as the first instance of a general resurrection of the dead and as a beginning of the revelation of the divinity of God in the non-existent, but also as the source of the risen life of all believers and as a confirmation of the promise which will be fulfilled in all and will show itself in the very deadliness of death to be irresistible."[142] Moltmann presents a crucifixion hope that accepts that life is full of suffering and death; it shows God's love for creation in God's participation in the hopelessness of creation; and it perseveres on the way toward God's open future of the full resurrection. He writes: "God in Auschwitz and Auschwitz in the crucified God—that is the basis for a real hope which both embraces and overcomes the world, and the ground for a love which is stronger than death and can sustain death. It is the ground for living with the terror of history and the end of history, and nevertheless remaining in love and meeting what comes in openness for God's future. It is the ground for living and bearing guilt and sorrow for the future of man in God."[143]

In order to connect crucifixion hope and resurrection hope, certain hope and open hope, the already and the not-yet, Moltmann uses his own version of the Hegelian dialectic. In *Theology of Hope*, he presents the cross and the resurrection as oppositional, held together in Christ: "The identity of Jesus can be understood only as an identity *in*, but not above and beyond, cross and resurrection—that is, that it must remain bound up with the dialectic of cross and resurrection. In that case the contradictions between the cross and the resurrection can neither be reduced to the cross, as showing its meaning, nor can the cross be reduced to the resurrection, as its preliminary. It is formally a question of a dialectical identity which

---

142. Moltmann, *Theology*, 211.
143. Moltmann, *Coming*, 278.

exists only through the contradiction, and of a dialectic which exists in the identity."[144] Moltmann names the end of God's kingdom as the site for the resolution of mutually negating and affirming cross and resurrection. He points to 1 Cor 15:28, to show how Christ's subjection to God's authority and God's gift of authority to Christ find eschatological unity: "What happened between the cross and the Easter appearances is then an eschatological event which has its goal in future revelation and universal fulfillment . . . Their dialectic is an open dialectic, which will find its resolving synthesis only in the *eschaton* of all things."[145] Moltmann's progression of theological themes moves from the hope of the resurrection, to the hope of the crucified God, and on to the Trinity. In this way, resurrection hope and crucifixion hope neither cancel each other out nor subsume one into the other. The cross reins in resurrection hope, when Christ draws God and creation through the crucifixion toward the anticipation of the eschaton. Then the Holy Spirit carries both hopes ahead as one hope, as God and creation prepare for the new, complete creation that will fulfill all hopes. Moltmann modulates a dialectical relationship into his theology of the Trinity, in which the Holy Spirit shares God's presence with creation and includes all of creation in the open Trinity of interpenetrating relationships.[146] The hope of the cross and resurrection dialectic finds resolution in the new creation's divine and human trinitarian relationships.

Although Moltmann aspires to dialectically balanced resolutions, his account of hope gradually moves away from Bloch's open future, in which nothing is yet decided, toward a more consistently confident hope, through the cross and the resurrection interpreted by the future: "Christianity is wholly and entirely confident hope, a stretching out to what is ahead, and a readiness for a fresh start. *Future* is not just something or other to do with Christianity. It is the essential element of the faith which is specifically Christian: the keynote of all its hymns, the dawn colouring of the new day in which everything is bathed."[147] The content of that future, the new creation shared by the Creator and creation, establishes the reconciliation of cross and reconciliation and God's loving justice on earth for all.

---

144. Moltmann, *Theology*, 200.
145. Moltmann, *Theology*, 201.
146. Meeks, "Foreword," xi.
147. Moltmann, *End*, 87.

Our Only Hope

Moltmann's eschatological hope ends with the new beginning of the kingdom of God here.[148] That kingdom does not sit high in the clouds, apart from this earth; nor does it stand on its own, apart from God. Moltmann explains that "the Creator does not remain detached from his creation. He enters into it, so as to make it his eternal dwelling. The whole creation becomes the temple of the Eternal One. Through this indwelling God interpenetrates everything with his livingness and his beauty, and all things will thereby be newly formed so that they conform to God and correspond to him in eternity. This new world will then become *God's eternal home country,* 'on earth as it is in heaven.'"[149] The end which is the beginning comes when God, the Creator, comes to the earth to be at home with the new creation on earth.

Moltmann interprets the Lord's Prayer to indicate that God's kingdom will come on earth, and it will be as God's kingdom in heaven. The Lord's Prayer as presented in scripture does not gain punctuation until subsequent translations. In English translations, commas contribute to the interpretation: "Your kingdom come, your will be done, on earth as it is in heaven." This is frequently understood as: "May your kingdom come, and may your will be done on earth as your will is done in heaven." Moltmann counters with a different emphasis. He understands the Lord's Prayer to be asserting that God and God's kingdom will come to earth; God will inhabit the earth which, made anew, will be the location for the kingdom of God; and this kingdom reflects God's incarnation in Christ. He argues that "the model for this view of the kingdom of God is Christ himself, for Christ is 'the kingdom of God in person,' as the New Testament emphasizes: 'In him the whole fullness of deity dwells bodily' (Col 2.9). What we have to expect of the coming kingdom of God on earth as it is in heaven is nothing less than the cosmic incarnation of God, in which divinity and humanity interpenetrate one another mutually as they do in the 'incarnation' of the eternal Word of God and in the 'outpouring of God's Spirit on all flesh.'"[150] Moltmann's account of the new creation fits within his distinction between God's initial creation and the coming creation for which both God and creation hope, the creation which establishes from the future the basis for and the ethics of eschatological hope.

Moltmann reconsiders the creation of the world narrated in scripture and theology in order to shift hope from a return to the goodness of God's

---

148. Neal, *Theology,* 216.
149. Moltmann, *End,* 158.
150. Ibid., 158–59.

Moltmann's Hope and Moltmannian Hope

pre-fall world to the anticipated arrival of a new and better creation. He presents an altered version of *creatio ex nihilo*, revised to cohere with God's passibility, in which God's act of creating is preceded by God's withdrawal of Godself, to make room for creation. Moltmann answers the question, "How can God create out of 'nothing' when there cannot be such a thing as nothing, since his essence is everywhere and interpenetrates everything?" by arguing that "*God's self-humiliaton* begins" with creation.[151] "God withdrew his omnipresence in order to concede space for the limited presence of the creation. In this way, creation comes into being in the space of God's *kenosis*."[152] Hence, even though God creates out of nothing, God lessens or diminishes Godself in the process by conceding space and moving aside. "The first act of all is not an act of revelation but one of limitation."[153] From God's initial withdrawal, God creates a creation born of God's lack, of a certain incompleteness of God. This creation is less than perfect and turns to the sin and corruption that precedes the great Flood.

According to Moltmann, Noah's story reveals God's dismay with God's initial creation. "God 'was sorry' for having created human beings and 'it grieved him to his heart' (Gen.6.6b)."[154] He reads the description of God's grief at the state of creation to mean that God suffers for God's mistakes.[155] "As God sees creation now [before the Flood], it is by no means 'very good,' (which was the way he initially saw it according to the end of the first creation account [Gen.1.31]). On the contrary; it is very bad. We might say that God's creation had gone wrong. God suffers from the corruption of what he has created. This grief has rightly been called 'the divine pain.' In order to surmount it, the Creator revokes his resolve to create, and lets his earthly creation perish. This is God's 'repentance'—his act of regret."[156] After the Flood's destruction, God's faithfulness to "his resolve to create" leads God to promise never to destroy creation again.[157] God recommits to sustaining creation, despite God's regrets about that creation and despite Creation's persistent corruption. Moltmann explains that "everything that comes and endures after the catastrophe and is not again destroyed issues from God's pain over the beings he has created,

---

151. Moltmann, Trinity, 59.
152. Neal, Theology, 142–43.
153. Ibid., 80.
154. Moltmann, End, 39.
155. Ibid.
156. Ibid.
157. Ibid., 40.

who are ruining themselves. God suffers the world in its contradictions, and endures it in his long-suffering, instead of annihilating it. He takes upon himself the dissonance between the world's creation and its corruption, so that in spite of its corruption the world may live."[158] God's faithfulness perdures, even though God must experience the worst of creation so that creation might survive.

Much of Christianity has narrated God's faithfulness in terms of God's promises and the fulfillment of those promises throughout the history of Israel, the life of Christ, the death and resurrection of Christ, Christ's ascension, the lives of the earliest Christians, and the presence of the Holy Spirit throughout the history of the church. Moltmann presents God's faithfulness in terms of God's promises and affirmations that those promises will be fulfilled. God's fulfilled promises will constitute God's kingdom. God's faithfulness confirms and extends God's promises eschatologically, while supporting Christian hope across time and locations. Moltmann explains that God's faithfulness does not indicate a static, unmerciful God, but God who is constant in faithfulness throughout history. God is the faithful God of promise (Heb 2:3; 11:11), and "his essence is not his absoluteness as such, but the faithfulness with which he reveals and identifies himself in the history of his promise as 'the same.'"[159]

Moltmann argues that the God of the new creation is the same God of the *creatio ex nihilo*, but the new creation will not be a return to the beginning of the first creation or a repeat of the first creation so far. Moltmann claims that there is no reason to hope for a return to the conditions of God's initial creation, established as it is through God's incompleteness, when the true and fulfilled creation is yet to come.[160] "The goal of this history of creation is not a return to the paradisial primordial condition. Its goal is the revelation of the glory of God. It is true that this end 'corresponds' to the beginning in the sense that it represents the fulfillment of the real promise implanted in creation itself; but the new creation of heaven and earth in the kingdom of glory surpasses everything that can be told about creation in the beginning."[161] Hence, according to Moltmann, eschatological hope looks toward the future creation in which God will be present within all of creation.

---

158. Ibid., 41.
159. Moltmann, *Theology*, 143.
160. Neal, *Theology*, 216.
161. Moltmann, *God in Creation*, 141.

In the beginning, Moltmann explains, God created the world out of a freedom determined by love.[162] God's love is God's essence, such that God could not be God without needing to create the world. "Creation is a fruit of God's longing for 'his Other' and for that Other's free response to the divine love. That is why the idea of the world is inherent in the nature of God himself from eternity."[163] Further, "it is in accordance with the love which is God that he should fashion a creation which he rejoices over . . . Not to do this would contradict the love which God is."[164] Moltmann recognizes that God's freedom in creating may be described as necessity, since God's love requires that God create, but he is more comfortable qualifying God's freedom than claiming the primacy of God's free will, untempered by love. Moltmann's rejection of an impassible God includes the rejection of an absolute, utterly independent God.[165] Moltmann's understanding of the creation by the passible God "is informed by the confluence of necessity, freedom, and love, which condition the divine nature."[166] Moltmann presents the apparently conflicting categories of God's freedom and the necessity of creation within the context of a dialectical relationship. If God is only free, then God may not have created the world; if creation is only a necessity, God is not free. In either extreme, there is no place for love. Therefore, God's freedom to create and the necessity of creation rely on each other and on God's essential character of love. The new creation will provide God's true freedom and creation's true freedom, through God's love.

> What concept of freedom is appropriate for God? If we start from the point of view of the created being, the Creator appears as almighty and gracious. His freedom has no limits, and his commitment to what he has created is without obligation. But if we start from the Creator himself, the self-communication of his goodness in love to his creation is not a matter of his free will. It is the self-evident operation of his eternal nature. The essential activity of God *is* the eternal resolve of his will, and the eternal resolve of his will *is* his essential activity. In other words, God is not entirely free when he can do and leave undone what he likes; he is entirely free when he is entirely himself. He loves

---

162. Neal, *Theology*, 135.
163. Neal, *Theology*, 134; Moltmann, *Trinity*, 106.
164. Neal, *Theology*, 135; Moltmann, *Trinity*, 58.
165. Neal, *Theology*, 136.
166. Ibid., 137.

the world in the surrender of his Son with the very same love which he *is*, from eternity to eternity (John 3.16; 1 John 4.16).[167]

In Moltmann's presentation, God hopes, along with creation, for the new creation, which will bring freedom for God and for creation. Neal explains that, for Moltmann, "eschatological justification does not return creation and humanity to the beginning as it was, but brings about what was never there, a freedom for the divine, instead of oppressing nothingness."[168]

Moltmann's God of hope is not perfect but needs the perfection that will come when God comes to creation in the midst of the new, completed creation of the fulfilled future. His God is not a simple, unified, and self-enclosed entity, because God longs to draw all of created life in to the perichoretic relationship of the Trinity.[169] The passible God of hope is infinite *and* subject to creation's limitations; God will be drawn into the finitude of redeemed creatures at the eschaton. In the end/beginning, the goodness of God enters into the evil and death of the imperfect creation, in order to recreate the entire world in a just and righteous universal salvation. "The consummation of creation is something *new* over against creation-in-the-beginning."[170] At times, Moltmann describes the circumstances of the new creation as the finite enveloping the infinite. At other times, he argues that the new beginning includes all that comes before: "The important point is to link the eschatological category *novum* with the anamnetic category of repetition in such a way that the beginning is gathered up into the end, and the consummation brings back everything that had ever been before."[171] Either way, God's coming in and to the new creation renders everything new, good, and intermingled with God. Moltmann notes that, "if we speak of the 'coming God,' his future becomes the source of the times. His coming constantly creates new time in history. If his creation at the end of history means 'Behold, I make all things new,' we are able to anticipate in it that his grace is 'new every morning.'"[172] The coming of God interrupts history and breaks into the repetition of the old that can constrain creation.

---

167. Moltmann, *God*, 82–83.

168. Neal, *Theology*, 216. Here, Neal cites Moltmann: "If we apply this to theology we are not able to speak of a 'becoming God' but only of the 'coming God.' This is the difference between eschatology and process philosophy" (*Experiment*, 52–3).

169. Moltmann *Crucified*, 249.

170. Moltmann, *Coming*, 265.

171. Ibid.

172. Moltmann, *Experiment*, 53.

Moltmann corrects Christianity's tendency to embrace a mythological circularity about time: "strictly speaking, this circle of the Christian drama of redemption would have to repeat itself to all eternity."[173] Instead, Moltmann argues, time begins with creation. Creation is changeable and open, "a temporal one, not yet an eternal creation. As a *temporal creation* it is projected towards a future in which it is to become an *eternal creation*."[174] The temporal creation we know will be opened to its future as the eternal creation of God's home, here with us.

The People of Hope

The anthropology that accompanies Moltmann's theology of hope promises that humanity will reach the coming new life through Christ's non-punitive judgment that includes all in love. People need not fear Christ's judgment, and they need not fear the loss of this world, since the new life will be here. Through his suffering and death, Christ has brought God to share suffering and, in the future, to share the world, with creation. The ethics of this hope calls for people who have experienced the love of God's godforsakenness in their own godforsakenness to reach out to those who are suffering and in great need.

Moltmann develops a theological anthropology that leans toward the more confident side of his open-future eschatology of hope. Through Christ's suffering and death for people, people are freed from history and opened to alternatives. In the alternative future of hope that Moltmann proclaims, God will come to this creation to make it new and God's judgment will embrace all in love. This hope requires a release from the limitations of history, so that people can catch a glimpse of the possibilities determined by the future. Moltmann critiques the common error of extrapolating from the present to the future: "Extrapolation sees the future as an extrapolated and extended present and it hence kills the very future character of the future. The only people who have any interest in prolonging this rule of the present over the future are those who possess and dominate the present. The have-nots, the suffering and the guilty, however, ask for a *different* future; they ask for change and liberation."[175] There is nothing to hope for in more of the same.

---

173. Moltmann, *Coming*, 263.

174. Ibid. Moltmann here affirms Augustine's claim that time begins with creation (*Conf.* 9.30, 40).

175. Moltmann, *Future of Creation*, 43. This point bears particular attention as it is

Moltmann explains that those who hope see past those who are mired in the present, toward a world not bound by current injustice. "The Christian hope, in so far as it is Christian, is the hope of those who have no future. It is therefore a hope in contradiction of self-satisfied optimists and of equally self-satisfied pessimists."[176] Moltmann's hope directly addresses the conditions of those whose lives are constituted by suffering. Christ's death and resurrection open a future beyond the reach of death and beyond the injustice of the present. He writes: "The resurrection of the crucified Christ, however, reveals a new justice, which is the justification of the godless. The hope in resurrection within Christianity is therefore no longer ambiguous, but straightforward and clear. It faces without fear God's future as a joyous hope in the power of divine grace, which *even death cannot resist*. It is indeed a hope for the hopeless. Through the crucified Christ the future of resurrection and life, of freedom, joy, and justice is opened up to those who live in guilt without hope and who must die in fear without a future."[177] Just as God transforms Christ from death to glory, so too will God transform the bodies of creation from death to eternal life.[178] The transformation of the crucified Christ affects the political structure of present life. The powerful authorities of government, finance, and the institutional church lose their strength, in the eyes of those who know Christ crucified, and hope now lies with the oppressed, "with a loving solidarity with the dispossessed."[179] The hope of the dispossessed, the future that the crucifixion opens up, is not only an alternative to the closed present, but a clear future of eternal resurrection life.

Moltmann describes the coming kingdom of the new creation as the kingdom of God's justice, the reconciliation necessary for the coming of God. Moltmann objects to a focus on how to punish and justify the guilty, "the only question asked in the Church's tradition [of the theological doctrine of justification]"; instead he attends to the victims of wickedness.[180] Therefore, God's justice brings comfort to the oppressed and righteousness to the oppressors, without fear of punishing judgment. He argues that "'The Last Judgment' is not a terror. In the truth of Christ it is the most

---

an aspect of Moltmann's theology that does not continue unalloyed into Moltmann*ian* theology of hope.

176. Moltmann, *Man*, 117.
177. Moltmann, *Experiment*, 57.
178. Moltmann, *Coming*, 57.
179. Moltmann, *Future of Creation*, 17.
180. Moltmann, *End*, 53.

wonderful thing that can be proclaimed to men and women. It is a source of endlessly consoling joy to know, not just that the murderers will finally fail to triumph over their victims, but that they cannot in eternity even remain the murderers of their victims. The eschatological doctrine about the restoration of all things has these two sides: *God's judgment*, which puts all things to rights, and *God's kingdom*, which awakens to new life."[181] He argues further that Christ's judgment to come does not divide people into sheep and goats, sending the worthy to heaven and the guilty to hell. God will not separate and then damn sinful people who do not make the standard of righteousness necessary for salvation. Instead, according to Moltmann, God will destroy the powers of evil that separate creation from God: "What will be annihilated is Nothingness, what will be slain is death, what will be dissolved is the power of evil, what will be separated from all created beings is the power of evil, what will be separated from all created beings is separation from God, sin. The ground is then prepared for the new creation of all things."[182] Christ's judgment, "God's creative justice," is not the end; it leads to the new creation.[183]

Moltmann explains that the people of hope contribute to God's creative justice by helping God's own justification. "Through the justice that creates and puts right, God anticipates the justice and righteousness of his coming kingdom through which he will redeem the world, and in this way he justifies himself to the world." "God justifies us, and we justify God."[184] In the coming kingdom, God and humans will live in righteousness together, in a creation free of limitations to God as well as limitations to humans. "Justifying faith is not just a faith through which human beings are justified; it is faith through which God is justified too."[185] Here, Moltmann appreciates that Bloch not only opens up the future, but also opens up humans to their God and God to humans. "Ernst Bloch puts it as follows[:] 'Only the wicked exist through their God, but the righteous—God exists through them, and in their hands is laid the sanctification of the Name, the name of God itself.' That is our justification of God in the

---

181. Moltmann, *Coming*, 255.

182. Moltmann, *End*, 145.

183. Ibid., 143. Also: "This divine justice is the lead-in to the new creation: "'Behold, I make all things new' (Rev. 21.5)'" (ibid.).

184. Moltmann, *End*, 78.

185. Ibid.

world."[186] In God's kingdom, the justified God will be all in all with the justfied creation.

The new creation of justified people and justified God embraces bodies and the world. Moltmann critiques Christian eschatology that hopes for the release of souls from bodies and the world.[187] His correction to Christian teaching names God as Redeemer *and* Creator, who necessarily redeems all of creation in a "human and earthly future."[188] "God would contradict himself if he were not to redeem everything he has made. The God who created the universe will one day be 'all in all' (I Cor.15.28). Why else should he have created everything? Cosmic eschatology is not required for the sake of some 'universalism' or other; it is necessary for God's sake. There are not two Gods, a Creator God and a Redeemer God. There is one God. It is for his sake that the unity of redemption and creation has to be thought." [189] Moltmann encourages Christians to think of the eschatological unity of redemption and all of creation so that they might express their hope through active care for the earth. Moltmann convicts traditional Christianity for its hope for life with God apart from this world, and he charges Christians to more responsible action for this earth and in the leadership of this world. He asserts that "Christianity will do this for the sake of a world which is developing toward the future of God,"[190] and he suggests that Christianity needs to do this, so that the world will indeed develop toward the future of God.

Moltmann counters Christian notions of apocalyptic devastation with his vision of a new creation created from this earth. Instead, Moltmann emphasizes that humanity's future with God *includes* this earth; God will come to this earth in the redeemed future of hope. "*This* earth, with its world of the living, is the real and sensorially experienceable promise of *the new* earth, as truly as this earthly, mortal life here is an experienceable promise of the life that is eternal, immortal. If the divine Redeemer is himself present in this earth in hidden form, then the earth becomes the bearer or vehicle of his and our future. But in that case there is no fellowship with Christ without fellowship with the earth. Love for Christ and hope for him embrace love and hope for the earth."[191] The hope Moltmann

---

186. Ibid.; brackets added.
187. Moltmann, *Coming*, 259.
188. Ibid.
189. Ibid.
190. Moltmann, *Experiment*, 41.
191. Moltmann, *Coming*, 279.

describes is a hope for the new creation of this world that embraces the material and the living bodies of earth and the historical circumstances and events of this world.

Moltmann posits that Christ crucified opens this world to the kingdom of God's coming, so that present history can be shaped, in hope, by the new creation of the future. Christ provides possibilities of newness now for those living in hope, by claiming the world as home and by liberating the oppressed. Moltmann asserts: "The crucified Lord embodies the new humanity which responds to God in the circumstances of inhumanity which oppose God. He incorporates home in the circumstances of alienation, and freedom in the midst of the chains of slavery. But it is just through this that men are empowered to alter these relationships, to make the world more homelike, and to abolish internal and external slavery."[192] Moltmann explains that people empowered by the crucified Christ to live out alternatives can bring about real change here and now: "Without the hope of faith, there is no ground for hope in action. Without hope in action, there are no results from the hope of faith. Without a presence for peace in the vicious circles, giving an account of our hope remains abstract and of no help to anyone. Without the growth and spread of the hope of faith, however, all programs for peace and campaigns for liberation fall short of their marks, become pragmatic, and quickly succumb to weariness."[193] Moltmann urges Christians to take action in hope to release people from oppression and to restore the abused earth to health. Without hope, the historical progress toward destruction, chaos, violence, and death seems inevitable. Hope for the resurrection of the world that will come through Christ's resurrection unlocks history from the powers that enclose it.

Moltmann argues that the powers that enclose the world, the mighty of history, have reasons to keep history from radical alternatives. "They have to extend their victorious present into the future in order to augment and consolidate their power. *Their* future is without an alternative, and devoid of surprises."[194] Moltmann stands with those who suffer and resist the mighty and their historical re-entrenchment of power; "God's messianic future" breaks into that history and its future bereft of possibilities and reveals perpectives for a future of hope.[195] "The deadliness of progress towards the economic, ecological, nuclear and genetic catastrophes

192. Moltmann, *Man*, 116.
193. Moltmann, *End*, 185.
194. Moltmann, *Coming*, 45.
195. Ibid.

is recognized; and the modern world's lack of future is perceived. The way becomes free for alternative developments. I should like to call this the redemption of the future from the power of history in the *kairos* of conversion. Only that will again make the theological eschatology possible, for through that, hope as a theological category will be redeemed from the ruins of historical reason."[196] Hope will then be freed from the constraints of the oppressors and oppressed of history. The people of hope can see alternatives to the history of power and then take actions otherwise unimaginable, to steer away from catastrophe and toward life, peace, and liberation; but Moltmann notes that this does not always happen: "If the world in which we live and hope presents a mixture of realities and possibilities, then we may not see it as a finished house of being but as an open process. Then the world becomes not a system with eternally repeatable structures, but an open history in which something new happens and can be realized. Then it is not a completed creation but an open creative process and the world is in itself a great experiment, *a laboratorium possibilis salutis* (a laboratory of possible salvation) as Bloch says.[197] A world open to possibilities beyond history is a world open to God's creative justice.

Moltmann presents an ethics of the hope that asks Christians to reflect "the redemption of the future from the power of history" and to accept the challenges of living as God's hope.

> Here we realize that God is not simply the point of our hope in heaven, but that we are his hope on earth. In such experiences man attains the unforgettable impression that he is, together with other people and this whole creation, the utopia of God. "God created all things with finality," says an old rabbinical commentary on the creation story, "but he created man in hope." With the experiment "man" and the experiment "world" God has joined a hope. That gives man an unambiguous certainty of hope precisely at the place and time when he can no longer see any future ahead of him. It simultaneously places him in the open question of how he wants to fulfill, personally and together with society, that hope which God has placed in him and this world.[198]

Moltmann holds open uncertainty together with certain future, and he settles the uncertainty on *how* people will engage with God's certain gift

196. Ibid., 45–46.
197. Moltmann, *Experiment*, 26.
198. Ibid., 27.

of certain hope. He names three practices to live out the certainty and openness of this hope in a social and this-worldly focus: "proclamation of the Gospel of the kingdom to the poor . . . ; founding of the Christian congregation; . . . creative, battling, and loving obedience ready to suffer in the everyday situations of the present world."[199] These practices demonstrate Moltmann's conviction that Christian hope must not settle into a complacent cooperation with "reality as it is." Resistance means disrupting, suffering, and conflicting with the world as a witness to an alternative to the world's determined commitment to the same.[200] As a group gathered into a congregation, Christians can show their hope that is not limited to the terms of society's current norms and governance. "Only where their resistance shows them to be a group that is incapable of being assimilated or of 'making the grade' can they communicate their own hope to this society."[201] Christian hope is not visible unless the sharp difference between that hope and "bodily reality" is visible. Those who cling to the way things are cannot see their way to break free of socially closed reality and the powers that try to perpetuate it.

Moltmann narrates the character of baptism in keeping with his arguments about the not-yet nature of Christ's resurrection.[202] Just as the resurrection affirms the promise of Christ's completed resurrection in the future resurrection of all, so too baptism promises the future unity of the body of Christ. At present, Christians can follow Jesus' life in hope through proclamation and obedience as a gathered community of promise. Moltmann urges Christians to turn from internal piety, from "a continual, self-absorbed repentance,"[203] to obedience to God's will in love and the hope of God's glory. "In taking his way to the cross, Jesus was also making his own decision: his active love for sufferers becomes his suffering love with sufferers."[204] Moltmann urges Christians to follow Jesus by loving and suf-

199. Moltmann, *Future of Creation*, 37–38.

200. Moltmann, *Theology*, 21–22.

201. Ibid., 324.

202. In contrast to a more sacramental theology, Moltmann argues that the efficacy of both baptism and Christ's resurrection lies in the future. Note also that Moltmann here refers to adult baptism, instead of infant baptism, which he rejects because he understands it to be involuntary, passive, and a reinforcement of Constantinianism. Presumably, his early years in Germany helped established this association, as well as his inclination toward Free Church and against Roman Catholicism. See Neal, *Theology*, 86–87.

203. Moltmann, *End*, 56.

204. Ibid., 69.

fering with those who suffer. Moltmann argues for a Christian ethics of hope that aims at a balance of independence (to decide freely to counter injustice) and empathetic responses to suffering (to love and stand with those who suffer): "In the midst of all struggle against inhuman and ruinous suffering and experience of pain, there also has to be developed a concept of meaningful human passion and an acceptance of meaningful human conflicts and suffering. An *ethic of the pathic*, without destroying the independence of the person, must teach people to allow themselves to be vulnerable, to allow themselves to be affected, and to develop their own spontaneity."[205] According to Moltmann, the church can only imagine the coming new creation when engaged in an "ethic of the pathic" that resists the powers of slavery (political, economic, military, and egotistic) and shares Jesus' love for and with the suffering.[206]

Moltmann directs the church to attend to God's suffering which frees both the oppressed and the oppressors from the past and the present: "Let us look at the image of God's pain. The suffering of God is important both for the victims of sin and for those who are enslaved by sin. To perceive this suffering releases the victims from the torment of remembrance, and frees the enslaved from the power of their repressions. Even God cannot make what is done undone, but he can loose the fetters which bind the present to this past, and open for the present a new future."[207] Moltmann argues that Jesus' suffering and death manifests God's suffering love for creation. He objects to the church's understanding of Jesus' death as self-sacrifice for our sins; his account shifts the focus from sins to people and their need for God's presence with them in their darkest despair. He writes that Jesus' sacrificial death

> has often been interpreted to mean that Jesus died as the vicarious victim for our sins, paying off our debts in a heavenly bank, so to speak, and transferring them from us to him. But this is just what it does not mean. Interpretations of this kind are only illustrations—more or less apt images—but they do not touch the heart of the matter. The one who "was put to death for our trespasses" (Rom 4.25) was not the one sacrificed for our sins by God, his Father; he is the one who was sent by his Father to those who had been given up for lost (Rom 1.24, 26, 28), so that God himself might be brought into the pit of godforsakenness and could thereby awaken these godless people for a new

205. Moltmann, *Experiment*, 16.
206. Moltmann, *End*, 117; *Man*, 104.
207. Moltmann, *End*, 73.

beginning. . . . The personal "for us" of Christ is primary; the object "for our sins" is secondary.[208]

Moltmann explains that when the future new creation establishes the basis for hope, then Christ would have nothing new to offer, and there would be nothing new to hope for. Hence, the passion, death, and resurrection of Christ effects not so much the exchange of sins for forgiveness, but the possibility of a new, different, better creation. "The hope of faith in Christ expects more of the end than there was in the beginning."[209] The people of this hope should therefore not wait for a return to the pre-fall creation; the end of hope, which is the beginning of God's kingdom, promises a better, unlimited creation-wide community of incorporation. God will embrace earthly life with God's presence, and creation will embrace God throughout the world.[210] "The hope of creation, in eschatological terms, is the future indwelling of creation by God, when 'the finite is able to contain the infinite.'"[211] People living in anticipation of the coming God demonstrate their hope in God's eschatological creation by protecting and restoring the abused earth, by moving governmental policies toward peace and justice, and by sharing the news of God's love in and as the church. People waiting for the new creation should worry less about what happens to their sins and love more: the godforsaken, the suffering, their own selves.

Moltmann reaches out to those who cannot see God's presence in the horrors of the Holocaust nor any reason for hope in God after the Holocaust. He describes God's love of the godforsaken, demonstrated by God's adoption of godforsakenness in God's own being. And he describes the possibilities for hope in the midst of hopelessness. Christ's acceptance of godforsakenness in his suffering and death draws God into godforsakenness. The crucified Christ can now accompany the godforsaken as a brother and friend.[212] The godforsaken God can now bring all of creation into God's new kingdom, having negated the negation of God's goodness through the experience of hopelessness and through the power of love.

---

208. Ibid., 56, 73–74. Also: "We understand his suffering obedience to God not as his sacrifice for the sins of the world but as his unreserved self-giving to the uttermost for the God-forsaken. Here Jesus reveals a love on God's part 'such as was never thought of in any God', as Bloch said" (ibid., 69).

209. Moltmann, "Theology as Eschatology," 29.

210. Moltmann, Future of Creation, 168–70.

211. Bauckham, 37.

212. Moltmann, End, 70.

Moltmann explains that someone in an utterly hopeless circumstance, someone who suffers and faces death abandoned by all others—even God—still has grounds for hope. First, God can be known most surely by someone who is in the depths of godforsakenness, because God has experienced that same hopelessness, that same godforsakenness, and is therefore most present. Second, the experience of God's presence in the midst of godforsakenness opens up an alternative to overwhelming, inescapable suffering. Third, that opening is the open future that is the coming kingdom of God. Hope does not depend on hopeful evidence in the physical and social circumstances of one's experience. Hope is not a matter of mustering possible alternatives when there are none. Moltmann names the source of hope as the coming of God's creation; to hope is to be open to the coming God. "Hoping does not mean to *have* a number of hopes at one's disposal. It means, rather, hoping to *be* open."[213] As an example, Moltmann points to those in Auschwitz who prayed in their hopelessness. "Anyone who later comes up against insoluble problems and despair must remember that the *Shema* of Israel and the Lord's Prayer were prayed in Auschwitz."[214] He is not proposing optimism or wishful thinking; Moltmann is talking about an openness to the possibility that God offers life even where death seems to have won.

Moltmann champions an eschatological hope that looks beyond the possibilities of history, through the crucified Christ who interrupts history, to the other-than-history new creation that establishes the basis for hope.[215] He writes that "eschatology is not a doctrine about history's happy end. In the present situation of our world, facile consolation is as fatal as melancholy hopelessness. No one can assure us that the worst will not happen. According to all the laws of experience: it will. We can only trust that even the end of the world hides a new beginning if we trust the God who calls into being the things that are not, and out of death creates new life."[216] Moltmann's picture of hope found in the worst experiences echoes his own experiences of war and prison camp. The hope he describes comes to the hopeless through Christ's suffering and brings God's love, and the

---

213. Moltmann, *Experiment*, 20.

214. Moltmann, *Crucified*, 278.

215. "Christian faith in God is shaped by the experience of the dying and death of Christ, and by the appearances of the Christ who was raised. Resurrection is not a return to this, or another, mortal life. It is entry into a life that is eternal. Christ's resurrection is therefore not a historical event; it is an eschatological happening to the crucified Christ and took place 'once for all' (Rom 6.10)" (Moltmann, *Coming*, 69).

216. Ibid., 234.

hopeless person finds some kind of strength to go on. "In the midst of the unbearable story of the passion of the world he discovers the reconciling story of the passion of Christ. This gives him the power to hope when there is nothing more to hope for, and to love, when he hates himself."[217] Moltmann connects Christ's resurrection—and the coming resurrection of all—with the resiliance of the hopeful. Anticipatory participation in the resurrection grants possibilities beyond those of current history and the strength to carry on. "Christian faith is faith in the resurrection, and the resurrection is literally just that: rising up again. It gives us the strength to get up, and the creative freedom to begin something once more in the midst of our ongoing history, something fresh. *Incipit vita nova*— a new life begins. That is the truly revolutionary power of hope. It is revolutionary because it is innovative. With it, we leave behind us the fatalism of non-success."[218] Hope-inspired people do not succumb to the world of no hope, Moltmann explains, because they are drawn toward God's coming success, the truly new and future creation: "Through the power of hope, we don't give up, and don't give ourselves up; we remain unreconciled and unaccepting in an unjust and deadly world."[219] People of hope are resolute in their persistence toward the success of resurrection and God's coming kingdom.

Moltmannian Hope: Reclaiming Hope from the Rapture

Moltmann's theology of hope was received appreciatively in the 1960s and 1970s by theologians who shared with him the conviction that theology needed to speak directly to the pressing social and political circumstances of the second half of the twenty-first century. Moltmann has continued to influence theologians, clergy, and lay people since. He has written dozens of books after *Theology of Hope*, and, like most theologians, his positions have shifted and developed across the past fifty years. Also like most theologians, he has not written a comprehensive account of the consistensies, inconsistencies, and changes his work displays. At the same time, a generalized impression of Moltmann-inspired hope has grown, and that impression now characterizes many theologians and members of the church who have not read Moltmann. I am calling this Moltmann-inspired hope

217. Moltmann, *Man*, 114.
218. Moltmann, *End*, 38.
219. Ibid., 90.

Moltmannian hope. It does not represent the nuances and more complicated arguments of Moltmann's work, and it often leans more toward an alliance with secular norms than toward Moltmann's critiques of the modern world. To a certain extent, the latter tendency could be connected to the way that Moltmann tried to work with the modern context as well as to critique it. It can be hard for his critiques of the world to win out over the more familiar ideologies of hope.[220]

To illustrate Moltmannian hope, I will cite a pair of lectures by Moltmann himself, which highlight themes from his theology of hope familiar to Moltmannian scholars, clergy, and church members. A lecture by Barbara Rossing, at the same conference, offers a Moltmannian argument about the dangers of the Rapture movement and its hope. Then, I turn to Ellen Ott Marshall's book about hope that demonstrates characteristics of Moltmannian hope.

In January of 2007, the annual Episcopal Trinity Institute Conference featured Moltmann and his work with the theme, "God's Unfinished Future: Why It Matters Now."[221] When the Rev. Mark Richardson, the director of the Institute,[222] introduced Jürgen Moltmann for the two central presentations of the conference, his introduction highlighted the celebratory nature of the event: the Institute wanted to honor Moltmann and his

---

220. I am using the word *ideology* to refer to a system of thought, imagination, and practices that implicitly shapes and constitutes shared truth. On the one hand, ideologies in and of themselves are not positive or negative, but formative and reflective of community identity and conviction. On the other hand, uncritical acceptance of an ideology risks an inability to consider or accept other possibilities. Of course, the position from which one might critique an ideology itself represents another ideology; however, the characterization of a truth system as an ideology makes space for the possibility of explicit claims and critical engagement with ideas previously presupposed to be outside such examination.

221. Trinity Institute occupies a unique position in the Episcopal church, as the most visible and accessible provider of current theological scholarship for the church. Since 1967, the Institute has been presenting conferences on theological topics. Churches throughout the country offer viewings of the event, so that people can listen together and then discuss the material. In the past few years, geographically-disparate audience members have been able to submit questions right along with those listening in Trinity Church. The speakers provide substantive resources from their own scriptural interpretation, theological study, and cultural gleanings, in ways that church leaders can use in their own teaching and preaching to congregations. Some recent topics include: The Church in a Postmodern Age, 1987; The Art of Conversation: Speaking of God in a Pluralistic Age, 1993; Ordered Freedom: An Anglican Paradox, 1997; Radical Abundance: A Theology of Sustainability, 2009.

222. He was then a professor at General Theological Seminary; now he is the dean of Church Divinity School of the Pacific.

long career as theologian, as he turned eighty years old. Richardson cast the conference in the context of Moltmann's life work of scholarship, with attention to the promise of God's not-yet fulfilled future. Now, forty-five years later, Richardson noted that Moltmann's work seems all the more relevant, as we face increased anxieties about the future of the planet and our civilization and as some Christians spread fears of an imminent and violent apocalypse.[223]

The conference addressed a topic of pressing concern to Episcopal clergy, lay leaders, teachers, and their mainstream Protestant colleagues: how to respond to the assertions about eschatology and hope popularized by the *Left Behind* series and related Rapture theologies. The Rapture has not traditionally captured the theological imaginations of Episcopalians. The lectionary spends relatively little time working through Revelation, and few Episcopal preachers focus on end-time issues, but parishioners do encounter the images and ideologies of the Rapture movement throughout their daily lives, outside of church. Instead of a future marked by imminent world destruction and otherworldly escape for the faithful, this conference championed the in-process, world-affirming future. Richardson explained that the conference's speakers would describe the promise of transformation for all things which takes hold of us now and leads to an entirely different kind of religion of and for this world. "What we envision about the future tells us something about what we trust as ultimate–'last things' for people of faith, are really 'things that last,' 'things worthy of God's creative transformation,' and this is why the stakes we place in future hope have practical urgency for how we live now. What picture of the future will motivate us?"[224] The conference gave the organizers, participants, and audience a chance to express their appreciation to Moltmann for his ongoing work on hope and the future.

In this context, Moltmann's presentations functioned on two levels. He was delivering lectures on a current topic of much interest to him: Rapture eschatology as a current manifestation of the other-worldly eschatology he has critiqued throughout all of his scholarship. This conference championed the in-process, world-affirming future, instead of a future marked by imminent world destruction and otherworldly escape for the faithful. Moltmann was also there as the figurehead of Moltmannian hope broadly accepted as normative. For those present (physically and remotely

---

223. Richardson, "Introduction."
224. Ibid.

via telecast), Moltmann embodied and affirmed a prominent ideology of hope familiar in Episcopal pulpits.

Conference participants included the Presiding Bishop Katherine Jefferts Schiori; author James P. Carroll, opening preacher; Barbara Rossing, a Lutheran pastor and New Testament professor; Moltmann; and Harvard professor and minister Peter Gomes, closing preacher. To give a sense of the Moltmannian hope displayed at the conference, I will note the main themes of Moltmann's keynote lectures, and I will describe Barbara Rossing's lecture.[225]

When Richardson introduced the speakers, he explained that the conference assumes a direct connection between our visions of the future and our present actions, and it reflects on how faith in Jesus' resurrection informs our expectations for the future of history and the cosmos.[226] "We will be asking if the future of hope is able to comprehend and liberate us from the cynicism and anxiety of our age."[227] Acknowledging that the conference participants are all leaders, "front line theologians in our respective congregations," he noted the pressing need for new ways to express the central images of God's future coming out of Christianity in the United States.[228] Richardson remarked that, as the popular books of the religious right fill the shelves of bookstores with apocalyptic visions of end times, "one can only wonder how this feeds a wartime frenzy, interpreting the present as setting the stage for holy battle."[229] Richardson, the attendees present, and the viewers far away, then turned to Moltmann for guidance on new ways to present God's future today.

Moltmann's first lecture, "The Final Judgment: Sunrise of Christ's Liberating Justice,"[230] features two themes characteristic of his theology of hope: judgment is universally inclusive and positive, and the end is the beginning. Moltmann critiques the characterization of eschatology as the site of God's final judgment, and he challenges the assumption that divine judgment involves condemnation, wrath, and punishment. He explains that people who expect an ultimate separation between good and

---

225. The description and quotations are drawn from the audio-video recordings of the conference on *God's Unfinished Future*, and from *Anglican Theological Review*'s abridged versions of the presentations, as marked.

226. Richardson, "Introduction."

227. Ibid.

228. Ibid.

229. Ibid.

230. Moltmann, "Final Judgment."

Moltmann's Hope and Moltmannian Hope

bad necessarily see everyone now on divisive terms, thereby furthering conflict and violence. He cites as examples the tendency of the *Left Behind* movement to see the world divided into believers and unbelievers and President G. W. Bush's administration's apparent division of the world into terrorists and antiterrorists. Moltmann argues that politics shaped by friend vs. foe images of judgment-oriented people accompanies an end-time fascination, sometimes aligned with the Armageddon of Rev. 16:16. In that view, God will finalize the division between good and bad with the global destruction of the godless. "The expectation of an exclusive final judgment justifies the exclusion of those who do not belong to us. Whoever is not for us or like us is against us—and we against them."[231] At the same time, Moltmann objects to views that place the responsibility for righteousness in the hands of humans, who can either follow or turn away from God's planned salvation for all. He argues that these images reflect the corruption of true Christian belief by ancient Egyptian expectations of Osiris' judgment and Roman law's criminal court system:[232] "It's high time to Christianize our traditional images and perceptions of God's final judgment and to evangelize their present effects on our lives and worldviews, so we may greet the coming judge with joy: 'Maranatha, come Lord Jesus, come soon' and may live already here and now in the sunrise of God's justice on earth (Rev. 21:20)."[233] Here he echoes his lifelong efforts to promote a theology of hope governed neither by mistaken tradition nor by modernity's perverted desires.

Moltmann agrees that some kind of final judgment is necessary, in order to grant peace to victims and rest to perpetrators. Jesus is the judge, but not an avenging judge. Moltmann dismisses as unrecognizable those images of Jesus as the coming judge in medieval paintings in which Jesus appears physically strong, an Olympian figure, a heroically powerful conqueror of death. That figure "couldn't be Jesus of Nazareth"; "Michelangelo's Jesus in the Sistine Chapel has nothing to do with the crucified Christ."[234] Moltmann explains that Christ's justice, rightly understood, establishes "God's creative justice which brings the victims justice and puts the perpetrators to right."[235] Victims and perpetrators of evil will all be born again to new life, having been cleansed in the fire of God, which

---

231. Ibid., 568.
232. Ibid., 568, 570.
233. Ibid., 569–70.
234. Moltmann, "Final," in *God's Unfinished Future*, DVD.
235. Moltmann, "Final Judgment," 571.

saves the people in love while burning away everything "in contradiction to God."[236] Although this judgment involves fire, cleansing and annihilation, Moltmann argues that it is not so much negative as the negation of the negative, and hence positive, saving, and fulfilling. "If death is no more and hell destroyed, the question of whether all or only a few shall be saved is irrelevant."[237] Sin and death are destroyed, not the people consumed by them. He claims that the universalism of Christ's judgment excludes no one; the Christian response should embrace all as believers, regardless of their belief or faith, while at the same time practicing preferential treatment of the poor and oppressed.[238] This preferential treatment will demonstrate our hope in God's coming new creation, in which inequities are corrected and wrongs are righted.

Moltmann resists what he perceives as the limitations and closure of final, eternal judgment. The divine judgment he proclaims is simply "the end of the old age," which is really the beginning.[239] "In my opinion, it was a fatal mistake of Christian tradition in doctrine and spirituality, to look only at final judgment and not through to new creation, not believing in new beginning of this end."[240] God is still curious, he argues, looking forward to new generations, waiting to see what will come.[241] An inappropriate rush to final judgment, the end of the world, misconstrues God's judgment as an assessment of the past, rather than as the establishment of a new creation that embraces everyone, victim and oppressor, believer and nonbeliever, in a new life of reconciliation and mercy for all. In this way, Moltmann counters Rapture theology and any theology and scriptural interpretation that dwells on the divine discernment of good and evil as an eternal division. He underscores the Moltmannian expectation that the new beginning (wrongly viewed as the end) extends this world through to its new creation; and he demonstrates the Moltmannian assumption that God is not so perfect as to know ahead of time what will happen in the future.[242]

236. Ibid.
237. Ibid., 574.
238. Ibid., 575.
239. Ibid., 572.
240. Ibid.
241. Moltmann, "Final," in *God's Unfinished Future*, DVD.
242. The *Anglican Theological Review* versions of the Moltmann and Rossing presentations appear to have been edited not only for length, but for content in a way that excludes most of the explicit references to panentheism, God's suffering, God's need for creation for God's own completion, and God's hope and curiosity.

Moltmann's second lecture, "The Presence of God's Future: The Risen Christ,"[243] continues his discussion of God's new beginning and considers the nature of resurrection hope. He picks up again the contemporary fascination with end-time, noting that it reflects our desires to be released from the pain and suffering and anxiety of this world. Images of global destruction may appeal to our need to know that what oppresses us will end, but those images do not illustrate Christian anticipation of God's future. Christian future, Moltmann argues, "has nothing to do with the final destruction of the world God has created and loves. Its focus is not the end, the end of life, the end of history, the end of all things. It is, rather, *the beginning*, the beginning of true life, the beginning of God's kingdom, the beginning of the new creation of all things."[244] Hope begins with the resurrection of Christ, he continues, "the presence of God's promised future."[245] Life after the resurrection of Christ is transformed life, and life now means living against death. Our hope in the resurrection of all fleshly bodies fills "us with a new spirit and life power already before death" and a new sensitivity to suffering.[246]

Moltmann reflects the earth-centered focus of his later books as he explains that this salvation of souls and bodies will occur here on earth, arguing that Jewish and Christian belief looks to redemption *of*, not *from*, the world we already inhabit.[247] "Christ doesn't lead people in the afterlife of religious escapism or flight from the world, but gives them back to the earth as her faithful people."[248] Christ was born, lived, and died on earth; therefore we should expect transformation of life here. While he still champions the future-oriented interpretation of past and present established in his earlier work, Moltmann now locates the future here, in these bodies, on this earth. Moltmann expects a Kingdom of God noticeably different from the current status quo; he has specific hopes for the character of God's unfinished future. He is sure that looking for God and God's future elsewhere than here reflects a foolish escapism that necessarily leads to the neglect and abuse of of the earth we now inhabit. It also leads to the poor stewardship of God's gifts of creation, which are the means with which we will receive the future.

243. Moltmann, "Presence," 577–88.
244. Ibid., 577–78.
245. Ibid., 585.
246. Ibid.
247. Ibid., 587.
248. Ibid., 588.

Our Only Hope

The Rev. Dr. Barbara R. Rossing is a New Testament professor and ordained Lutheran pastor, with a background in natural science. Rossing has written a book that rebuts the Rapture movement series with an alternative reading of Revelation, *The Rapture Exposed: The Message of Hope in the Book of Revelation*. In the book, Rossing traces the history of the Rapture movement, which she describes as a racket, invented in the nineteenth century, evolved through dispensationalism in the early twentieth century, revived by Hal Linsday's *Late Great Planet Earth* in the 1970s, and now popularized in the *Left Behind* books by Lahaye and Jenkins. Her book focuses on an interpretation of Revelation as a text of hope and reconciliation, not devastation.

Rossing's lecture, "Prophecy, End-Times and American Apocalypse: Reclaiming Hope for Our World,"[249] begins with thanks to Carroll's homiletic vision of God's Unfinished Future and with deep appreciation for Moltmann's body of work, especially his theological engagement with environmental concerns. She dismisses *Left Behind* theology as "Nuts!", while acknowledging that a sense of "end" does permeate our culture.[250] In response to concerns about continued life on this planet, Rossing sets out to reclaim the Bible and the Apocalypse as "a diagnosis of the sickness of our imperial world, and as an urgent wake-up call about the future—a vision of hope for this planet earth and every one of us."[251] She does this through four steps: reconfiguring sin as illness, looking for the end of empire rather than the end of the world, attending to the long-term health and life of creation, and welcoming God to the New Jerusalem which is our healing earth.

First, Rossing draws a powerful connection between humans and all of creation by naming *illness* as the one crisis that infects all of creation. She notes that while the grammar of sin, guilt, and repentance may still be important, she (and many others) prefer a theology of illness and healing. A focus on sickness highlights the healing which all of creation needs, and which scripture addresses through the healing stories of the Gospels.[252]

Second, she names *empire* as the cause of the illness that consumes all of creation. She argues that we, like the earliest Christians, must "try to envision a way of life beyond empire"—both the Roman Empire which

---

249. Rossing, "Prophecy," in *God's Unfinished Future*, DVD.

250. Ibid.

251. Rossing, "Prophecy," 553.

252. Rossing shares with Moltmann a conviction to narrate judgment non-punitively.

threatened their world, and the imperialism which pervades and sickens our world today. Rossing analyzes the three Greek words often translated as "world," (*gê, kosmos*, and *oikoumenê*) and proposes that the New Testament uses *oikoumenê* negatively, to represent the domination of world powers; in Revelation, *oikoumene* refers to the Roman Empire and its eschatology of an eternal imperial world order, *Roma aeterna*, attained and sustained through the capture and torture of other peoples and lands.[253] In Rossing's reading, Revelation repudiates this empire and proclaims the end of its age. Rossing argues that the end that Revelation proclaims is the end to this age, and the whole book leads up to the "city of beauty, welcome, ecological renewal, with enough for everyone."[254] The New Jerusalem image illustrates Rossing's Moltmannian "earth-centered vision of hope for this world."[255]

Third, Rossing identifies *healing the creation* as the final word of the Bible and the central message of Revelation: God's will is not to destroy our world, but to heal us, and that healing comes "not directly from God but from the leaves of the tree of life, noting that it is an image common to many of the world's religions, and can therefore be an image that unites all as God's people.[256]

Fourth, Rossing highlights the importance of *welcoming God to the earth*. Rossing's Revelation centers on a vision of hope for this world and not on a world-clearing Rapture. Representing Moltmannian hope in the continuation of this earth, she suggests it might make more sense to consider that Revelation offers "a vision of God being 'raptured' down to earth to dwell with us on earth (Rev 21), to dwell with us in what is called New Jerusalem."[257] She stresses the ethical ramifications of this vision, calling for human efforts to protect and save the world before it is too late.

Rossing offers the above tools for reclaiming in order to show that, despite the claims of *Left Behind* theology, the idea of the apocalypse may indeed play a healing role in our culture. She can imagine that this might be the case, especially if someone can write a novel to counter the *Left Behind* series, a novel about people of the world, living with ecological care and protecting the earth's resources. This novel's heroes could be living in sustainable communities, maybe practicing permaculture

---

253. Rossing, "Prophecy," 557–58.
254. Ibid., 560.
255. Ibid.
256. Rossing, "Prophecy," in *God's Unfinished Future*, DVD.
257. Rossing, "Prophecy," 560.

gardening—sharing in the river of life, tending the nation-healing tree of life. Such a story could be just as thrilling as the *Left Behind* story—but instead of carrying guns to battle the Antichrist and his forces, our little band of heroes carries seedlings, or solar panels; they rescue farmers about to be bulldozed by developers; they foil the evil forces of polluters and greenhouse gas emitters—today's most dangerous manifestations of the Antichrist. In defense of her reading, and against the Rapture-focussed exegesis of Revelation, Rossing declares, "It's all there in the Bible! I'm not making it up!"[258] It is a story of "a world that will not be left behind."[259]

Rossing offers a passionate, angry, but rational and this-worldly response to the passionate and popular biblicism of the apocalyptic Christians she describes. Her position as mainstream seminary professor, her authorship of a book that debunks the "Rapture Racket," her background in science, her hermeneutical alternatives to unsophisticated literalism, and her references to Greek etymology all establish her as a solid resource to whom church leaders can turn to counter their parishioners' possible attractions to the *Left Behind* movement. She warns against the mainstream Christian tendency to avoid Revelation whenever possible, noting that it is a part of the Bible *and* a part of public rhetoric. "We may try to ignore it, but the fundamentalists came in with a vengeance to teach our parishes what it really means!"[260] Rossing provides the ammunition needed for anti-Rapture congregations to reclaim Revelation and eschatological hope.

Moltmannian hope critiques eschatology that distracts from the realities of this world and fails to appreciate the goods of this world. Rapture eschatology is currently the most obvious form of the otherworldly hope that Moltmannian hope resists. The ethical force of Moltmann's and Rossing's argument against the Rapture movement presupposes that the primary theological goods are inclusion, democracy, nonviolence, ministry to the poor, and environmental activism. They claim that the Rapture movement, with its priority of life with God in heaven for the selected faithful, fails to support any of these goods, fostering exclusivism and division between believers and nonbelievers, and between creation to be saved and creation to be abandoned. Moltmann and Rossing argue that the very concept of election defies democracy and reeks of empire. They assert that the anticipation of God's wrathful destruction of the ungodly and unclean

258. Ibid., 562.
259. Ibid.
260. Rossing, "Prophecy," in *God's Unfinished Future*, DVD.

supports war and violence among people and the earth. An obsession with other-worldliness detracts from the preferential option for the poor. A heart that longs to live in heaven cannot be bothered to nurture or restore this world. Hence, according to this ethics, the chief fault of the Rapture movement lies in its misdirected priorities that exacerbate rather than ameliorate the very troubles that the coming God aims to heal. Those who fall under the spell of and then propogate the *Left Behind* ideology pervert and impede hopes to address the greatest concerns of the world today.

The second great fault of the Rapture movement, according to the Moltmann and Rossing critique, is that it encourages exciting feelings but little human agency. Rossing deplores the persuasive attraction of Rapture anticipation that counts on God's angelic forces to do the work. Hopeful and responsible resurrection life (Moltmann) or anti-empirical healing life (Rossing) calls for rational action based on sound biblical scholarship and on theological reasoning that reflects the sensibilities of this age. The Rapture movement, these speakers argue, encourages believers to sit back, focus on personal salvation, and leave the condition of the world to God who will soon set all things right. An uninformed and literal reading of Revelation supplies these believers with the assurance that a wrathful God comes to judge, saving the godly and destroying the rest, leaving little for the faithful to do in the meantime. In contrast, Rossing reads Revelation from a perspective that interprets the Armageddon passages of Revelation as hortatory persuasion in the service of the most important message of book: Jesus the Lamb comes to establish the New Jerusalem on this earth. Drawing on her exegetical determination of the original connotations of the Greek, Rossing explains that God intends to dismantle empirical structures, not to destroy the earth or the rest of the world apart from those unhealthy power structures. Moltmann counters the Rapture movement and eschatological hope that expects punitive divine judgment with corrections based on his own scholarship: Christian eschatology needs to be freed from the corruptive influences of ancient Egyptian and Roman beliefs, from the mistaken Christology of artistic representations; from outdated doctrines of God, from a static sameness of eternity (toward an open-ended continuation of unfinished time), and from notions of the Kingdom of God apart from this world. *True* Christianity, they argue, rejects *Left Behind* and embraces God's good creation.

The God of Moltmannian hope is the God of love, whose love is so great that God the Father (and God the three in one) suffers in the godforsaken experience of his crucified Son. In resurrection life, God, the godforsaken and godforsaking, will come to this recreated earth, this time, these bodies, this creation, and in and with us for ever. Moltmannian hope is universally inclusive not only because it is for all of creation, but because it is about the inclusion of God in the universe and the universe in God. Hope in God's unfinished future rests on God's coming to bring the end of all divisiveness, including the divisions between creation and the Creator. Moltmannian hope offers a liberating spirit and a power that can be tapped into in order to prepare this creation for the new creation God promises. It is a bold hope, relying on God's promises of future fulfillment to make sense of the present and to determine how to proceed. And, this hope is positive, trusting in God's negation of all that is negative to produce an undefeatable positive future in which everything life-affirming is affirmed by God, and everything that is not life-affirming is rendered life-affirming.

The Moltmannian hope of God's unfinished future matters, its proponents argue, because with this hope, we can begin to establish the New Jerusalem here and now. This Moltmannian hope seems better for the planet than more traditional doctrines of hope, because it focuses on the earth as the future home of God, which is worthy of preservation and care. It is better for humans, because it does not exclude anyone from God's just and merciful future, but instead anticipates that God will cleanse and heal as necessary in the recreation of the cosmos at God's coming. No one will be left out, and the world will not be left out. Heaven will be renewed life here on the earth we know, and the earth and all of creation will be created anew, filled with God's presence. This Moltmannian hope contrasts with the hopes of escapists who put the health of the earth in peril while yearning for a false heaven, the hopes of the judgmental who divide this world the way they imagine God will divide the world to come, and the hopes of the optimists who think things are getting better for them and their empire every day—but at the expense of others. This hope matters because suffering needs to be relieved now, the environment needs to be saved now, and society needs to be rescued from the evils of empire and fanatical and charismatic leaders.

Moltmannian hope tries to correct what it understands to be the problematic aspects of both Rapture theology and traditional Christian theology. Moltmannian theology claims nothing is more primary than that God is love, and love necessarily means suffering-with; whereas traditional doctrine does not pay sufficient attention to God's love and mercy. God loves the world so much that God will come to the world, recreate it, and dwell within it and within its continuing time. Just as God will come, God did enter into human history on the cross in love and suffering. Because God will come to renew and participate in this world, rather than end it or abandon it, Moltmannian hope promotes the care for and preservation of this world. Because God will come to heal and unite everyone in merciful love, people should love and live without division now. This future of life with and in God's love, made available to us through Jesus' crucifixion and resurrection, is what we should rightly hope for; and that hope carries a power that can help us prepare ourselves and all the world for the coming fulfillment of all hopes.

MARSHALL'S MOLTMANNIAN RESPONSIBLE HOPE

Ellen Ott Marshall was not one of the participants in the Trinity Institute conference, but she reflects and builds on a Moltmannian theology of hope in her book, *Though the Fig Tree Does Not Blossom: toward a Responsible Theology of Christian Hope*. She is an ethics professor who draws from Moltmann's incorporation of the new and the not-yet into history, in order to establish Christian hope within the priorities of social justice activism for the life of the earth and its inhabitants. Marshall identifies herself with a feminist and process theology of God, in which humans share power with God and focus their hopes on this life. She considers the categorization of hope as a virtue; she appreciates contemporary objections to eschatological hope that precludes adequate attention to tragedy; but she balances those objections with what she understands to be a more positive hope; and she charges hope with the task of generating and sustaining moral agency and activity.

Marshall feels that the traditional view of hope as a theological virtue does a disservice to hope, humanity, and the world.[261] Traditionally, as a theological virture, hope (along with faith and love) receives a divine infusion of grace which helps humans direct their hopes toward their true end in God. Marshall finds the idea of infused grace to be a distracting and dis-

---

261. Moltmann has expressed no interest in joining the discourse of theological virtues. When he does mention theological virtue, it is in the context of his delight in curiosity, which is decidedly not a virtue—theological or otherwise—in the Thomistic account from which Marshall dissents. "Right down to the present day, theology (curious search for God) has continued to be for me a tremendous adventure, a journey of discovery into a, for me, unknown country, a voyage without the certainty of a return, a path into the unknown with many surprises and not without disappointments. If I have a theological virtue at all, then it is one that has never been recognized as such: curiosity" (Moltmann, *Coming*, xiv).

empowering move that hands over to an overbearing God the power that rightfully belongs to responsible human agents. She wants to free hope from its glorified position in Christian tradition, where it "assumes an air of royalty" and where its "status as a theological virtue has overshadowed its everyday employment, such that we treat it like a show horse rather than a workhorse."[262] Marshall argues that hope, as a theological virtue, merely serves as a one-way conduit for power that flows from a commandeering God to a puppet-like human. In the process, that theological hope narrows the gaze of the those who hope, turning them away from the world and their responsibilities to the needy. In contrast, Marshall proposes a hope that is more responsible and ethical, because it recognizes and accepts the work of hope. "Hope has a job to do. In the continuous and far-reaching labor of the moral life, hope is the sense of possibility that generates and sustains moral agency."[263] The work of Marshall's responsible hope must be done by humans who claim this responsibility by exercising their freedom, and by sharing power with God and others in mutuality.

Marshall's account of hope looks to the *basileia tou theou,* "a community of peace and justice," which she identifies as the Christian tradition's highest good.[264] She claims the *basileia tou theou* as a vision of faith constructed both by interpretations of its descriptions in scripture and by present desires for the future. As a faith claim, this *basileia* does not rest on evidence (on scientific or social-historical terms) to establish its contents nor its plausibility. Instead, the *basileia* both shapes and is shaped by hope for what might be, and Marshall explains that she is able to "construe a source of hope through the lens of this faith claim."[265] Marshall does not feel she can ground her vision of the *basileia tou theou* on concrete examples of documented manifestations, because she sees more lived experiences of suffering, oppression, and injustice than glimpses of actualized *basileia* communities. Therefore she wants hope to be grounded on and governed by practices that will bring about the social changes necessary for the eventual *basileia*. She shares with Moltmannian hope the importance of the changes humans need to make so that the new kingdom will be appropriately constituted:

> The violence, displacement, disparity, degradation, disease, and oppression that mark our world demand steps toward conflict

262. Marshall, *Fig Tree,* xiii.
263. Ibid.
264. Ibid., 7.
265. Ibid., 8.

transformation and reconciliation, guarantees of protection and freedom from persecution, social change and economic restructuring, sustainable ecological practices, scientific research and affordable health care, active opposition to authoritarian regimes, and movements to create space for freedom. The depth of destruction and sadness caused by these historical conditions should give pause to anyone who speaks of hope today, and the concrete steps necessary to address these problems should serve as a corrective to abstract references to the *basileia* vision.[266]

Her account illustrates the priorities of Moltmannian hope: recognizing suffering, avoiding other-worldly distractions, and taking steps to address systemic injustice.

With the *basileia* in place as the end of hope, Marshall designs a framework for hope that nods to the virtue ethics of Aristotle and Aquinas, but makes significant alterations to both. Aristotle's *Nicomachean Ethics* describes the virtues of a man who occupies a position of privilege and prestige in his world and strives toward the good of ultimate happiness. In order to reach the excellence of virtue and happiness, Aristotle's ethical subject aims both for a balance of all virtues (*x* without *y* or *a* without *b* benefits little) and for a balance, or mean, of each virtue. The Christian engagement with ethics narrates a different list of virtues than Aristotle's, since the goods of disciples of Christ differ from the goods of the Nicomachean man of excellence. In addition, Aquinas describes the scriptural attributes of faith, hope, and love as *theological* virtues, which aim beyond that which can be attained naturally, with one's own human resources. In the theological virtues that Aquinas articulates, God draws humans into a glimpse of the supernatural end Christ has prepared; in faith, hope, and love, God helps humans aim toward and approach, however partially, the end of eternal happiness with God. Most Christian virtues aim toward that which leads to God, and as measures of human capacities and effort they are tempered by means, as are Aristotle's virtues. The theological virtues, however, aim toward God, whose possibilities are endless, whose power is unlimited, and whose goodness exceeds far beyond human finitude and imagination. Thus the mean does not apply to theological virtues. It is impossible to hope in God too much, since "too much" does not apply to God. The theological virtue of hope in God is not constrained by human limitations; it is defined by the unconstrained breadth of possibility that is God.

266. Ibid.

Marshall appreciates the open possibility of Aquinas's theological virtue of hope. The responsible hope she champions is strengthened by increased awareness of possibilities for change and by increased assurance that the difficult good is possible to attain; yet Marshall does not accept the essential distinction between God and creatures, between God's infinite power and the finite capacities of humans, that Aquinas and his tradition assumes. She is more persuaded by a theology of shared power between God and creatures, neither of whom can claim a limitless power, since each must depend on cooperation from the other to effect change. In this scenario, the measure of a mean still applies, and Marshall asserts that "hope does indeed observe a mean between optimism and despair. Thus, we cultivate hope by preserving the tension between promise and sobering experiences."[267] Further, she argues, regarding hope as virtue of mean as does Aristotle, balanced between the two potentially excessive extremes of optimism and despair, offers a broader vision of hope than afforded by the theological hope that claims infinite possibilities in God. According to Marshall, hope rooted in a God differentiated from creation narrows the possibilities for hope by looking to God alone and not to creation. Where Aquinas describes the role of persons as instrumental agents of hope, secondary to God the primary agent, Marshall perceives an unfortunate denial of resources for hope in creation.[268] In this way, Marshall claims the primacy of human freedom from God and the importance of this-worldly, rather than other-worldly hope.

With Aquinas, Marshall names the object of hope, the passion, as "a future good, difficult but possible to attain."[269] Marshall, however, does not embrace the distinction Aquinas makes between hope as "contending emotion"[270] and hope as a theological virtue, a future good that is difficult and impossible to obtain without God's help. Marshall names the emotion, appetite, or affect of hope *as* theological, using a different definition of "theological."[271] Marshall makes this shift because she prioritizes human agency, which she understands to be disempowered by a reliance on the infused grace of (traditional) theological virtue. "Classifying hope as an act of appetite is essential because of the connection between hope and

267. Ibid., 30–31.
268. Ibid., 32.
269. Ibid., 17.
270. Ibid.

271. Munztel, "Hope," argues that Thomistic hope offers an affective hope that is at the same time a divinely participatory hope that perdures with love and might provide the sort of basis for an ethics of hope to match Marshall's theology of hope.

[human] agency."[272] Since hope's job is "to generate and sustain moral agency," Marshall needs human hope to be motivating human efforts for social change.[273] She observes that both Aquinas and Augustine distinguish between God and creation when discussing the attainment of hope and its ends. Augustine makes clear, in *City of God*, that hope must rest with God and not with human efforts. Aquinas names theological hope as a theological virtue because it looks to its end in and through God, with persons as instrumental agents rather than competing or comparable ends. Marshall agrees with Aquinas that God helps us realize possibilities we otherwise might not imagine. God's help points us toward the highest good, Marshall's *basileia tou theou*, and with God's help, we are able to "expand our sense of possibility."[274] At the same time, however, Marshall's commitment to autonomous human agency and shared human-divine power leads her to reject the notion that God's help is necessarily different or more important than human help. "Because I understand God's help to be relational, I do not make a substantive distinction between divine and human helpers."[275] Here, Marshall is using the particular connotation of "relational power" that emphasizes cooperation and mutuality. The argument that God's power is relational grows from a perception that much of traditional theology teaches that God dominates creation with a detached and iron will from far away and from outside of history. This domineering God denies humans the comfort of divine companionship and shared suffering, while simultaneously denying humans their own freedom, agency, and power.

Marshall, who has already defined hope in terms of human ethical action, finds little hope in God-driven Creator-creation dynamic. "With many feminist and process theologians, I assert that God acts with creation, rather than upon it, as though from a distance, or even through it, as though creation were a passive vessel."[276] Instead, Marshall champions a dynamic that more evenly distributes power, and thereby more evenly distributes the source, activity, and ends of hope. She argues that relational power "is shared and persuasive rather than controlling and coercive. There is consequently no *substantive* distinction between God's power and human power; I cannot mark a line that separates them from one another,

272. Marshall, *Fig Tree*, 19.
273. Ibid., xiii.
274. Ibid., 24.
275. Ibid., 33.
276. Ibid.

let alone place trust in one and not the other."[277] Relational power supports Marshall's understanding of hope as an aspect of human freedom and a human capacity to effect change. The proper end of hope is the *basileia tou theou*, a vision of a community of peace and justice for this creation; the work of hope is the ethical task of expanding possibilities toward the *basileia tou theou*; God and creation cooperatively exercise their powers to perform the work of hope and effect the hoped-for change.

This understanding of power respects the freedom of each member of a relationship. Marshall champions shared power over forms of domination and control, in which one party remains a passive participant. In models of shared power, no one is a secondary or instrumental agent passively carrying out the will of another. There is always the freedom to refuse the job, to resist the order, to say no. In process theology, she argues, God lures and influences, but does not exact a tyrannical will. Feminist theology claims for women freedom and will, despite systemic political and hierarchical structures of exclusion. Human beings have the freedom to say no, as well as the propensity to misunderstand or misappropriate God's influence. So, we cannot hope for change without hoping in human ability to discern God's influence accurately and in human will to respond appropriately. When the power that effects change is cooperative in nature, we must hope that all necessary parties will perform their functions well in order for that power to be realized.[278]

Marshall's presentation of a hope fueled by relational power places God and humans on the same playing field, sharing similar categories of freedom, will, responsiveness, and interdependence. God and humans together contribute to the fulfillment of hope with comparable resources. "If we understand God's power to be relational, to be shared with creation, then one hopes in God by hoping in creation also."[279] God as relational encourages care for others and for the earth.[280] The hope of relational power also locates the end of hope *here*, in the midst of this creation that we know, rather than somewhere beyond our experience and imagination. Marshall explains that a hope oriented toward God does not call for us "to distinguish between hope for God and hope for history or creation. Affirming God's presence within creation, as I do, dissolves such a distinction. One hopes for the reunion of the separated, the flourishing of

277. Ibid.
278. Ibid., 33–34.
279. Ibid., 33.
280. Ibid., 52.

creation; this is the beatific vision and *summum bonum*."[281] God's presence within creation renders eschatological hopes for another life, somewhere *other* than here, contrary to the aim of hope, a distraction from the proper focus of hope: "hope for this life."[282] In fact, Marshall worries that the very discussion of eschatology risks drawing our attention away from "this world and its problems."[283] "We cannot talk about hope without talking about eschatology, but this turn to 'the last' things threatens the very possibility of a responsible hope, one that generates and sustains moral action on behalf of this planet and people."[284] Marshall thus aligns herself with those who feel that the church has over-emphasized the otherworldly character of our ultimate end in God,[285] and she supports the assertion that hope in a future life beyond this one leads to irresponsible neglect (or even outright harm) to the known created world and its inhabitants. She rejects "otherworldly visions that direct our attention away from this world and its problems, and I insist in a 'hope for this life.'"[286] With Rosemary Radford Ruether, she deplores the dualism "reinforced by an eschatological understanding that severs the tie between history and nature and thus envisions the culmination of human history in one salvific point at the end of a linear process."[287] Having established that eschatology distracts from the reality of lived experience and inhibits appropriate engagements with that reality, Marshall explains that responsible hope sustains the tension between the way things are and the way things might change to become.[288]

Marshall places the tension of hope between her claims that God is good and her realization that tragedy calls that claim into question. She asserts that God is "good and loving," and she points to God's activity in the world as evidence of the "particular moral quality" we can know about God.[289] In what stands out as her strongest assertion about God, Marshall argues that "in this world of absolute horror, God must be good to be worthy of worship," and we can know God's goodness because "God is at work in the world clearing space for freedom."[290] She justifies her claim

281. Ibid., 32.
282. Marshall, 45, citing Cone.
283. Marshall, *Fig Tree*, 45.
284. Ibid., 46.
285. Ibid., 44, referring to Moltmann, *Coming*, 50.
286. Marshall, *Fig Tree*, 45, citing Cone.
287. Marshall, *Fig Tree*, 46, citing Ruether.
288. Marshall, *Fig Tree*, 56.
289. Ibid., 53.
290. Ibid.

that "God is neither absent, malevolent, nor utterly unknowable," but acting for good in the world now, on similar claims made by "countless liberation theologians."[291] The fact that she feels compelled to defend God's goodness indicates the depth of her commitment to give an account of suffering, violence, and tragedy to those who challenge Christian claims of divine goodness in the face of human suffering. Marshall describes Wendy Farley's objections to Christianity's story of suffering explained by sin through the fall and ending with eschatological harmony: that story locates God and hope in the future, while providing insufficient justice and compassion here and now.[292] According to Farley, a more tragic—and therefore more appropriate—theology resists the tendency to presume the explanation or atonement of suffering.[293] Marshall adds to the importance of tragedy Kathleen Sands's rejection of eschatological assumptions that good can triumph over, or at least be separated from, evil: such narratives of God's goodness distract us from the reality of tragic existence, where there is no divine participation or clarity among the messiness of suffering.[294] For Sands, hope comes from God's compassionate presence with us as we resist evil and stand in solidarity with those who suffer. Sands trusts that God stands with us in suffering, and this faith moves her to claim that we can stand with others who suffer. Her hope rests not so much in relief from suffering but from companionship in suffering.[295] Like Sands, Farley finds hope in the sharing of pain: "Hope, therefore, rests not in a future salvation, but in the copresence of God and other persons within lived painful experience. In those moments, one learns that evil is not absolute."[296]

Like Farley and Sands, Marshall argues that hope must not ignore suffering, and that suffering can be resisted with the notion of an accompanying God who shares in our suffering as we share each others' suffering. Marshall then presents a hope that moves beyond resistance to suffering and motivates moral action: "Hope must not only enable resistance to suffering but also empower one to work for change. That is, hope must draw on the immediate strength offered through acts of compassion and on the prophetic visions that insist that real change in circumstances is possible. We must resist what we know and also envision something else."[297] In or-

291. Ibid.
292. Marshall, *Fig Tree*, 58–59, citing Farley, *Tragic*.
293. Marshall, *Fig Tree*, 53, citing Farley.
294. Marshall, *Fig Tree*, 61, citing Sands, *Escape*.
295. Sands, *Escape*.
296. Marshall, *Fig Tree*, 62.
297. Ibid., 63.

der for hope to be responsible, according to Marshall, it must both attend to present realities and effect future change. "We must remain accountable to the way things are *and* envision alternatives that cultivate a revolutionary disposition."[298] Hope, as the mean between despair and optimism thus acknowledges suffering with compassion and looks to improve the conditions that cause suffering, without succumbing to disconsolate paralysis or naive presumption.

Marshall's responsible hope relies on a present God who shares our suffering and our power, and on the human capacity to develop ethical practices in response to God, but without the assistance of divinely-infused virtue. She calls attention to those who demonstrate such ethical practices, because "we need a theological anthropology that celebrates these figures as individuals who chose to collaborate with God on behalf of the flourishing whole rather than questionable creatures whom God managed to utilize in spite of themselves. In order to survive and resist, we need a theology that affirms human potential to engage goodness and holds us responsible for doing so. We also need a theology that affirms God's unfailing and unbounded presence with all of creation such that the *theological* virtue of hope deepens and broadens our vision instead of redirecting our gaze."[299] Marshall urges us to "insist that such goodness reflects human potential and outlines human responsibility rather than humbly celebrating a momentary appearance of the Divine."[300] If we mistakenly attribute demonstrations of responsible hope to the infusion of divine virtue, Marshall argues, we are denigrating human potential and failing to hope in humanity.

Conclusion

Moltmann defends hope from superficial selfishness and from a spiritual, otherworldly escapism, with his theology of hope, born of a revelation of God's presence in his experience of godforsakenness. Moltmann narrates his theological hope with help from Bloch's philosophy of future possibility, which he uses to extend God's promises toward their fulfillment in the future of God's coming. Hope rests on the presence of God who suffers with the suffering, thereby promising relief from suffering with God in the new creation. Jesus Christ's crucifixion brings God to the suffering;

298. Marshall, *Fig Tree,* 64.
299. Ibid., 86–87.
300. Ibid.

his resurrection opens up this life to God's future. Moltmann articulates the tension of crucifixion and resurrection, of the uncertainty of death and the certainty of the future; in his latest work, his dialectic subsumes crucifixion and uncertainty into resurrection and the certain future of new creation. The people of this hope are justified in Christ's reconciliation of all. Their lives of care for each other and all of creation help prepare for God's arrival with the new creation of love and freedom.

Moltmannian hope reflects Moltmann's theology and highlights, especially the assumption of a passible, compassionate God and the value of investing in on-the-ground improvements to social injustice and ecological preservation. Freed from the distractions of Rapture, apocalyptic, and heavenly bliss eschatologies, Christians can hope for God's new creation of God's good creation and express that hope through responsible practices that make a difference in a world of suffering.

Moltmannian hope performs a theological response to doctrines that do not seem to fit with today's constructions of identity and agency, contemporary sensibilities about the character of God, and current life circumstances. The benefits of that response come with losses that might not be recognizable to adherents of Moltmannian hope. Exclusive dependence on Moltmannian hope detaches Christians from a wealth of resources within the broad river of tradition's doctrines of hope and deprives Christians of a theological hope sturdy enough to survive through and beyond the devastation and death of the world we know. Chapter 2 names some of the costs incurred by Moltmannian hope's dismissal of apparently irrelevant doctrines; these losses call for a reconsideration of resources for hope now discounted and forgotten.

2

The Costs of a Moltmannian Theological Hope

The legacy of Moltmann's theological hope abides as a contemporary doctrine, loosely articulated and broadly accepted. The broad outlines of his eschatological hope shape the presuppositions and imaginations of many theologians, clergy, and lay Christians, including some who have never engaged with his work directly. I have identified the legacy of Moltmann's theology of hope as *Moltmannian*, because it reflects his work, at least indirectly, even though it does not attend to all of the particulars of his theological scholarship. When this Moltmannian hope constitutes the exclusive resource for eschatological hope, the costs are great.

Moltmann offers Christians fresh access to theological hope, timely reconsiderations of hope in the midst of suffering, and an eschatology that embraces the future new creation of this world. His theology meets contemporary Christians where they stand with a way to reconnect with God, eschatology, and hope. Moltmannian hope demonstrates that connection through support for ecclesial commitments to inclusivity, ministry to those in need, care for the environment, resistance to injustice, and active reconstructions of social structures. Moltmannian hope reflects Moltmann's theology as it affirms efforts to rescue and sustain this world in preparation for God's transforming arrival. Moltmannian hope encourages freedom from the constraints of closed hierarchical institutions and political systems; it redirects people from the distractions of apocalyptic and other-worldly end-times speculation; and it authorizes detachment from doctrine that might seem inappropriate for today. It prioritizes action over theory, cooperates with secular social activism, and provides an appealing and relevant way to make sense of eschatological hope in contemporary circumstances. Moltmann draws together resurrection life and the trinitarian God with the new creation of the known world, to produce an eschatological hope that has been appreciatively adopted, adapted, and embraced. The decisive mark of Moltmannian hope's widespread popularity is its ideological normativity; Christians teach, preach, and presume a Moltmannian theological hope, even when they have no conscious awareness of Moltmann's scholarly influence.

Despite the appeal of Moltmannian hope, an exclusive embrace of this hope renders largely invisible many rich theological resources, the reasons for their dismissal, and possible rebuttals to that dismissal. Almost fifty years into the era of Moltmann-influenced hope, many Christians have lost track of those aspects of hope that Moltmann drops to make room for his construction of a relevant hope for the post-Auschwitz twentieth century. Moltmann's negative appraisals of church teachings about hope are now comfortably familiar; and yet, his critiques and reconstructions do not all stand up to examination. His readings of doctrine are at times uncharitable, inattentive to systematic theological context, and narrowed by his modern and ecclesial investments. When Christians accept uncritically Moltmann's theological discernments, they lose contact with a wealth of wisdom about life lived in eschatological hope. Responses to Moltmann's theological constraints and to Moltmannian presuppositions abound within Christian tradition and doctrine; but if those responses are not acknowledged or consulted, they are not accessible as resources. Hope loses strength and fortitude.

Moltmann's scholarship features constructive work on theological loci. He challenges and often leaves behind the theological teachings with which he disagrees. He does not invest his efforts in doctrinal continuity in difference. Stanley Grenz and Roger Olson observe that

> by his own confession Moltmann intends his theology to be "biblically founded, eschatologically oriented, and politically responsible." However his methodology is somewhat more complex. In fact, there is reason to doubt whether he has a coherent theological method in any traditional sense. This lack of systematic approach arises partly from his lack of interest in correct doctrine. "I am not so concerned with pure theory but with practical theory." He sees the task of theology not so much as to provide an interpretation of the world as to transform it in the light of hope for its ultimate transformation by God.[1]

---

1. Grenz and Olson, 20*th Century*, 175.

Moltmann works to transform the world in the light of hope from the midst of his particular situatedness in twentieth- and twenty-first-century modernity; and his theology both reflects and speaks to the modern imagination.[2] There is no single, agreed-upon list of characteristics from which to discern the theological sensibilities of modernity. For the present purpose, I note three: newness, the authority of experience, and stand-alone biblical hermeneutics.[3]

Moltmann's initial writing on hope in 1965 celebrated the new and the future.[4] Over the course of Moltmann's scholarship, his focus of hope shifted from the completely other eschatology of radical newness to a more continuous development of new upon new. (Moltmannian hope now reflects this later emphasis.) In 1969, Moltmann emphasized the discontinuity between history and the new creation: "If, for the sake of this God, Christians hope for the future, they hope for a *novum ex nihilo*."[5] In 1979, he argued for a balance of eschatological otherness, distinct from history, and a continuum of history and the eschatological completion of history.

> The more faith interprets Christian transcendence eschatologically, the more it will understand the boundary of immanence historically and give itself up to the movement of transcending. But the more it interprets this eschatological transcendence in Christian terms—that is, with its eyes on the crucified Jesus—the more it will become conscious that the qualitatively new future of God has allied itself with those who are dispossessed, denied and downtrodden at the present day; so that this future does not begin up at the spearheads of progress in a "progressive society," but down below, among society's victims. It will have to

---

2. In Moltmann's earliest work, he sets out to establish connections between secular modernity and the contemporary church. He tries to legitimize each one to the other, so that theological hope can be relevant and recognizable in the twentieth century. In his later work, he presents his theology as more resistant to and critical of modernity, while continuing to sustain a hope that addresses the current circumstances of Christianity, but popular Moltmannian hope has not received those nuances.

3. Adam, *Making Sense of New Testament Theology* and *What is Postmodern Biblical Criticism?*, describes the priority of the new, and addresses the detachment of biblical interpretation from pre-modernity in *Faithful Interpretation*, 11–36. Rossi addresses modernity's construction of the authority of experience in "The Authority of Experience."

4. Moltmann, *Theology*.

5. Moltmann, *Religion*, 171; Neal, *Theology*, 211.

link hope for the eschatological future with a loving solidarity with the depressed.[6]

In 1996, Moltmann described a continual progression from history to its end (which is its beginning): "Raising [of the dead] is not a new creation; it is a new creating of this same mortal life for the life that is eternal."[7] In 2007, he noted that Jewish and Christian belief looks to redemption *of*, not *from*, the world we already inhabit. "Christ doesn't lead people in the afterlife of religious escapism or flight from the world, but gives them back to the earth as her faithful people."[8] Hope leans toward the newest version of the now we know.

Moltmann consistently prioritizes the new in his readiness to dismiss older theology at will; only those doctrines that support his theology of hope warrant attention. Moltmannian hope readily sets aside wisdom of the past in favor of the new. Moltmannian hope detaches itself from what it understands to be the outdated and mistaken theology of hope offered by the classical tradition. It also detaches itself from Moltmann's concerns about secular hope and instead elides eschatological hope with the popular modern model of hope in steady improvement. Eschatological hope thus manifests as the expectation of a continuing trajectory from new improvements to an even newer and divinely-improved version of this creation here on earth. The particular character of modern newness embraced by Moltmannian hope entails an ever-developing, new-and-improved version of the present: things are getting better every day.

Moltmannian hope's priority of the future illustrates an extreme form of modernity's focus on time and its life-determining force. The future establishes hope and gives the past and present meaning. History gains importance through its incorporation into the future; the present is empty without the presence of the future. This future is not detached from current time; Moltmann corrects the "understandable misconception" of the Apostles' Creed that imagines Christ in heaven, "waiting for a time when he will all at once 'come again' to judge the living and the dead. That is the picture behind the saying about Christ's 'coming again.'"[9] Instead, Moltmann argues, "if we talk about 'Christ's coming,' then he is already in the process of coming, and in the power of hope we open ourselves today with all our senses for the experiences of his arrival. By arrival we mean a

6. Moltmann, *Future*, 17.
7. Moltmann, *Coming*, 75; Neal, *Theology*, 211.
8. Moltmann, "Presence," 587.
9. Moltmann, *End*, 88.

future which is already present, yet without ceasing to be the future. 'Jesus is in the process of coming.'"[10] The image of being in process matches contemporary expectations of personal, economic, and social development.

Rossing reflects Moltmannian hope's commitment to a particular understanding of time when she argues against the end-time theology of Rapture movements, in favor of God's continuing time. Sermons that stress hope for the future—in our children, social service, or care for the environment—often cast that hope in the context of an eschatological future, such that human efforts now will facilitate the arrival of a future that elides historical future with eschatological future. Throughout a Moltmannian theology of hope, the future claims priority as the end (although it does not itself actually end) and the beginning, and it shares in the agency of change for God and for creation.

Future-determined hope suggests that the God of hope is defined by the future and God's participation in time. The church's understanding that God is out of time and yet works within time thus gives way to an understanding of God bound by time who brings the future to a future-oriented humanity. One cost of that shift is that hope loses the assurance of a God not driven by time's limitations, not daunted by current events or future catastrophe, and not pressured by the ticking clock of earth's demise. Hope loses the open possibilites and unknowable mysteries of an eschatology shaped by the imagination of God, the creator of time who is therefore not contained in time.

Modernity's focus on newness depletes the resources for eschatological hope, by downgrading the past presentations of theological hope from the cumulative wisdom of the church to unnecessary preambles. The priority of new hope turns God's fulfilled promises to the people of Israel and Christ's resurrection into affirmations that God *will* fulfill the promises. The continually progressing, upward trajectory of hope displaces the circular, cyclical ecclesial year, in which the hope of the resurrection is celebrated on Easter and in every eucharist, and the hope of the eternal life of Christ is nurtured by participation in the liturgical year. The ongoing progression of the new toward the even newer overshadows hope in an eternal life that is entirely of God, for whom nothing is new or old.

The authority of experience stands as another marker of modernity that characterizes Moltmannian hope. Moltmann's theology of hope grows from his own particular experience of sharing with God the experience suffering abandonment; and that experience determines, includes,

10. Ibid., 89.

absorbs his own identity and God's. His experience of suffering with God who suffers defines God's experience on the terms of his experience, and that experience resonates with a broad societal sense of loss. In this account, divine experience is close enough to human experience that it can be shared and understood as a shared experience. Moltmann explains that "if a person once feels the infinite passion of God's love which finds expression here, then he understands the mystery of the triune God. God suffers with us—God suffers from us—God suffers for us: it is this experience of God that reveals the true God."[11] Moltmann here refers to the whole of the Trinity, and in so doing he has, as Paul Molnar observes, "blurred the distinction between human experience and God's experience."[12] Who God is and what God can do fits within the realm of human experience. Moltmannian hope affirms personal experience and grants authority of that experience over the wisdom and guidance of some teachers and teachings.

There are some drawbacks to claiming the revelatory authority of this particular experience of theological hope. People who do not share the experience Moltmann describes evidently do not have access to knowledge of the true God. All other knowledge of God, which is to say, all other experiences of God, do not receive the same stamp of authority. This revelation is confined to those who share (or desire to share) the particular experience of suffering as described. The description becomes a definition; experiences of hope in God that do not feature God's suffering are suspect. God's transcendence is scaled down to fit within the sphere of human experience; and without a sense of God's radical transcendence, human experience determines the possibilities of hope. Moltmann's revelatory experience exemplifies the modern sense that personal identity contains experience, even when the experience is an encounter with God. Philip Rossi draws on K. Schmitz's work on interiority to illustrate this containment: "Schmitz contends that modern understandings of subjectivity and interiority 'yield only a muted sense of trans-human reality and a muffled transcendence' inasmuch as 'various post-Cartesian strategies have absorbed reality into the horizon of subjectivity, giving us at best a shadowy and indeterminate transcendence.' As a result, any 'positive appreciation of transcendent depth and breadth. . .must capitulate to human terms and be absorbed and refracted into the horizon of human immanence before it is acceptable.'"[13] When hope is founded on proscribed

---

11. Moltmann, *Trinity*, 4.
12. Molnar, "Function," 684.
13. Rossi, "Authority," 275.

individual experiences of shared suffering with God, God's transcendence is lessened to fit within human experience, and the people who do not have or desire those particular experiences are excluded from the sphere of recognized eschatological hope.

Moltmann's biblical hermeneutics stands as a third modernity marker, as it displays some of the effects of modernity's prioritization of the new and (a particular sort of) experience. Moltmann's theological work coincides with an explosion of biblical interpretation methods: from textual, form, redaction, and literary criticism to structural, narrative, feminist, and postmodern criticism; however, he does not claim involvement in or debt to any particular method. He draws on some of these, but his interpretations chiefly reflect his new insights and his experience of God's love through shared suffering. Moltmann eschews those passages about law, gender, final judgment, and eschatology that apparently conflict with his theology of hope.[14] A new-and-now, experience-supported approach to interpretation cannot account for multiple senses, multiple interpretations of scripture, challenging biblical passages, or challenging biblical interpreters.

Moltmannian hope follows Moltmann's appreciation of Old Testament passages that speak of God in anthropomorphic terms. Moltmann's theological attention to such passages complements the work of Terence Fretheim and Open Theism theologians who consider anew biblical indications that God does indeed change. Christian doctrine has long grappled with the wide range of biblical accounts of God, the interpretations thereof, and the ramifications for theological hope. Moltmannian hope that takes as given recent support for a God of lessened transcendence and increased suffering misses out on centuries of debate and discernment.[15]

---

14. For example, Moltmann cannot make sense of Matthew's description of the last judgment. The idea that the Son of Man would send some people to eternal punishment and others to eternal life does not fit his theology of hope, in which the coming future brings new creation to humanity without punitive judgment; so he cannot accept the plain sense. He cannot discern a metaphorical sense for this separation, either. As a result, Moltmann downplays the sheep and goats image and Jesus' pronouncement of separation, in favor of the exhortation to care for the needy, in whom Christ is present. See *Coming*, 165, 250–51.

15. More than twenty-five years ago, John Barton expressed concerns about Moltmann's language for God, noting his fear that "Moltmann has not registered sufficiently that he is making some extraordinarily bold moves by applying to God terms such as 'suffering,' 'history' or 'experience.' It is difficult to escape the impression that Moltmann finds talk of God fundamentally unproblematic" ("Moltmann," 6). Since then, Moltmann's bold moves have become normative. Moltmannian hope

Moltmannian hope supports its characterization of God with an incoherent hermeneutical practice of selective literalism. The God of Moltmannian hope is affective, loving, sometimes moved to anger and disappointment with creation, but primarily responsive, compassionate, and restorative. This characterization of God comes from specific biblical passages, interpreted literally. Of course, no biblical literalism is consistently literal; readers always need to make the same sorts of discernments they make every day with spoken and non-spoken interactions. Concurrently, no biblical interpretation avoids some degree of plain-sense assessment. Moltmannian readers of scripture, like most other readers, make sense of what they read through combinations of plain sense, metaphor, allegory, community formation, and pre-existing expectations; yet Moltmannian readers often claim the authority of their interpretations based on "what the text says." As noted in the previous chapter, when Barbara Rossing argues for the authority of her interpretation of Revelation, in correction of Rapture eschatology's interpretation, she claims that what she is saying is *in* the Bible.[16] She does not, however, offer an explanation for the fact that the fundamentalist literalist Christians she opposes authorize their interpretations the same way. Attempts to cancel out one literalism with another reflect an ill-considered hermeneutics.

Moltmann adopts (without claiming) a literalist translation of many passages of the Old Testament that use anthropomorphic descriptions of God's feelings and actions in time and in responsive relationship with God's people; he understands God in the Gospels to take on human suffering. Moltmann argues that the passionate and compassionate God feels the pain of a father abandoning his son on the cross, feels the pain of the son abandoned by his father, and then feels the suffering of humanity as well.

Moltmannian hope that follows Moltmann's hermeneutics and ties itself to his particular interpretation of the character of God retains hope in a largely anthropomorphic image of a God of love. Moltmann does make a distinction between God's feelings and human feelings (as noted in chapter 1), but his literal account of some biblical passages—and the authority he grants that account— gives the impression that God is moved

---

now presumes that biblical accounts of the God of hope can be unproblematically understood in a plain sense interpretation (when that interpretation supports God's passionate experience of suffering).

16. Rossing, "Prophecy," 562.

by feelings the way people are and that God is buffeted by emotions the way people are.

Moltmannian hope appreciates scriptural presentations of God that describe God as loving, kind, merciful, fair, and gentle; it rejects understandings of God as sovereign and almighty, preferring instead God who shares power and weakness with humanity. John Sanders, an Openness theologian strongly influenced by Moltmann, advocates a God who takes risks, who exposes Godself to vulnerability for the sake of a particular kind of give-and-take relationship with humans. Sanders describes

> a personal God who enters into genuine give-and-take relations with his creatures. Neither an impersonal deity nor a personal deity who meticulously controls every event takes risk. The portrait of God developed here is one according to which God sovereignly wills to have human persons become collaborators with him in achieving the divine project of mutual relations of love. Such an understanding of the divine-human relationship may be called "relational theism." By this I mean any model of the divine-human relationship that includes genuine give-and-take relations between God and humans such that there is a receptivity and a degree of contingency in God. In give-and-take relationships God receives and does not merely give.[17]

Sanders argues that we learn about what God is like and how to speak of God through metaphorical and anthropomorphic language of the Bible[18]; and he objects to representations of God as sovereign (impassible and immutable), and non-contingent.[19] According to Sanders, God listens, responds, and changes in response to prayers; an impassible God would mean "there is no place for imprecatory prayer."[20]

Sanders sees different interpretations of scriptural passages about God in terms of different models of God: the best model affords the best

---

17. Sanders, *Risks*, 12.

18. Ibid., 15.

19. Sanders cites James' exhortations to submit to God, rather than to internal conflicts and external disputes: "You do not have, because you do not ask" (4:2). According to Sanders, this passage makes no sense within a model of the sovereign God who does not listen and change course in response to prayers: "if the God of specific sovereignty wanted you to have it, then he would ensure that you asked for it." James' next sentence could be understood as clarifying the previous: "You ask and do not receive, because you ask wrongly, in order to spend what you get on your pleasures" (4:3). However, Sanders reads that to mean that "we sometimes petition God from wrong motives and so we do not receive" (ibid., 270–71).

20. Ibid., 271.

interpretation, and scripture supports the best model. Sanders' hermeneutical approach presents a portrait of God similar to the God of Moltmannian hope, and Sanders provides a more explicit narrative of his method of interpretation. However, while Sanders recognizes different interpretations, he does not accept the possibility that scriptural passages about God may point to divine characteristics and actions through radically different metaphors.

Without a framework, or a grammar, for making sense of scriptural assertions about God and God's actions, Moltmannian hope relies on an unarticulated and unaccountable determination of what scripture "really means." The authority of Moltmannian hope rests on an idiosyncratic hermeneutic determined more by ideology and preference than by a narratable connection with the rest of scripture and the rest of scriptural interpretation. A hermeneutics without patience for making sense of apparently conflicting scriptural assertions about God makes no room for the memory of communities who have adopted scriptural passages and claimed them as their own, through interpretations specific to their immediate crises and faithful to the trusted interpreters who precede them.[21] When passages are rejected from scripture, hope can be relinquished along with the verses. A passage that seems inappropriate today might seem a welcome resource in radically changed circumstances. God's constant presence continues to provide hope regardless of the limits of human perception and imagination.

The content and method of Moltmann's scholarship trickle down into Moltmannian hope such that adherents see no reason to reconsider the possible value of the doctrine he has set aside. The first cost of a Moltmannian theology of hope is the loss of *interest* in making connections with previous and differing claims taught and received by the church across time and geography. Further doctrinal costs include: God's impassibility, Jesus Christ's two natures, heaven beyond this world, theocentric anthropology, and discipleship. When hope is difficult to sustain, and when the resources of hope are chiefly provided by one, narrowed, theological account, it is time to pay attention to what is lost.

---

21. I recently heard an Episcopal preacher explain to the congregation that the gospel reading from Matthew 24 did not belong with the truth about the God he knows. He was unhappy with the images of God gleaning the people from the fields, entering homes like a thief in the night, causing weeping and gnashing of teeth. He pronounced: "This is not a God I can believe in." He encouraged the congregation to join him in excising the passage from the Bible; and he continued with a description of the God he can accept, who is gentler, more inclusive, less judgmental.

Lost: Divine Impassibility and Perfect Compassion

Moltmannian hope rests on the belief that God shares human suffering in loving compassion and in response to human need and prayer. This hope assumes that God must be capable of changing emotions and actions in order to be a caring, comforting God; hope depends on a God who experiences what we experience and brings relief from those sometimes overwhelming experiences. This hope expects God to be in a non-hierarchical relation to creation. The fulfillment of this hope involves God and human collaboration. God *needs* creation for ultimate, eschatological fulfillment. The cost of this claim is God's perfect compassion that abides undaunted in the face of the suffering, despair, and death.

Moltmann's personal discovery of hope comes through his revelation of God's suffering presence with him. His theology of hope reflects that experience of divine passibility manifest in God the Father's experience of suffering and loss in the crucifixion. Moltmann argues that the resurrection victory over death is God's victory over the very absence of God. In Moltmann's account of the Passion, Jesus Christ's experience of being abandoned by God is the ontological absence of God; God the Father actually abandons the Son. Further, since God suffers when Christ suffers, God, Godself, is abandoned by God. The resurrection marks God's victory over God's own abandonment, so that humans will no longer be abandoned by God as God was abandoned by God. God embraces within Godself the brokenness and godforsakenness of creation through Christ's suffering and death on the cross. God consoles creation by sharing in the depths of total divine abandonment.

Dietrich Bonhoeffer's claim, written while he was in prison, that "only the suffering God can help," has become a familiar marker of Moltmannian hope, broadly understood to mean that: there is no hope in God who does not suffer; God suffers and therefore God is worthy of our hope. Bonhoeffer presents this claim with the specification that it is Jesus who is suffering, but both he and Moltmann understand God to be participating wholly in the passion, in abandoning and being abandoned on the cross, and in weakness. Moltmann underscores Bonhoeffer's phrase: "A God who by reason of his essence cannot suffer, cannot suffer with us either, or even feel sympathy. The *Deus impassibilis* is a God without a heart and without compassion, a cold heavenly power."[22] Moltmannian hope stands in opposition to divine impassibility.

---

22. Moltmann, *End*, 70.

Moltmann's criticism of divine impassibility depends on the theory of malign Greek philosophical influence. He imagines that Greek thought imposed itself on the otherwise wholly separate Hebrew theology and constrained early Christian theologians who could not see the true God because of their Hellenistic blinders.[23] This premise bears investigation, since it is largely based on particular claims of mid-twentieth century biblical criticism that have not been as predominant in scholarship before or afterward. Paul Gavrilyuk describes the position Moltmann adopts:

> It has become almost commonplace in contemporary theological works to pass a negative judgment upon the patristic concept of the divine impassibility. Superficial criticism of the divine apatheia on purely etymological grounds, without any serious analysis of its actual function in the thought of the Fathers, has become a convenient polemical starting point for the subsequent elaboration of a passibilist position. Such a dismissive attitude towards the patristic heritage is guided far more by the contemporary climate of opinion on the issue of divine suffering than by any serious engagement with the theology of the Fathers.
>
> A standard line of criticism places divine impassibility in the conceptual realm of Hellenistic philosophy, where the term allegedly meant the absence of emotions and indifference to the world, and then concludes that impassibility in this sense cannot be an attribute of the Christian God. In this regard, a popular dichotomy between Hebrew and Greek theological thinking has been elaborated specifically with reference to the issues of divine (im)passibility and (im)mutability. On this reading, the God of the prophets and apostles is the God of pathos, whereas the God of the philosophers is apathetic.[24]

The Hebrew/Greek dichotomy theory Gavrilyuk critiques is not socially plausible: coexisting, intermingled, and hybrid communities demonstrate more of a fluid and partial influence of ideological influences than the imposition of opposite concepts from one portion of a community on another. The theory is also contradicted by the ways that early Christian theologians worked to articulate distinctly Christian accounts of available philosophical thought. Certainly early Christian theology engages with

23. Moltmann's reading of the historical church does not allow for the possibility that early Christian theology might have been influenced by the intellectual culture of the day *and* have worked with familiar philosophical thought to articulate distinctly Christian accounts of the distinctly Christian God.

24. Gavrilyuk, *Suffering*, 3.

The Costs of a Moltmannian Theological Hope

secular ideas, with greater and lesser degrees of discernment and wisdom. Hellenistic thought did indeed influence Christian thinking about God, but twenty-first century theological discourse would benefit from a more complicated than dichotomous account of Hellenistic influences.

The church sometimes tries to describe God who is Creator of all, the great I AM, *and* intimately related to creation, in covenant, incarnation, and salvation in terms of paradox, such that God is *passibly impassible* or *impassibly passible*. Moltmann's approach is to choose passibility over impassibility. Nancy Bedford explains:

> The Christian tradition has struggled with various ways to reconcile the *impassiblity* of God understood as a safeguard of God's transcendence and "wholly other" character, and the fact of God's necessary involvement in the passion of the Son, in order to safeguard the soteriological dimension of the cross. This led to formulations such as the 'suffering of the impassible God.' Moltmann believes that this sort of paradoxical formulation concedes too much to natural theology, particularly because in his view the more weight given to the axiom of God's impassibility, the weaker becomes the ability to identify God with the Passion of Christ. This fundamentally Trinitarian rationale (that is, the conviction that in the cross "God was in Christ reconciling the world into Godself") is what pushes Moltmann to recast the "axiom of impassibility" (*Apathieaxiom*) into the "axiom of God's passion" (*Axiom des leidenschaftlichen Gottes*), in the double sense of "suffering" (*Leiden*) and of "ardent love" (*Leidenschaft*).[25]

Moltmann determines that God cannot love without suffering; suffering expresses God's love; passibility outweighs impassibility.

The priority of passibility reflects Moltmannian hope's rejection of the grammar for speaking of God that Aquinas offers in the beginning of the *Summa Theologica*,[26] in the midst of questions about the essence of God and the nature of the Trinity. There, Aquinas presents six words, often referred to as *attributes*, as indicators of a grammar that guides speech about God. These are familiar words which, analogically, point to what God is not.[27] The six are listed in an order that demonstrates how the words work together. The first is simplicity: God is not made up of various

---

25. Bedford, "God's Power," 106.

26. I, q. 3–11.

27. These are not, properly speaking, *attributes*, since they are not properties that God holds.

parts. The second is perfection: God's simplicity is not a lack of complexity or multiplicity, but the whole of perfect goodness. Third, God's simplicity and perfection are not limited in size or breadth or extent because of God's infinity. God's infinity, perfection, and simplicity, do not change, cannot be depleted or added to, as indicated by the fourth, God's immutability and impassibility (frequently identified simply as impassibility), which affirm that God neither needs more nor experiences loss. Fifth, eternity marks that God's simplicity, perfection, infinity, immutability and impassibility do not bind to a particular time. Finally, God's unity shows that these attributes are not separable. God's oneness is completely perfect, limitless and endless, unchanging and unmovable. Hope for eternal life in the company of this God is hope in a life more abundantly good than any creature can fully imagine.

Moltmannian hope understands these attributes in relation to modern and anthropocentric accounts of the good, such that God's transcendent abundance seems insufficiently supportive of human needs. Thus, simplicity seems less than complexity; perfection seems to cut off possible growth and improvement; and infinity seems to downplay on-the-ground reality. Immutability and impassibility seem to separate God from human change and feelings; eternity seems to downplay the importance of the historical here and now; and oneness infringes on unique individuality. Impassibility causes the most offense to Moltmannian hope, as it seems to contradict God's identity as the God of love whose compassion grows in response to human need.

Hope that depends on a passible God and rejects these attributes loses contact with a traditional grammar for God without establishing an alternative grammar to show continuity and difference. The loss of fluency in the grammar of attributes makes communication between that grammar and different accounts of God all the more challenging. Eschatological hope that is defined by divine passibility trades in a life with God that is undeterred, undiminished, and undercut by the crises, failures, disasters, and sins of this world for hope in a passible God who loves, cares for, and shares suffering with. If God is subject to suffering, then God is not perfect, and hope must depend on an imperfect God. If God changes in response to creation, then God is neither perfect nor simple, God cannot be infinite or eternal, and unity is impossible as well, since the substance of unity is variable and inconstant. Hope in a passible God displaces the sovereignty of the Creator God with a God like us, and the divine fulfillment of creation with an eschatological end of our own design. The resulting Moltmannian theology of hope embraces this formula and loses the possibility that the God of hope suffers in love without diminishing Godself in simplicity, perfection, infinity, impassibility, eternity, and unity. Hope in God's perfect compassion fades as hope in God's contingent suffering becomes the single, established truth. When Moltmann categorically dismisses accounts of divine impassibility as outdated descriptions of a distant, unsympathetic, cold God who cannot offer hope to creation, he oversimplifies a long theological history of careful speech about what cannot be contained in speech; and he reifies that oversimplification into a non-negotiable foundation for theological hope.

Moltmannian hope reflects Moltmann's conclusion without an appreciation of what Moltmann rejects and why. In the process, hope provided by a God who is perfectly compassionate *and* greater than the limitations of suffering and death is set aside as woefully inadequate. Moltmannian hope depends on a God who experiences what we experience and brings relief, soon. If God does not seem to prevent or alleviate suffering and despair, then it seems that God must at least *feel* that pain along with those who suffer and then, perhaps, regret and repent God's own errors which led to human suffering. Hope thus arises from the confidence that God knows, feels, and reacts to human experience with ready relief or at least comparable shared suffering. Moltmannian theology embraces the God whose love is suffering love, but it loses the God of hope who suffers in constant love through Jesus Christ and remains transcendent, in simplicity, perfection, infinity, impassibility, eternity, and unity. Moltmannian hope expects that the fulfillment of hopes involves God and human collaboration[28] and that God needs creation for eschatological completion.[29] Moltmannian hope opts for a recognizably anthropomorphic and anthropocentric God with limitations instead of a God whose divine compassion is unmoveably perfect *and* whose incarnation, Jesus Christ, shares all human suffering and dies a human death.

Lost: The Two Natures of Christ

The God of Moltmann's theology of hope is the trinitarian God of love who, on the one hand, absorbs into the whole of God all the particularity of Jesus Christ, and, on the other hand, demotes Jesus Christ to the role of

---

28. Moltmann, *Creation* 87; Molnar on Torrance, "Function," 80.
29. "God 'needs' the word and man. If God is love, then he neither will nor can be without the one who is his beloved" (*Trinity*, 57–58).

facilitator, such that Jesus' suffering and death on the cross make possible God's access to humanity. (Moltmann does not always clarify whether he means God the first person of the Trinity or God the One in Three.) He sets aside the two natures of Jesus Christ and downplays the efficacy of the incarnation, crucifixion, and resurrection, such that Christ is no longer *the* hope but the affirmation of God's promises, extended into the future. He declines a Christology wherein Jesus Christ lives, suffers, and dies as fully human *and* as fully divine.

Moltmann's work on the Trinity has helped stir up a renewed attention to trinitarian theology in the last few decades. His particular contributions present the Trinity as an open set of relations, into which creation will be drawn. Moltmannian eschatological hope looks toward God's indwellng of creation and creation's participation in the perichoretic relations of the Trinity itself. In the meantime, it seems, the Trinity longs for its completion through the inclusion of creation in its multiple and unified identity. The God of this Trinity shares in the human condition directly; Jesus' role on the cross is to bring God to human suffering.

Moltmann's trinitarian theology presents a social Trinity that directly engages with creation. God, Christ, and the Holy Spirit share all, and Jesus' suffering and death are trinitarian experiences. Instead of a Christology of two natures, wherein Jesus Christ is fully human and fully divine and suffers as fully human and remains fully divine even as the incarnation of God, Moltmann prioritizes God the Father (while claiming non-hierarchical trinitarian relations) and places shared human suffering chiefly in the person of God. Bauckham observes that, "eschewing two-natures Christology in favor of Jesus' being-in-relation and being-in-history, Moltmann seems to see Jesus as a human being whose relationship to the Father in the Spirit makes him the unique Son of God."[30]

Moltmann narrates the two-natures Christology as another ramification of (his perception of) the problematic Hellenistic influence on Christianity; he argues that Christianity developed the two natures of Christ in order to counteract the problems raised by the distant, static, philosophical God. Without these problems, Moltmann posits, the two natures would not be necessary or appropriate. He acknowledges that early church liturgy did attend to the passion and the cross,

> but theological reflection was not in a position to identify God himself with the suffering and the death of Jesus. As a result of this, traditional Christology came very near to docetism,

30. Bauckham, 208.

> according to which Jesus only appeared to suffer and only appeared to die abandoned by God: this did not happen in reality. The intellectual bar to this came from the philosophical concept of God, according which God's being is incorruptible, unchangeable, indivisible, incapable of suffering and immortal; human nature, on the other hand, is transitory, changeable, divisible, capable of suffering and mortal. The doctrine of the two natures in Christ began from this fundamental distinction, in order to be able to conceive of the personal union of the two natures in Christ in light of this difference.[31]

Moltmann's alternative establishes the Passion as primarily a divine event in which the Trinity is the agent and participant in the cross: "If the cross of Jesus is understood as a divine event, i.e. as an event between Jesus and his God and Father, it is necessary to speak in trinitarian terms of the Son and the Father and the Spirit. In that case the doctrine of the Trinity is no longer an exorbitant and impractical speculation about God, but is nothing other than a shorter version of the passion narrative of Christ in its significance for the eschatological freedom of faith and the life of oppressed nature."[32] Salvation requires the complete absorption of Jesus' suffering, which is the suffering of all creation, into God, as the content of the Trinity. "Only if all disaster, forsakenness by God, absolute death, the infinite curse of damnation and sinking into nothingness *is in God himself*, is community with this God eternal salvation, infinite joy, indestructible election and divine life."[33] By shifting the suffering of Jesus Christ into "God himself," Moltmann turns away from the human and divinely redemptive suffering of Jesus Christ and instead places God and people together as those who suffer.[34]

Moltmann's narrative of the salvific trinitarian Passion translates Jesus' suffering and death into solely divine suffering and defers Christ's role in redemption to the future fulfillment of God's promises. The key players become the suffering God and the human individual who is abandoned

31. Moltmann, *Crucified*, 227–28.
32. Ibid., 246.
33. Ibid., italics added
34. Weinandy notes that "this co-suffering of God with the suffering victim is intended to engender hope and consolation. At times one feels that what they wish is a God who feels sorry for them because of their plight—a God who authenticates and justifies their self-pity. Actually, such a view . . . radically diminishes the salvific significance of Christ's redemptive suffering and so the import of his body, as the whole church and as individual members within it, which actively co-suffers with him for its own sanctification and for humankind's well-being and salvation" (*Suffer?*, 281).

and unloved. Moltmann asks: "If the believer experiences his freedom and the new possibility of his life in the fact that the love of God reaches him, the loveless and the unloved, in the cross of Christ, what must be the thoughts of a theology which corresponds to this love?"[35] His answer involves the love of God who draws the individual into God's inner life, through the cross of Christ:

> [The believer] is in fact taken up into the inner life of God, if in the cross of Christ he experiences the love of God for the godless, the enemies, in so far as the history of Christ is the inner life of God himself. In that case, if he lives in this love, he lives in God and God in him. If he lives in this freedom, he lives in God and God in him. If one conceives of the Trinity as an event of love in the suffering and the death of Jesus—and that is something which faith must do—then the Trinity is no self-contained group in heaven, but an eschatological process open for men on earth, which stems from the cross of Christ. By the secular cross on Golgotha, understood as open vulnerability and as the love of God for the loveless and unloved, dehumanized men, God's being and God's life is open to true man.[36]

The event of the Trinity draws God and humanity into interpenetrating life together, through the cross. Jesus Christ himself need not embody humanity or divinity or both, because God and humanity fulfill each other.

Moltmann opens the Trinity to include creation in salvation, but he also narrows the Trinity by rendering the humanity of Jesus and the efficacy of Christ's salvation secondary to the assumption of suffering into God's experience. In Moltmann's account, the end of hope for humanity is full participation in the Trinity. God has taken on human suffering in order to bring humans into fellowship with God; Jesus Christ serves that end. Moltmann's theology of hope emphasizes salvation as the union of the Trinity and humanity, through God's suffering, and God's need for humanity to join the Trinity. The cost of this account of hope is hope in Jesus Christ as the model of the fulfillment of humanity in relationship with God. Humanity no longer lives in unity with Christ now, in hope of the fulfillment of humanity through Christ to come. Hope no longer rests on Jesus, who, as Kathryn Tanner notes, is God-with-us, "the one in whom

---

35. Moltmann, *Crucified*, 248.
36. Ibid., 249.

God's relationship with us attains perfection."[37] Tanner describes the hope in Jesus Christ that Moltmannian hope deflects:

> By way of this perfected humanity in union with God, God's gifts are distributed to us—we are saved—just to the extent that we are one with Christ in faith and love; unity with Christ the gift-giver is the means of our perfection as human beings, just as the union of humanity and divinity in Christ was the means of his perfect humanity. United with Christ, we are thereby emboldened as ministers of God's beneficence to the world, aligning ourselves with, entering into communion with, those in need as God in Christ was *for us* in our need and as Christ was a man for others, especially those in need.[38]

Tanner counters Moltmann's assumption that God's experience of Jesus' experience of abandonment by God is the determinative event of salvation, with the claim that Jesus' oneness with God is never broken, even by death. Through the divine perfection of humanity which is Jesus Christ, humanity is drawn into constant and eternal connection with God, through all suffering and death and beyond. "United with Christ, we too are inseparable from God."[39] Through the two-natures of Christ, Jesus' human life funds hope that full humanity, life with God, is possible. Jesus' death and resurrection accomplish that possibility. Tanner explains that "the perfect correspondence of identity that is Christ's life remains our hope. Already achieved by Christ, who as the very same one is both the Son giving and the human being receiving, we aim toward this unity or identity by efforts, never completed in this life, to eradicate sin and match the life intended for us by Christ's assumption of us. Not simply a future yet to be for us and not simply the past achieved by Christ but not by ourselves, our future is present in us as Christ shapes us in accordance with himself."[40] Eschatological hope looks toward the full accordance of human life in Christ.

Moltmannian hope loses the perfection and efficacy of Christs' incarnation, life, death, and resurrection, and thus loses Jesus Christ as the anchor of hope, the priest and sacrifice who leads the hopeful through the veil to God's heavenly kingdom. Moltmannian hope bypasses the already/not yet identity of the ecclesial body of the two-natured Christ, and looks

---

37. Tanner, *Jesus*, 9.
38. Ibid.
39. Ibid., 107.
40. Ibid., 59.

instead to God's shared experience with humanity and God's dependence on humanity for God's own completion. In these circumstances, human hope loses any anchor but its own limited resources. In order to sustain the primacy of God's suffering over the two-natured Christ who suffers as human and is fully divine as well, Moltmann attributes to the two-nature doctrine the dualism it was designed to avoid.[41] Moltmann dismisses out of hand any positive possibilities of Chalcedon's engagement with the identity of Christ. He further rejects any Christology that does not accept the primacy of the suffering of God.[42] In so doing, Moltmann separates himself and his theology of hope from any connection with the many strands of Christian theology which conflict with his. His hope, and subsequently, Moltmannian hope, lose fluency in the christological grammar that is not defined by the suffering of God. Daniel Castelo finds this singlemindedness of Moltmannian doctrine a lost opportunity for a closer conversation and sharing of wisdom with differing and alternative accounts: "Quite simply, the theological implications stemming from the identity of the one called Jesus of Nazareth are absent from Moltmann's program as it is articulated in his speculative doctrine of God; an account of the incarnation that would have created greater coherence and exchange between divinity and humanity within Christ's person is sorely missing in his project. In this instance, as in others, Moltmann has lost an opportunity to claim and be claimed by the tradition with its original parameters and warrants."[43] Hope that draws its strength from an emphasis on God and the Trinity, could be strengthened further with increased attention to Jesus Christ, beyond what he provides to God.

Moltmannian hope that hinges on God's suffering has difficulty making sense of scriptural claims about Jesus Christ and the salvific efficacy of his death and resurrection. Christ's death and resurrection stand as promissory notes to the redemption to come, the redemption that God, in passibility, is bringing. Thus theological hope loses the challenge and assurance of passages such as Paul's words to the Romans about redemption through Christ Jesus: "But now, irrespective of law, the righteousness of God has been disclosed, and is attested by the law and the prophets, the righteousness of God through faith in Jesus Christ for all who believe. For there is no distinction, since all have sinned and fall short of the glory of God; they are now justified by his grace as a gift, through the redemption

---

41. Castelo, *Apathetic* 119–20.
42. Ibid., 120.
43. Ibid.

that is in Christ Jesus, whom God put forward as a sacrifice of atonement by his blood, effective through faith" (3:21–25a). When eschatological hope depends on God's diminished transcendence and absorption of human suffering, living into the body of Christ becomes irrelevant. Moltmannian hope does not appreciate Paul when he reminds the Ephesians that Christ's gifts of prophecy and teaching are intended to bring the body of Christ to its true identity in Christ, "until all of us come to the unity of the faith and of the knowledge of the Son of God, to maturity, to the measure of the full stature of Christ" (3:10–13). Moltmannian hope does not resonate with the hope of the Hebrews, the hope in Jesus Christ, who is pioneer, mediator, high priest and sacrifice, who leads us into the sanctuary and through the curtain which is also his flesh (10:19–22), through judgment, to the throne of God. Moltmannian hope bypasses Jesus Christ, God incarnate, to make way for the suffering God.

Lost: Heaven Unlimited

Moltmannian hope counts on God to bring a new creation that preserves, protects, and reconfigures the world into a better version of the one we know now. Moltmannian hope rejects both an end-time devastation of this world and a heavenly life beyond this world. It assumes continuity between this world and the next determined more by the potential goods of this creation than by God's constant, unwavering, relationship with God's creation. This reconfiguration of Christian hope turns away from misguided creation-nostalgia and heavenly escapism; but the cost is eschatological hope for God's fulfillment of creation beyond the limits of human effort and imagination.

From his earliest work on, Moltmann exhibits a tension he cannot resolve between the open-ended future of Bloch and his own confidence in the universal salvation of the world. While Moltmann does not explicitly address his struggle with this conflict, his work leans increasingly toward the assurance of a recognizable future, in which God comes to join the world, and the Trinity opens up to include creation. Bloch's startling and unsettling open future of infinite potentialities that excited Moltmann in his early work loses its ominous possibilities in favor of assured universal conservation. Moltmann still sustains some sense that God's future—which is the future of creation—cannot be fully grasped by humans now; but Moltmannian hope has settled firmly into the conviction that a God worth paying attention to will provide an end that encompasses and perpetuates the life we know, albeit with some significant improvements. The eschatological promised land foretold and foretasted by the people of God loses its divine design in favor of a human design, to be completed by God. The expectation that hope will be fulfilled in this creation rules out the possibility that God might wipe the creation slate clean through annihilation or a cosmic battle of good and evil, because a loving God would not destroy that which God has created. It also rules out an eschatology of return to the original, pre-fall creation. At the same time, confidence in a coming kingdom of preservation and improvement risks over-confidence that humans are capable of preparing themselves and the world for God. Eschatological hope then expects a tamer and more domesticated future than much of scripture and the witness of the saints claim. Miroslav Volf illustrates this expectation: hopes for continuity "between the present and future orders are theologically inseparable from the Judeo-Christian belief in the goodness of divine creation (which is a rededication not only of the original but also of the present creation, the reality of evil in it notwithstanding). It makes little sense to affirm the goodness of creation and at the same time expect its eschatological destruction."[44] Hope that depends on the continuation of what we know displaces hope that depends on the constancy of God's faithfulness more than perpetuation of geography, climate, and social structures.[45]

The persistent expectation that God will come to this world, bringing new creation to that which God has created, assumes a continuing future for this world in the face of much apparent evidence to the contrary. A creation-long lifetime of human efforts toward repentance, reconciliation, and recuperation from sin has not reversed brokenness and alienation

---

44. Volf and Katerberg, *Future of Hope*, 29.

45. One indication of the widespread acceptance of Moltmannian hope and its confidence about the particulars of eschatological life is N. T. Wright's *Surprised by Hope*. Wright is about twenty years younger than Moltmann, an evangelical Anglican, and a New Testament scholar. He is more conservative than Moltmann on matters of sexuality and marriage, and his account of eschatological hope sustains stronger connections to early and persevering Christian doctrine than does Moltmann's. Wright tries to bring together the apparently disparate hopes of beyond-earth heaven and of anti-heaven Social Gospel, noting the inadequacies of each on its own. Yet Wright's theological hope shares with Moltmannian hope the conviction that eschatological fulfillment will happen (is happening) on this earth, in these bodies. Wright equates hopes for heaven unbound by this (transformed) world with a dismissal of the bodily resurrection, the kingdom of Jesus, and the life of discipleship as citizens of heaven. By so doing, he diminishes hope for the transformation of creation beyond the possibilities of this world we already know.

among humans and between humans and God. A wide variety of efforts by humans to live with and care for the rest of creation has not led to a healthier planet. A broad range of polis constructions and governance has not corrected social disparities or cured humanity's dedication to violence and war. Ongoing medical advances and discoveries have not stopped illness, aging, or death. Humans created in the image of God and members of the body of Christ are non-negotiably called to live lives shaped by these efforts toward the kingdom of God, but God will not necessarily bring our efforts to fruition on the terms we anticipate. When eschatological hope is so focused on a conceivable future in which God comes to this improved creation, the assurance of God's forgiving, transforming grace can lull us into assuming that we can be certain about *how* God will right the wrongs of this life and establish the just and righteous life effected by Christ's death and resurrection. Hope in the resurrection of the body includes the very real death which precedes resurrection, and there is no guarantee that creation will never die. Dedicated stewardship and care of creation are essential performances of gratitude for God's gift of creation and practices of witness to hope in the resurrection of all life; but these human actions do not determine the location or character of the fulfillment of eschatological hope.

Moltmannian hope overestimates human knowledge of and readiness for life eternal with God, while underestimating God's wondrous gift of life beyond that which we can ask or imagine, and while downplaying God's awe-full gift of merciful judgment to prepare creation for that life. By focusing on the world we know as the location of the fulfillment of hope, Moltmannian hope loses touch with what we know about this world: it is finite. Tanner observes that

> the best scientific description of the day leaves little doubt that death is the end towards which our solar system and the universe as a whole move. Our sun will one day exhaust its fuel, annihilating life on this planet. The universe will either collapse onto itself in a fiery conflagration or dissipate away its energy over the course of an infinite expansion. If the scientists are right, the world for which Christians hold out hope, the world they hope to minister to as the agents of divine beneficence, ultimately has no future. Hope for an everlasting and consummate fulfillment of this world, a fulfillment of the world that would imitate the fullness of the triune life through incorporation into it, seems futile since destruction is our world's end. Because of its cosmic scope, this last failure of hope would bring with it all the others.[46]

---

46. Tanner, *Jesus*, 98.

Tanner notes that Moltmannian hope appears to be undaunted by such predictions, as it claims instead a continuity granted by God greater than "purely natural processes."[47] This hope asserts confidence in God to surpass the limitations of material finitude, and at the same time limits God's surpassing power to the continuity of the known world. Thus, creation depends on God's grace to continue life by moving the world "without any great interruption to its consummation,"[48] but that consummation is determined by human constraints on God's power, imagination, and possibilites.

Advocates of a this-world-oriented hope may find it relatively easy to condemn theologies of hope that anticipate global destruction in preparation for eternal life with God; but they may find it more challenging to sustain a world-based hope in the face of the persistent decline of resources on which the desired continuity depends. Gradual global devastation may become increasingly hard to ignore as its effects begin to reach the affluent global North and West. Moltmannian eschatological hope in a continuous, improved future of this world will falter when the ramifications of a faltering earth hit home. Tanner counters the over-reliance on an even better future:

> At the most fundamental level, eternal life is ours now in union with Christ, as in the future. It is therefore not directly associated with the world's future and not convertible with the idea that the world will always have a future or further time. Here the eschaton cannot be primarily understood as what comes *from* the future to draw the time of this world ever onward. It is not especially associated with any particular moment of time (past, present or future) and therefore such an understanding of the eschaton has no stake in any reworked, theological account of temporal relations in which a coming future is given primacy over present and past times.[49]

Moltmannian hope draws heavily on the perpetuation of contemporary circumstances. Hope built exclusively on this foundation loses the vision of life grounded in divine possibility, unbound by human experience, imagination, or time.

---

47. Ibid., 99.
48. Ibid.
49. Ibid., 111.

Lost: Transcendent Human Flourishing

The received version of Moltmann's eschatological vision joins God and humanity into trinitarian relationship. Moltmannian hope relies on God's panentheistic identification with creation and inflates humanity's free and effective agency on a trajectory toward trinitarian status. Such hope presupposes a more humanist than theocentric anthropology and thereby loses humanity's utter dependence on God as well as theological hope in human flourishing beyond this world.[50]

Shortly before the Trinity Institute Conference featuring Moltmann, he participated in an interview to promote the event. At one point, the interviewer asked Moltmann how he might explain eschatology to his eleven-year-old son. Moltmann responded, "Eschatology is the . . . name for the life-power of hope. The life-power of hope is to stand up after defeat."[51] Moltmann then showed the interviewer a "stand-up man" children's toy, a *Stehaufmännchen*, which is a little person that can be tipped over but always rights itself "to new life, to freedom."[52] Moltmannian hope similarly focuses on humans as stand-up figures who bounce back in the face of adversity and who effect improved physical, social, and environmental circumstances in this world. Hope for human flourishing loses horizons beyond the conditions we aim to achieve here and now (or soon). It constrains hope to the divinely-assisted completion of human aspirations and efforts for creation, rather than opening hope to the possibility of human flourishing in the fullness of resurrection beyond human efforts and projections.

Moltmannian hope presupposes an anthropology that emphasizes freedom from hierarchical ecclesial authority and freedom for independent human agency. Hope based on this understanding of the human de-emphasizes the character of hope funded by creaturely dependence

---

50. Weinandy critiques Moltmann's panentheism: "Theologians who argue for a suffering God (process theologians and Moltmann being the prime, but not exclusive, examples) readily admit, and rightly so (and those who do not miss the logic of their stance), that their theodicy is panentheistic. Since panentheism holds that, while God's being is more than all else and is not exhausted by all else, his being includes all else, these theologians clearly perceive that if God is to suffer he must share in the same ontological order as everything else. However, to place God and all else in the same ontological order has disastrous philosophical and theological consequences" (*Suffer?*, 154).

51. Trinity Wall Street, "Moltmann."

52. Ibid. This German toy resembles the once-popular American Weeble toy, which was advertized with the proclamation: "Weebles wobble but they don't fall down!"

on God, salvation through Christ, the sustenance of the Holy Spirit, and sacramental worship. Moltmannian hope champions non-hierarchical relations between people and with God, and yet a certain elitism is at work in this hope which champions independent effective agency. Moltmannian hope prioritizes those actions oriented toward on-the-ground social change, to improve lives for the needy who are not in positions to make those changes themselves. The ability to help oneself and others, to move from depending on others to becoming an agent of hope for others, stands as the primary marker of successfully fulfilled hope. Attempts by the more fortunate to shape life in the image of the kingdom of God faithfully follow the words and actions of Jesus; but without accompanying hopes for that which far exceeds human effort and achievement, hopes for human flourishing remain tied to the actions of agents who make a visible difference in the world. Further, those who cannot act as agents of hope thus configured cannot fully participate in hope, and their hopes are best focused on what already-empowered agents can accomplish for them. Those who *can* act, but who dedicate their lives to prayer, worship, and hopes for the divine justice, seem to display insufficiently responsible and compassionate hope. In this context, the unfortunate and unnecessary conflict between on-the-ground and beyond-this-world hope thrives.

The anthropology that shapes the imagination of Moltmannian hope primarily reflects the humanism that developed in the West during the turn of the seventeenth to the eighteenth century. Charles Taylor narrates the circumstances of the shift from a time in which humans were understood exclusively as creatures dependent on their creator God to a time when the idea of an exclusively secular humanism was ideologically possible: "It had always been thought that God had further purposes as well in his creation; that these were largely inscrutable, but that they included our love and worship of him. So that a recognition of God and our dependence on him places immediately on us a demand which goes beyond human flourishing. But now a striking anthropocentric shift occurs, around the turn of the seventeenth/eighteenth centuries, give or take a couple of decades."[53] Taylor charts the developing possibility of exclusive humanism in the context of social restructuring. Warlords lose their positions of power, obtained by conquering tracts of land and the people of those tracts, and sustained by bloody battles. In the place of violent and somewhat chaotic feudal territorialism, cities set up civil structures of a more peaceful nature. A well-ordered social system serves the interests

---

53. Taylor, *Sources*, 221–22.

of the city's high-ranking leaders, and they begin to establish guidelines for all municipal inhabitants to support that order. Society's noble elites share social status with "well-placed commoners."[54] Guilds for artisans organize those who produce material goods for the city, and peasants lead lives largely unchanged except for the decrease in injury, death, and crop destruction previously caused by rampaging hordes. The goals for society are now politeness and civility, since these dispositions support the economic interests of the elite and the interests of safety and stability for all the city's population. The virtues of disciplined work and harmony increase productivity which increases economic stability (for the elite) and peaceful security (for the entire community). The priorities of freedom, beneficent order, and the anthropocentric turn made religion that was not geared toward those priorities seem inadequate and threatening.[55] Secular comes to mean the ordering of time measured in ages, as opposed to God's time, eternity. Its meaning expands to include the condition of living in that ordered time of ages, in politically governed states, under regimes of property.

Taylor lists four changes in the general theological imagination, which he names as the eclipses of future purpose, grace, mystery, and "the idea that God was planning a transformation of human beings, which would take them beyond the limitations which inhere in their present condition."[56] With these four eclipses, human plans for this life on human terms replace a reliance on God's plans for humans beyond this life. No longer does it seem necessary to respond to God's larger purpose with worship, because "worship shrinks to carrying out God's goals (= our goals) in the world."[57] Taylor's account of the factors that opened the door to secular humanism highlights the shape of the anthropology later reflected by Moltmann's theology and then presupposed by Moltmannian hope.

Arne Rasmussen desecribes Moltmann's secular humanist/Christian understanding of humans as autonomous, individual, free, and eventual members of the Trinity.

> We thus find that, just as his history of freedom is an attempt to integrate Christian and Enlightenment understandings, his

54. Ibid., 236.

55. Ibid., 264. Taylor's narrative corrects the account of the subtraction story in which unbelief comes from the arrival of science and rational inquiry.

56. Ibid., 224.

57. Ibid., 233.

> systematic account of freedom is constructed in a way that makes it open for the Enlightenment ideas of autonomy, both seen (in the version advocated by Moltmann) as personal self-realization and globally as humanity being the subject of history striving to "attain their unhindered humanity." First, when he criticizes the liberal view of freedom as rule, he associates this especially with property, but not with the idea of autonomy, which he defends. Second, in his account of freedom as community it is first of all a question of accepting and being accepted as one is, not of being formed through the community. Third, in describing freedom as a project, freedom is understood as the striving for the future realization of humanity. Fourth, in his trinitarian doctrine of freedom the concept of friendship with God is the "highest" dimension. The importance of this is that, in Moltmann's interpretation, it makes it possible to redefine the relation between God and humanity in non-hierarchical terms.[58]

Moltmann's account of human thriving in terms of autonomous freedom and non-heirarchical relationships with God, leads to a Moltmannian eschatological hope that anticipates the goods of secular humanism in an extended (and improved) version of known life on earth now.

Even though Moltmann champions the poor and needy as the appropriate focus of hope, and even though he underscores the shared and communal character of hope, the Moltmannian emphasis on the goods of the here and now supports an expectation of steadily improving social conditions for people through human efforts. Hopes for human flourishing are limited to city and state contexts for economic and social advantages. When humanity's identity is not grounded in dependence on God, it is particularly difficult to consider the hope of the imitation of Christ's self-denying, service discipleship. It is even harder to consider what hope there might be for those whose needs are so great that they cannot be fulfilled in this world or in any world we can imagine. Hopes for peace cannot reach beyond trying to support some warring powers over others. Actions of hope that make a difference count more than those that witness to God's goodness without improving anything. Hope loses its resources in the lives of saints, humble servants, martyrs, and the faithful unsung witnesses to life not constrained by this world.

When human flourishing is framed within the context of Christianized secular or secularized Christian humanism, eschatological transcendence seems an unfortunate distraction from the desired fulfillment of

---

58. Rasmusson, *Church*, 97–98.

that humanism in new beginning, joined by God. A humanism-based hope limits eschatological imagination, reduces resources for human flourishing to human relationships and social order, and replaces God's transformative resurrection power with human potentiality.[59] When hope for human thriving embraces autonomous freedom and non-hierarchical friendship with God without concurrently embracing dependent creaturely reliance on God, eschatological hope rests on whatever human effort and earthly circumstances can provide. Hopes for the fulfillment of human thriving end with human resources.

Lost: Irresponsible Discipleship

Moltmannian hope invests in responsible actions that make a difference. It values on-the-ground ethical practices that address suffering and needs with effective measures. Responsible hope requires independent action for common goods. Ellen Ott Marshall describes this hope as affirming of but not dependent on God: "A responsible hope takes root in a relational concept of power, insisting that human effort is required to realize the possible. This is not a hope that relinquishes agency to the unidirectional control of an omnipotent God. Rather, this hope is born when we feel empowered to act."[60] Marshall's Moltmannian hope helps remind people that hope is not simply a sentiment, but more importantly a disposition toward particular habitual actions. However, in the attempt to dodge the dangers of an oppressive God, responsible hope names humans themselves as the agents of hope, and the end of hope becomes that which able-bodied and able-minded humans can expect to achieve as humans.

Moltmannian hope resonates with the hopes of the Social Gospel movement and of (North American Protestant appreciations of) liberation theology; these hopes focus on conditions in the world around us and they are performed in the sphere of socio-political ethics. This ethics of hope resists what it understands to be irresponsible, end-times, eschatological hope, working instead for responsible this-world hope manifest in ethical (on-the-ground care for the world around us) human action. James Cone explains: "I situate myself in the trajectory of social gospel and liberation theology because I reject otherworldly visions that direct our attention away from this world and its problems, and I insist in a 'hope for

---

59. Taylor, *Sources*, 251.
60. Marshall, *Fig Tree*, xiv; see also 78.

this life.'"⁶¹ Hope for this life requires a frank assessment and acceptance of the constraints of this life. As Marshall clarifies, "We need to cultivate a sense of the possible without glossing over the real losses and limits of life. This is what I mean by a responsible hope."⁶² Human agency determines the scope of eschatology and the range of God's participation.

Moltmannian hope tends toward a continuum between humanity and divinity (rather than a line of ontological difference between creation and God); and that continuum excludes an impossible, unearthly, and distant eschatological world. Accordingly, hope in an eschatological life beyond what humans can imagine as possible undermines and contradicts responsible hope for the world now. Marshall posits that "visions of another and more permanent and desirable existence above and beyond this one devalue this world and all that is in it. The person who subscribes to this view envisions the future—the desired future—as apart from the earth. Since the future rests elsewhere, the future of the planet seems less important.⁶³ Elizabeth Johnson makes the point more emphatically: "By focusing on life to come in a distant place that is considered our true home, eschatology displaces our identity as 'earthlings' and undermines care for this planet, the only home we and future generations as living, historical beings actually have."⁶⁴ Responsible hope aims at feasible actions to accomplish urgent goals for the immediate sustenance of this world, here and now. Agents demonstrate hope by assessing needs, resources, and strategies and then doing what can be done for creation.

In a context of Moltmannian hope, the detrimental effect of heavenly visions on responsible, creation-valuing action is obvious: people with other-worldly hopes will not perform that hope in ways that make the sort of difference in the world that facilitates the new creation God is bringing to the world. Congregations regularly hear exhortations to be different from those other people who really believe in life in the clouds, or the Rapture, or utopian release from the cares and struggles of this world. Few preachers or congregants pause to wonder if it is *necessarily* so that hope for eternal life with God in a world outside human imagination or accomplishment discourages or disables hopeful care for each other and this planet. Even fewer consider whether an ethics of hope must choose hope in earth over heaven in order to participate in hopeful practices. When

61. Ibid., 45, citing Cone, *Black Theology, Black Power*.
62. Marshall, *Fig Tree*, 13.
63. Ibid., 46.
64. Ibid., citing Johnson, *Friends of God*.

hope is assessed by how effectively it can improve present circumstances, the best agents of hope seem to be the most independent, free, and influential. Those who are not empowered to act, those who do not have the resources necessary for realizing possible hope cannot participate fully in that hope. In order to bear hope to the hopeless, friends and neighbors then need to fix the causes of suffering and death. The prioritization of effective ethical action risks dismissing practices of discipleship fostered by eschatological hope in Christ.

When discipleship is marked by hope in what Christ can do, hope for the hopeless does not depend on the capacity of others to fix or remove suffering. As Stanley Hauerwas and Charles Pinches observe, claiming and bearing hope in the face of suffering does not depend on human efforts to remove suffering, but on the refusal to accept that suffering and death are most truly defined by Christ's victory over death: "We can endure because we have confidence that though our enemies may kill us they cannot determine the meaning of our death. Christians have been given the power to overcome oppression, not by retaliation, but by the stalwart refusal to be defined as victims by the oppressor."[65] Christian discipleship can witness to eschatological hope by being present with those who suffer, even and especially when relief can only come through death and new life. Hauerwas and Pinches describe discipleship that shares hope through shared suffering and death:

> We endure because no matter what may be done to us we know that those who threaten our death are powerless to determine the meaning of our lives by killing us. Likewise, our decisive service to our neighbor is to open to her a place where she is no longer a victim, of others or of herself. If we can relieve her suffering, we should, but more importantly we offer her the endurance to live with her suffering, now no longer meaningless, since it is carried by an eschatological hope that is confident in what it has already witnessed, namely Christ's victory over death.[66]

In the discipleship of steadfast presence, Christians can share the hope of Christ's victory over death with those who have not yet witnessed it themselves. This may seem an irresponsible or inadequate expression of hope if the goals of discipleship are more oriented toward effective leadership than toward servant-companionship. Hope chiefly invested in

---

65. Hauerwas and Pinches, *Christians*, 123–24.
66. Ibid., 124.

eradicating suffering hides possibilities for outcomes beyond the humanly practical when it forgets that it is Christ who accomplishes hope. Christ, who is fully human and fully divine, is not constrained by practicality.

Discipleship practices of following and serving others in Jesus Christ, fully human and fully divine, can expand eschatological hope beyond the familiar routines of the home we have now. The Moltmannian hope of practical responsibility and making a difference undervalues hope shaped by our (imperfect) imitation of Christ's humility. Castelo argues that "if one is to take the *imitatio Christi* seriously as a way of discipleship, then it is clear that the Son's taking on the human predicament freely and out of love is a paradigm for Christian existence. As the synoptic verse suggests, the call of discipleship suggests that believers deny themselves, take up their cross, and follow Christ."[67] To follow Christ is to follow through this life, through death, and into the fulfillment of hope beyond this life. Christian hope developed in responsible, strategic policy renders almost invisible discipleship grown in precarity, radical humility, and the eternal life that that foreshadows. Discipleship formed in foolish and irresponsible hope can take follow Christ by picking up some of the less appealing tasks of witnessing to the fulfillment of hope. Hope for peace can be nurtured by accepting that an argument is not worth winning. Hope for healing can be expressed by sitting with those who are dying, who cannot be saved by better food distribution or medical procedures. The beginnings of hope for broader reconciliation might involve finding the patience to build a relationship—perhaps even a friendship—with the Christian neighbor one does not like, the one who is completely wrong about biblical interpretation, eschatology, ecclesiology, and politics.

If some Christians are worried that others who anticipate imminent heavenly release seem insufficiently concerned to redress systemic poverty or slash energy consumption, persuasive witness is definitely called for. However, the blanket dismissal of other-worldly eschatology because it can inhibit effective ethical action devalues an impractical hope in Christ that fosters hopeful practices of discipleship. When hope for the health of the earth is considered chiefly in terms of human strategies for the protection and renewal of resources, our desires of the moment and near future outweigh God's ordering of creation. Sarah Musser finds in the story of Job a critique of this disordered relationship with God and creation: "Job holds creation itself to be chaotic, lacking any moral logic. This self-centered

---

67. Castelo, *Apathetic*, 145.

estimation manifests itself most strikingly in Job's futile attempt to undo creation in chapter 3. Thus, both Job and his friends understand creation in terms of how they experience it: it is either a means of divine blessing or curse. It is not fundamentally a gift of a generous Creator."[68] She argues that human efforts to control the earth for our own benefit call for repentance and for a humble acceptance of our identity as creatures of the God of wisdom. Without acknowledging our self-serving damage to creation and our lack of God's wisdom, there is no reason to think that present day environmental policies and practices will improve the flourishing of creation and all creatures of creation. Musser continues:

> Just as Job experienced the futility of ordering creation through personal righteousness, so too should we expect to suffer the consequences of our flawed attempts to order and domesticate our environment. In our efforts to make life safe, we have unwittingly made it more dangerous—for ourselves and for our fellow creatures . . . [The book of Job] offers a critique of human manipulation of God and creation that should cause us to repent from our habits and practices of undisciplined management. This call to repentance is particularly urgent now that we have knowledge about the fragility of ecosystems and the disproportionate negative impact environmental calamities exact on the poor who are least responsible for them.[69]

Repentance for disregarding God's ordering of creation and God's end for creation reveals possibilities for hope in wiser human environmental care and in God's perfection of creation beyond our on-the-ground efforts.[70]

Practical hope values this world and its possibilities; and it desires God's good gifts of an eschatological future for this earth. It is a hope that drives the responsible and faithful practices that redistribute resources, provide urgent care for the needy, improve government social policies, protect the oppressed, nurture the earth and its creatures, and resist violence. Discipleship in eschatological hope calls Christians to follow Christ in these ways and to hold each other accountable for persevering *regardless* of results. When hope invests too heavily in favorable results, when practicalities chain hope to the limitations and frailties of this world, we lose sight of the hope that remains undiminished by our earth-bound

---

68. Musser, "Comfort," 288.
69. Ibid., 293.
70. See also Northcott, "Blowout."

circumstances and our creaturely capacities. Pope Benedict XVI, in his encyclical on hope, sets hope apart from the realm of responsible realism:

> Our daily efforts in pursuing our own lives and in working for the world's future either tire us or turn into fanaticism, unless we are enlightened by the radiance of the great hope that cannot be destroyed even by small-scale failures or by a breakdown in matters of historic importance. If we cannot hope for more than is effectively attainable at any given time, or more than is promised by political or economic authorities, our lives will soon be without hope. It is important to know that I can always continue to hope, even if in my own life, or the historical period in which I am living, there seems to be nothing left to hope for.[71]

Hope that begins when we feel empowered to act will fade when challenges increase, our empowerment fades, and our efforts prove inadequate to the cause. Hope that follows Christ in stumbling, unreasonable service relies on the perfection of hope that exceeds our effort and imagination.

Conclusion

Moltmannian theological hope provides alternatives to areas of theological doctrine that may seem outdated today. It reflects and extends Moltmann's account of hope with the accessibility of a less transcendent God and an open Trinity, with a focus on this world and human efforts to preserve it for renewal, and with the vernacular theological grammar of modernity. It looks toward an eschatology in which God comes to renew and join in this world and it rests on a changeably compassionate God who shares the human experience of abandonment and suffering. An exclusive reliance on those alternatives beggars the doctrine of God, the expectations of theological hope, and the anthropology and ethics of the people who hope. The modernity-situated understandings of time, experience, and biblical interpretation squeeze out the breadth and depth of Christian wisdom and resources of hope. Moltmannian hope turns away from the theological grammar that supports ongoing unity in difference. The doctrine of God loses God's undiminishable perfect compassion. Christ loses full humanity and full divinity. Theological hope loses eschatological possibilities beyond this life and this earth. It discards theocentric anthropology and servant discipleship. Moltmannian hope assumes that the aspects of theological

---

71. Benedict XVI, *Spe salvi*, §35.

hope that it has replaced are disposable without further engagement. The substance, practice, and sustenance of Christian eschatological hope must draw on more resources than Moltmannian hope offers, in order to witness to the hope of Jesus Christ in a faltering world.

3

A Thomistic Grammar of Hope

CHAPTER 1 DESCRIBED THE distinctive characteristics of Moltmann's theology of hope and the subsequent construction of Moltmannian hope. Chapter 2 examined some of the costs of an exclusive reliance on a Moltmannian theology of hope. This chapter considers the theology of hope presented by Aquinas that Moltmannian hope misunderstands and dismisses,[1] in order to recover some resources for contemporary theological hope. Chapter 4 will investigate resources from discourses not often considered in conversations about theological hope.

Moltmann's prioritization of colloquialized theology in a modern and secularized time reflects his conviction that Christian theology can suit contemporary concerns and terms, and it helps explain much of the appreciative response to his theology of hope. Moltmannian hope participates in the overriding presumption of contemporary society that what *has* been does not need to be carried through into the present day. In its rejection of the content and shape of central streams of Christian theology, Moltmannian hope cedes some of the distinctiveness of Christian hope to

1. Adherents of Moltmannian hope do not necessarily specify the source of the theologies of hope they reject. The assumption that theological history and past doctrines are disposable contributes to some confusion about whether the objectionable doctrines of hope draw on the early church, Aquinas, or various traditions within Roman Catholicism, Reformation churches, millenialism (Dispensational Premillenialism, Amillenialism, Postmillennialism, or Historic Premillennialism), or the *Left Behind* novels. I will address Aquinas's theological virtue of hope and the doctrine of God on which it depends, because it articulates widely embraced church doctrine since the earliest church, and because it provides a grammar for hope and God that most of Christian theology has engaged with, one way or another.

contemporary secular hope. Theological hope does not sustain its distinctively Christian character by attempting to preserve a mythical moment of just-right doctrine; nor does it attain correctness through the most up-to-date perspective. The shifting particularities of language, circumstance, and imagination challenge the church to discern continuity in the midst of difference and to receive wisdom in new forms.

Christians often divide into camps that claim to be authorized by either the old or the new. These divisions do not accurately represent the ongoing life and teaching of the church, and they can inhibit the work of the Spirit in the body of Christ. Chapter 2 described some ways that Moltmannian theological hope closes off conversations with the presentations of hope with which it disagrees. This chapter offers a charitable engagement with one resource that Moltmannian hope has largely discarded: Aquinas's teaching about the theological virtue of hope.[2] The aim here is not to demand that all scholarly engagements with theological hope embody the times and customs of previous centuries but rather to call into question Christian hope that does not sustain a lively connection to doctrine. Tanner underscores the benefits of avoiding premature closure to traditional teaching:

> To uncover an interpretive context for the coherence of traditional Christian theology is to overcome the closure to which a modern viewpoint is susceptible. Indeed this is the only general way to overcome closure once finite human understanding renounces the Cartesian dream of an external, neutral vantage point for self-scrutiny. One overcomes calcified or rigid pre-judgments, not by suppressing either prejudgement or the historical determination of context, but by continually extending and enriching one's point of view. This happens through open conversations and subsequent understanding of the alternatives for thought presented by other, not least past, traditions of discourse.[3]

This chapter brings to the table a doctrine of theological hope currently lost to adherents of Moltmannian hope, so that critical reconsiderations of apparently outdated resources for hope may challenge, clarify, and strengthen ongoing constructions of Christian theological hope.

---

2. A more in-depth study would benefit from an account of the major schools of Thomistic theology and the ramifications of those differences on understandings of theological virtues.

3. Tanner, *Creation*, 7.

Our Only Hope

A Thomistic presentation of hope relies on the impassibility of God, the two natures of Jesus Christ, and eternal life unbound by earthly limitations. Familiarity with a Thomistic grammar of language about the God of hope may facilitate connections between variant theologies of hope. Each section of the chapter begins with selected lyrics from a song or hymn from the distinctly non-Thomistic canon of old-timey gospel/blues/bluegrass music about hope and heaven. There is not room here to analyze these lines for theological soundness, but they point toward one of the discourses of theological hope which perseveres outside the realm of Moltmannian hope and is nonetheless worth attending to. An exclusive reliance on Moltmannian hope dismisses not only other streams of doctrine, but also the Christians throughout time and geography who have sung and lived out those non-Moltmannian doctrines of hope. Exposure to non-Moltmannian expressions of Christian hope might help complicate and invigorate theological hope in daunting times. As Tanner notes, complexity provides possibilities and resources otherwise forgotten:

> Knowledge of Christian complexity works generally to draw the theologian's viewpoint beyond the narrow confines of the present situation. So much of contemporary academic theology seems blinkered by current common sense and the specifics of a particular location; without availing oneself of a knowledge of what Christians have said and done elsewhere and at other times, what Christianity could be all about thins and hardens, unresourceful and brittle. Knowledge of Christianity in other times and places is a way, then, of expanding the range of imaginative possibilities for theological construction in any one time and place, a way of expanding the resources with which one can work. Placing one's own efforts within this ongoing and wide stream, one grows in appreciation for the two-thousand-year, global history of efforts to say what Christianity is all about, for the theological insights that might be contained within that history or be working themselves out there.[4]

Here follows an effort to place contemporary theological hope within the ongoing and wide streams of Christian tradition that it skirts, to expand the range of possibilities for theological hope beyond the limitations of Moltmannian hope.[5]

---

4. Tanner, *Jesus*, xviii.

5. I make no claim to be representing all resources of Christian theological traditions of theological hope. Other projects might look to the martyrs of El Salvador, Japan, and Iran; the desert fathers, religious mystics, and medieval beguines; or the

God

The Perfectly Compassionate, Impassible God of Hope

> Yes God, God don't never change
> He's God, always will be God.[6]

God's great compassion depends on the impassibility of God. The grammar of language about God, begun in the earliest conversations of the church, clarified and practiced throughout many systematic streams of doctrine, identifies the passibility of God within the almighty impassibility of God. Theological hope thus looks to God who is greater than all suffering, unchanged by catastrophe, and constant in goodness, regardless of the circumstances of creation.

The conviction that impassibility means an uninterested, uncaring, unloving God stands firm in Moltmannian hope, which counters with a suffering, changeable God to substantiate eschatological hope. The early ecclesial councils demonstrate similar concerns about apparently conflicting claims about God; attention to their work offers contemporary theologians the benefit of their wisdom and discernment. Castelo argues that, "in light of the experiences of older voices within the tradition, the axiom of divine impassibility provides an opportunity for theologians to reconsider basic questions and conventions surrounding long-held tenets of the theological enterprise. Such a reconsideration or reevaluation creates, in turn, a conversation that neither ignores nor dismisses possible continuities and parallels within the area of Christian theological reflection."[7] In this light, we can see the ways that the divine impassibility rejected by Moltmannian hope reflects a misunderstanding of the early church's engagements with the doctrine of God.

As noted in chapter 2, part of the misunderstanding reflects an oversimplified assessment of the relationship between Hellenistic philosophy and the development of Christian doctrine. That complex relationship played out in biblical translation and interpretation as well. Supporters of divine passibility often support their position with passages from the Old Testament that use words of human affect to describe God. The apparent

---

bearers of hope in oppression and devastation throughout the world—the wisdom and teaching of theologians often drowned out because they are not from the global north and west.

6. Johnson, "God."
7. Castelo, *Apathetic*, 20.

contradictions between God's sovereignty and God's involvement with creation have challenged scriptural interpretation for centuries. Castelo describes anomalies in LXX translations of Old Testament passages that suggest confusion about whether to interpret descriptions of God as more "anthropathic" or impassible: "Such aberrations within the LXX demonstrate that the ancient Hellenized world had great difficulty in maintaining certain aspects of the biblical witness since these clashed with what was perceived to be proper ways of speaking and thinking about God. One sees this tendency perpetuated among early writers and thinkers of the ancient world, including those who would have a lasting impression upon the early efforts at theologically systematizing the Christian faith."[8] At the same time, Castelo notes that the passages of the Old Testament that seem to support a contemporary passibilist understanding of God do not overshadow the unmoveable, unchangeable God of the covenant.

> For whatever one wants to make of the passibilist passages in the Old Testament, this strand of testimony makes up only one facet (and a non-dominant one at that) of a more general Jewish understanding of God that tends to privilege God's majesty, glory, transcendence, holiness, and otherness. Yahweh and Israel are two intimately linked covenant partners, but within its intimacy this relationship does not ignore the vast difference that exists between them. After all, it is Yahweh who both *initiates* and *sustains* the covenant relationship. Israel, on the other hand, constantly breaches and calls into question the covenant, suggesting that at points in which the narrative reaches a tense and critical moment, God not only is but shows his righteousness, holiness, and mercy.[9]

It can be easy for contemporary Christian accounts of the character of God to forget that Old Testament stories assume and do not contradict God's complete distinction from creation and the passions of creation.[10]

8. Ibid., 28–29.

9. Ibid., 34.

10. "At the risk of oversimplification, the limits and possibilities of God-talk within modern, conventional sensibilities and those detected in *Tanakh* can be illustrated by the adjective of choice used in describing God. When pushed, modern Christians would tend to conclude the phrase 'God is . . .' with the predicate adjective 'love.' This tendency is largely due to the contemporary favoring of the Johannine witness as well as certain cultural presumptions about viable and healthy relationships. One could argue quite convincingly, however, that the Old Testament portrayal suggests different adjectives, many of which are difficult for interpreters to understand today. Certainly, one finds the theme of 'love' in the Old Testament, but it is not as prominent as in

Even the staunchest supporters of divine passibility today struggle with the divine/human distinction. The tendency is to claim, on the one hand, that God has changing emotions in ways different from the ways humans do, and yet on the other hand, to lapse into an elision of human and divine natures. Gavrilyuk observes: "One important thing to be grasped from the very beginning is that the choice between an unrestrictedly impassible and an unrestrictedly passible God implied in the modern theopaschite consensus presents a false dilemma. This becomes more or less obvious if we realize that all the contemporary advocates of theopaschitism would agree that significant qualifications apply to their assertion that God suffers and has emotions."[11] Contemporary passibilists may be surprised to learn that these questions of language about God have been a topic of Christian discussion for two millenia, and along the way, the cumulative wisdom of the church has come up with some consensus about a grammar for the discussions.

A Grammar of God

He's my lighthouse, He's my bridge over troubled waters.
He's the old ship of Zion out on the raging sea.[12]

The earliest Christians struggled to find a language to name and to describe God: "I AM"; "the Lord your God"; God the Father; Jesus, the man in history, the Son of God, the messiah; Christ who lived died, was resurrected, and ascended; God the Trinity of perfect relations; the Holy Spirit who fills Christians with the presence of the resurrected Christ. The vast majority of theologians before, during, and after the Councils of Nicea and Chalcedon assumed and asserted the impassibility of God. There were disagreements about how to make sense of the relationship between the impassible God and the human Christ who suffered and died, but few Christians imagined that God might be subject to suffering and change that would deny divine impassibility. Their efforts to articulate (but not necessarily resolve) the paradox of passibility and impassibility developed into a grammar of divine transcendence and immanence, for example, from the fifth century *Lenten Triodion*: "Without changing Thou has emptied Thyself, and

---

the New Testament in that it is usually accompanied with other notions when used" (ibid.).

11. Gavrilyuk, *Suffering*, 5–6.
12. "He's My Lighthouse."

impassibly Thou has submitted to thy Passion."[13] God's impassibility includes, but is not superceded by, God's passibility, manifest in Jesus Christ, fully human and fully divine. Contemporary claims about passibility and impassibility have much to gain from attention to the grammar the early church established, as well as the related conflicts and agreements.

Chapter 2 described a way of speaking of God through six indications of what God is not. An expansion of that description will help demonstrate its ramifications for hope in the God of unchanging compassion. In Aquinas's theological grammar, hope seeks the attainment of the good with the assistance of the good. God *is* good and the source of all goodness. Creatures cannot know God's goodness perfectly, but humans can know something of goodness in God's creation and can analogously signify the goodness that pre-exists in God more perfectly than creatures can imagine or comprehend. Humans know God by recognizing perfections flowing from God to creatures and forming conceptions proportionate to those creature-scale perfections. "The perfections pre-exist in God unitedly and simply, whereas in creatures they are received, divided, and multiplied."[14] Humans assert, analogously and imperfectly, that God is simple, perfect, infinite, impassible and immutable, eternal, and one—all of which humans are not. Each of these cataphatic markers for God affirms an apophatic negativity: God is not complex, God is not incomplete, God is not limited, God is not temporal, God is not changeable, God is not divided. None of these attributes apply to God in ways that creatures can fully comprehend. At the same time, since all the goods that creatures know flow from God, humans can speak of God using a kind of relational grammar, in which words analogously—and truthfully—name God. "Whatever good we attribute to creatures, pre-exists in God, and in a more excellent and higher way."[15] Aquinas is not here positing an ontological relatedness between the created world humans can describe and the existence of God; he is demonstrating how to participate in the order of creation God has created, by recognizing human limitations and praising God's lack of limitation, even when human imagination cannot fathom what that means. These expressions fulfill certain roles in the grammar of analogy, thereby showing, indirectly, that God is beyond logic and createdness.

---

13. Gavrilyuk, "Select Quotations."

14. Aquinas, *Summa Theologica*, I, q. 13, a. 4. All subsequent Aquinas quotations will also be from the *Summa*.

15. I, q. 13, a. 4.

God's *simplicity* signifies that God is not composed of various parts; it is not the case that portions of God pertain to portions of creation, or that God has conflicting feelings that manifest in inconsistency. Theological hope does not appeal to a God of power in times of war and a God of generosity at harvest time (or at end of year salary bonus time). God is not complicated as are humans and idols.

God is simple and *perfect*; there is nothing about God that might be improved, fulfilled, or completed. Theological hope does not anticipate a better God who has grown and developed since the old days.

God is simple, perfect, and *infinite*. Space, quantity, and shape do not apply to God. Hope need not be tempered by the frameworks of mathematics, science, reason, or any conceivability that human understanding relies on.

God is simple, perfect, infinite, and *impassible and immutable*. As not-compound, not-improveable, not limited, and not in time, God is not moved or diminished, weakened, or impaired. God does not become more or less, God does not move from here to there, God is not daunted, surprised, or constrained.

God is simple, perfect, infinite, impassible and immutable, and *eternal*. God does not begin or end, and God is not defined by or limited by time.

Finally, God is simple, perfect, infinite, eternal, impassible, and *one*. God cannot be divided. God the Trinity is not separable into three individuals; Jesus Christ who is fully human and fully divine is one God. Hope in Christ, infused by the Holy Spirit, is hope in God, the one God, the Trinity.

This grammar establishes a narrative of hope that embraces but does not explain away a number of paradoxes, the most challenging of which today may be the paradox of impassible passibility. Hope for divine compassion rests in God's perfect compassion; God is already and forever complete compassion. Therefore God's perfect compassion in no way contradicts or undermines God's simplicity, infinity, impassibity, eternity, or oneness. Moltmannian hope prioritizes God's passibility and worries that claims of divine impassibility prevent or detract from God's compassion and God's suffering in solidarity, not understanding that the grammar of language about God described above renders unintelligible any suggestion that God does not care for humans. The impassible God rejected by Moltmannian theology represents a perversion of the doctrine presented here.

Castelo recommends the definition of divine impassibility that claims that God "cannot be affected against his will by an outside force."[16] Castelo also offers G. L. Prestige's observation that, "Impassibility means not that God is inactive or uninterested, not that He surveys existence with Epicurean impassivity from the shelter of a metaphysical insulation, but that His will is determined from within instead of being swayed from without."[17] As perfect, God's compassion cannot be increased, lessened, or improved upon; God's perfect compassion exceeds all limitations, and certainly human imagination. The Thomistic grammar of God posits that God is merciful, God does indeed care for creation, but not in the passionate way that humans are passionately merciful. While people express sorrow when others are sorrowful, God does not participate in that lack which sorrow and misery represent. For humans, empathy and compassion may be the best we can do, since we cannot remove the misery of others. God, however, is greater than sorrow and misery, overflowing in grace and mercy. Hence, God's "response" to sorrow is to dispel it. This is not a response on human terms, since God does not change from unmerciful to merciful. God already knows our misery and already meets that misery with goodness and mercy. Aquinas explains: "To sorrow over the misery of others does not belong to God; but it does most properly belong to Him to dispel that misery, whatever be the defect we call misery. Now defects are not removed, except by the perfection of some kind of goodness, and the primary source of goodness is God."[18] Thus in eternally constant and complete compassionate care for creation, God does not suffer, which is to say, God's impassibility is not diminished or nullified by God's compassion or passibility.

A theology of hope that retains no connections with this grammar of language about God, either directly or indirectly, lacks the tools for communication with other theological accounts of hope. D. Stephen Long argues for a strict adherence to Aquinas's grammar for God, asking for Christianity to retain and to teach the "traditional" Thomistic grammar for God, even as it considers "alternative ways of speaking about God."[19] He worries that the beliefs most Christians share (or at least engage with) may become divisive, instead of uniting, if Christians can no longer share a language about God. In the context of a seminar entitled, "The Sover-

---

16. Castelo, *Apathetic*, 16, drawing on Creel, *Divine Impassibility*.
17. Castelo, *Apathetic*, 16–17.
18. I, q. 21, a. 3.
19. Long, "Response," 183–84.

eignty of God Debate," Long writes: "To my knowledge, every presenter in this debate adheres to the basic confessions of the Christian faith, that Jesus is the incarnation of God; fully divine and fully human, united in one Person; that God is Triune; that God raised Jesus bodily from the dead and that God is love. We have so much upon which we agree."[20] He then argues for a common language that reflects these agreements: "My concern is that what we hold in common will be lost if we neglect the traditional language in which it was forged. If we lose this langague, we will lose one of the Bible's greatest gifts to all of humanity—the demythologization of God. Language that speaks of God's suffering and death and that demands a necessary relationship between God and creation can only finally remythologize God and turn him into a creature who needs us for his own intelligibility."[21] The question of God's impassibility determines the character and possibility of theological hope. A Thomistic systematic grammar shows that God is the end of hope and the means to hope. If God is passible without impassibility—less than perfect and susceptible to suffering, diminishment, and limitation—then hope looks to an eschatology provided by a God who is solely constituted by imperfection, suffering, diminishment, and limitation, and the means to hope is likewise constrained.

The grammar of divine impassible compassion names a paradox about what cannot be known or spoken about God. Anselm's deceptively simple statement in *The Proslogium* articulates a grammar for speaking about what cannot be known or spoken about God: "God is that than which nothing greater can be conceived." Long adds Robert Sokolowski's interpretation of Anselm: "this means that God plus creation is not greater than God alone."[22] This mind-boggling assertion reflects some of the earliest language instruction received by the people of God. Long claims that Anselm's assertion was "the logical articulation of a basic Christian (and Jewish) understanding of God that comes through the Bible and the Church Fathers. We find it in the first two commands revealed to Moses: 1. I am the Lord your God; you shall not have strange gods before me. 2. You shall not take the name of the Lord your God in vain. . . . If anything is placed before God, it becomes greater than God and thereby sets us up to worship that thing instead of God."[23] If there is no other God greater

20. "While others who adhere to the various theologies presented here may not confess these basic doctrines, all those invited to participate in Garrett's debate on God's sovereignty by the forum for evangelical theology adhere to them" (ibid., 183).

21. Ibid., 183–84.

22. Ibid., 184; Sokolowski, *Christian*.

23. Long, "Response," 184–85.

than the Lord God, who is greater than limitation or change, then any description of God as diminished, improved, or changed at all undermines and misrepresents the greatness of God.

Long worries that the suffering of God might define God and become greater than God. An application of Long's concerns to a theology of hope suggests that a language about God apart from a comprehensive grammar of systematic theology risks becoming idolatry when it holds God's impassibility or the suffering of the forsaken God outside a grammar that takes into account the debates, wisdom, witness, and scriptural interpretation that precede us and continue now.[24] The interpretation, translation, and application of grammars of God never stand alone in closed systems of people and meaning, set apart from other systems, people, and grammars. Fluency or familiarity with one grammar does not exclude fluency with others, but instead allows for hybrid languages and critical connections among discourses. A grammar for God language that discounts the grammatical discernments of the church to date effects closure and risks idolatry, as well as incomprehensibility, to the those in relation to the grammars outside the closure.

The theological grammars articulated by the early church and by Aquinas gather and express ecclesial wisdom of God's passibility/impassibility, with an appreciation of Christian theology's long-term confession that human language for God needs to be apophatic as well as cataphatic: divine mystery and paradox cannot be resolved by human reason. Moltmannian hope relies on resolving many of the paradoxes that have been and could be resources for eschatological hope by limiting God's mercy, judgment, suffering, compassion, and perfection to a grammar appropriate for human capacities. Moltmannian hope closes the window of hope in God's possibilities beyond human imagination, in favor of a certain future of universal salvation of this world, in this world. Christian paradox places the fulfillment of our lives in the window of hope in God's infinite goodness that far exceeds our capacities to achieve, reason, or imagine.

Paradox can only be narrated partially, and partial narratives still require care and caution. Mystery cannot and need not be explained, and mystery still needs to be recognized. The monastic traditions of silence in the presence and to the glory of God illustrate one performance of hope in God without the presumption of humanly reasoned resolution of God's nature. Castelo describes a narrative that sets suffering within

---

24. Of course, if a particular systematics does not include the commandment about idolatry, the grammar would work differently, and the theology would be hard to narrate as Christian.

A Thomistic Grammar of Hope

God's eternal love: "Divine impassibility points to God's power, wisdom, and love that are prior, contemporaneous, and subsequent to moments of humanly embodied suffering. Although affirming divine impassibility does not explain away the mystery of evil, which ultimately requires eschatological resolution, it does affirm by faith the mystery of God in whom the former will be resolved. Since pain and suffering surround us while it is in God that creation lives, moves, and has its being (Acts 17:28), the two mysteries must be maintained."[25] Jon Sobrino offers another expression of the God who suffers impassibly. While addressing questions about the suffering of God from the perspective of the poor and oppressed, Sobrino describes God as powerful *and* close to the suffering of the neediest. He identifies salvation as dependent upon the mystery of God as unimaginably transcendent and wholly immanent:

> Some theologians are reluctant to speak of God as suffering; others are not. In my opinion, the different theoretical views of such a serious problem are less important than how the world's poor and victims think about it ...The poor turn to God to save them with [God's] power, and in that they see God's effective love. But they also turn to God when they find [God] close to their own suffering, and in that they see credible love.... Those who do not declare God dead must bear the burden of [God's] mystery. In my opinion, the mystery is that human salvation presupposes a God with alterity (a different, omnipotent and therefore distant God) and a God with affinity (like us, crucified, close by).[26]

Theological hope that ignores the grammatical ways that the church has narrated the paradox of God's passibility and impassibility risks incoherence as Christian theology. A Christian theology of hope fed by an awareness of previous ecclesial struggles about the nature of God and the ways that God provides hope for creation has resources for discerning what is distinctive about Christian theological hope. The addition of patristic and Thomistic determinations about the God of hope can help contemporary theologians evaluate familiar Moltmannian themes in connection with ongoing practices of speaking about God. Perhaps the most crucial grammatical component of theological hope is Jesus Christ, the foundation and the fulfillment of hope.

---

25. Castelo, *Apathetic*, 145.
26. Sobrino, cited in Bedford, "Power," 109.

Christ, the Perfect Hope

> May my spirit be a ransom on your behalf, and my bonds as well, which you did not despise, nor were you ashamed of them. Nor will the perfect hope, Jesus Christ, be ashamed of you.[27]

> My hope is built on nothing less
> than Jesus' blood and righteousness.
> I dare not trust the sweetest frame,
> but wholly lean on Jesus' name.
>
> On Christ the solid rock I stand,
> all other ground is sinking sand;
> all other ground is sinking sand.[28]

The account of the God of hope who is compassionate and nevertheless impassible relies on the person of Jesus Christ, the incarnation of God, who is fully human and fully divine. Jesus Christ, through his death and resurrection, effects the transformation of humans into the fullness of their creatureliness in eternal life with God. In this way, Christ is the perfect hope. The doctrine and grammar of the impassible God and the two natures of Christ developed through a few centuries of theological arguments, debates, and conciliar documents, each in relation to problems raised and consensus gained. The span of theological conversation on the topic cannot be covered here[29]; here follow a few brief examples from the early church. Philo of Alexandria (a Jewish scholar of the first century CE) argues that God's mercy does not detract from God's unchangeableness, because God's constancy is not bound by the limitations of human efforts at constancy.[30] Ignatius of Antioch (a second century martyr) embraces God's impassibility and the passibility of God in Christ who is passible and impassible.[31] Justin Martyr and the Apologists (also second century) insist that God's care for creation is unchangeable, exceeding the greatest care that humans can imagine.[32] The Apologists in general try to use Hellenistic philosophical resources to explain to their Hellenic audiences how God is both transcendent and enfleshed in Christ, and how God is not the same

---

27. Ignatius, "Smyrnaeans," 10.2; 190–91.
28. Mote, "My Hope."
29. See Weinandy, Castelo, and Gavrilyuk.
30. Castelo, *Apathetic*, 29–30.
31. Ibid., 47.
32. Weinandy, *Suffer?*, 85.

as speculative philosophy or the wide array of deities available for worship.[33] Irenaeus of Lyons (late second century) counters Gnostic claims with an emphasis on God's transcendence, creation's dependence on God, and the unified person of the divine and human Christ.[34] Tertullian (second to third century) claims that God is impassible and passible, and he recommends describing humans in the ways that they (imperfectly) resemble God, rather than describing God in human terms.[35] Origen and his student Gregory Thaumaturgus (third century) give mixed signals, stating sometimes that God is impassible and at other times that God is passible. Gregory Thaumaturgus explains that God demonstrates God's impassibility by taking on "the crippling effects of the passions."[36]

In the fourth century, the Arians argue impassibility and passibility co-exist through the distinct separation of Christ and the High God. The first Council of Nicea constructs a grammar to account for both the unity of the persons of the Trinity and the divine impassibility that includes passibility. The Nicean Creed asserts that the Father and the Son are one and that the human suffering of the Son does not compromise the impassibility of God.[37] Nestorius and Cyril continue the argument through their writings: Nestorius claims that impassibility excludes any suffering, by definition, so the impassible God and the passible Christ must be separate. Cyril claims that God is one, so that the passion of Christ must be one in the impassible God. Cyril's grammar demonstrates the paradoxical oneness of God that includes impassibility and passibility, without diminishing either one. In this way, their disagreement is not an argument about whether or not God is impassible, a claim which they both assume to be true, but a conflict of grammatical narration: how to articulate God's impassibility with Christ's passion.[38] Through councils and onward, the church names the paradox of God's impassibility and passibility by narrating the incarnation of God as Jesus Christ.

The Council of Chalcedon (451) affirms the consensus it perceives that Christ is fully human and divine. The Council articulates the two

---

33. Castelo, *Apathetic*, 52. Note that their engagement with Hellenistic philosophy is a pedagogical and evangelical one.

34. Ibid., 53.

35. Ibid., 54–55.

36. Ibid., 57, citing *To Theopompus*, 9.

37. Gavrilyuk, *Suffering*, 132–34.

38. Ibid., 135–71.

natures of Christ, establishing a grammar for narrating divine passibility within divine impassibility.

> We, then, following the holy Fathers, all with one consent, teach people to confess one and the same Son, our Lord Jesus Christ, the same perfect in Godhead and also perfect in manhood; truly God and truly man, of a reasonable [rational] soul and body; consubstantial [co-essential] with the Father according to the Godhead, and consubstantial with us according to the Manhood; in all things like unto us, without sin; begotten before all ages of the Father according to the Godhead, and in these latter days, for us and for our salvation, born of the Virgin Mary, the Mother of God, according to the Manhood; one and the same Christ, Son, Lord, only begotten, to be acknowledged in two natures, inconfusedly, unchangeably, indivisibly, inseparably; the distinction of natures being by no means taken away by the union, but rather the property of each nature being preserved, and concurring in one Person and one Subsistence, not parted or divided into two persons, but one and the same Son, and only begotten God, the Word, the Lord Jesus Christ; as the prophets from the beginning [have declared] concerning Him, and the Lord Jesus Christ Himself has taught us, and the Creed of the holy Fathers has handed down to us.[39]

In the thirteenth century, when Aquinas gathers the wisdom of the patristic fathers with more recent theology and his own discernment, he names Christ as one of three persons within the one Trinity. The persons are equal, one and three, and coeternally in a relationship of generation and spiration,[40] while at the same time the mission of the Son sends him as incarnate gift to humanity for its salvation. In order to be perceived by humanity, the Son is sent as the visible author of salvation.[41] The Holy Spirit, in accordance with its mission, is sent as the sign of sanctification, a gift proceeding in love, which appears visibly as needed.[42] Jesus Christ, Son of God, remains fully and eternally divine and one with the Trinity, while living, suffering, and dying as fully human in created time.

Aquinas's presentation of Christ as the foundation of hope makes clear that hope rests in Christ and in Christ's salvific acts. In Aquinas's commentary on Hebrews, he explains that the transcendence of Christ

39. Chalcedon.
40. I, q. 43, a. 2.
41. I, q. 43, a. 7.
42. Ibid.: "in the confirmation and propagation of the faith by such visible signs."

is the subject matter of the Epistle; and in his discussion of Heb 6:18-19, Aquinas explains that Jesus places the hope set before us, the anchor of the soul, firmly where he has gone, behind the veil. "Christ has entered for us, into the inner sanctuary of the tent and has there made firm [*fixit*] our hope."[43] Christ grounds, fixes, and sustains the hope of believers, as the one through whom fulfillment has been effected (the "already," as professed in faith) and will be perfected (the "not yet," as professed in hope).

The hope of beatitude rests in Christ, who makes possible the fulfillment of those blessed by God: "God alone makes souls blessed through participation in him; but Christ is the one who leads us to beatitude."[44] Christ leads by virtue of his complete participation in human life, suffering, and death, and by his completion of humanity in his resurrection, which already and not yet effects the resurrection of all. Romanus Cessario describes Aquinas's claim that Christ establishes the efficacy of human hope: "Since God communicates His redeeming mercy through the sacrifice of Christ, the mystery of the Incarnation grounds every exercise of theological hope. Aquinas recognized that the New Testament explicitly points to Christ as the one who guarantees hope's efficacy: 'But I am not ashamed, for I know whom I have believed, and I am sure that he is able to guard until that Day what has been entrusted to me' (2 Tim 1:12). At the same time, the virtue of hope enables each believer to participate already in the promised eschatological salvation."[45] Christ, the perfection of hope, leads believers to full participation in beatitude through their hope in Christ. Aquinas identifies Christ as the foundation and the motivation of the virtue of hope.

Moltmannian hope downplays Christ's efficacy in providing hope when it emphasizes God's participation in Christ's crucifixion suffering, and when it casts Christ's resurrection as an affirmation that God's promises will be fulfilled, instead of the fulfillment of promise and means of salvation.[46] Moltmannian hope further downplays hope in Christ by narrating human participation in divine trinitarian perichoretic relations as the highest good instead of participation in Christ's triumph over death and sin. Tanner, countering Moltmann, writes that "The idea that human

43. Pieper, *Faith*, 106.
44. III, q. 59, a. 2.
45. Cessario, "Theological," 236.
46. Nieuwenhove, "Bearing," 277–78. Nieuwenhove attributes to Moltmann a diminution of the efficacy of Christ's resurrection by too much weight given to suffering. Nieuwenhove criticizes Schillebeeckx and Rahner for downplaying of the efficacy of the cross in favor of Christ's primary faithfulness.

relations should take on [the character of the persons of the Trinity] becomes an end in itself, apart from any more concrete consideration of what those relations among divine persons are actually doing for us in the economy—for example, bringing about the end of death, sin, and suffering in human lives."[47] Aquinas argues that while the principal agency of salvation is God's; the instrumental agency of salvation is Christ's: "Since Christ's humanity is the *instrument of the Godhead*, as stated above (Q.43, A. 2), therefore all Christ's actions and sufferings operate instrumentally in virtue of His Godhead for the salvation of men. Consequently, then, Christ's Passion accomplishes man's salvation efficiently."[48] Hope rests on the efficiency and efficacy of Christ's death and resurrection.

Thomistic christological hope sees hope even in Christ's judgment.[49] Benedict narrates Thomistic hope in Christ as "the creation of justice in a way we cannot conceive, but can begin to grasp through faith.[50] "Yes, there is a resurrection of the flesh. There is justice. There is an "undoing" of past suffering, a reparation that sets things aright. For this reason, faith in the Last Judgement is first and foremost hope."[51] God cares so much about creation that God deems it worthy of judgment and grace. God does not simply gloss over the world's pains and wrongs with a grace that ignores injustice. Human sin and error, the horrors of historical conflict and abuses of power, the woundedness no one else notices, and the disparity of goods no social program can resolve—all this and more is made right—has been made right—in Jesus Christ, "the Judge and Saviour," "the fire which both burns and saves."[52] Christ brings justice to the Psalmist, the martyrs, the victims of genocide, and all those deprived of the goods and benefits of others. Christ imposes a punishing justice on the oppressors, torturers, the powerful, and the wealthy; and Christ draws the people of hope through lives of virtue, through suffering and death, through resurrection, judgment, and to beatitude. "Christ Jesus our hope" (1 Tim 1:1) is perfect in

---

47. Tanner, *Christ*, 234.

48. III, q. 48, a. 6.

49. Moltmannian hope rejects images (biblical passages and doctrine) of Christ's final judgment that suggest punishment of sinners, preferring instead images of justice obtained through the righting of injustice itself. Christ's judgment becomes a way of clearing out the problematic aspects of humanity, while leaving the rest of humanity intact, as though sin were an addition to one's persona that can be deleted.

50. Benedict XVI, *Spe salvi*, §43.

51. Ibid.

52. Ibid., §47.

divinity, the perfection of humanity, and the perfector of humans, to the fullness of their creaturely identity.

Hope

God's gift of grace, manifest in the theological virtues, grants humans the possibility to imagine and attain life with God through the hope that is Christ Jesus. Aquinas's theology of hope casts the compassion of God within a grammar of the perfect compassion of divine impassibility, and it places the end of human hope beyond the known limitations of this-worldly life and its imagined extension.

The Theological Virtues

> Lord, lift me up and let me stand
> by faith on Heaven's table land
> A higher plain than I have found
> Lord, plant my feet on higher ground
>
> I want to scale the utmost heights
> and catch a gleam of glory bright
> but still I'll pray 'til heaven I've found
> Lord, lead me on to higher ground[53]

Thomistic systematic theology and some of the theologians in conversation with Aquinas identify hope as a theological virtue, a particular category of virtue which is infused by divine grace and directed by God toward God. The end of this hope is beatitude—the blessed vision of God. The certainty of this hope rests on God's past and present activity in history and as incarnate in Christ. God's goodness—not creation—is the continuity of this world to the next.

Aquinas names hope as a theological virtue directed toward God, by God, and fulfilled in eternal happiness, beatitude.[54] The theological virtues are gifts by grace, from within, that guide toward God, and manifest—in this life—as habitual pratices to perform. Aquinas interprets Aristotle's discussion of virtue in terms of the one God of Christian scripture and tradition. Aquinas rewrites Aristotle's observation that, "the virtue of a thing is that which makes its subject good, and its work good likewise,"

---

53. Oatman Jr., "Higher."

54. Wawrykow discusses the relationship between Aquinas's presentation of theological virtue and those of his contemporaries, in "Grace," 193–95.

claiming instead that the good of a human act is the extent to which it "attains [God's] reason or God Himself."⁵⁵ God's grace transforms the human act of hope into a theological virtue, a habit of mind that "flows from grace alone."⁵⁶ These virtues are not emotions, universal human traits, or an exercise of will power: they are habits with the divine assistance necessary in order for humans to surpass the limitations of their own nature. In theological virtues, humans can reflect God's nature as they are being perfected as creatures, "as kindled wood partakes of the nature of fire."⁵⁷ Peter of Poitiers defines a theological, infused, virtue as "a good quality of mind by which one lives righteously, of which no one can make bad use, which God works in us without us."⁵⁸ Theological virtues draw humans through their natural state into the supernatural possibility prepared for them by Christ. Josef Pieper explains: "Theological virtue is an ennobling of man's nature that entirely surpasses what he 'can be' of him. Theological virtue is the steadfast orientation toward a fulfillment and a beatitude that are not 'owed' to natural man. Theological virtue is the utmost degree of a supernatural potentiality for being. This supernatural potentiality for being is grounded in a real, grace-filled participation in the divine nature, which comes to man through Christ (2 Pet 1:4)."⁵⁹

The theological virtues of faith, hope, and love, Aquinas posits, aim for God, while other virtues aim for that which leads to God. While moral virtues try for a mean between extremes of human practice in the natural order, the theological virtues progress toward the divine end of humans in the supernatural order, an end which has no mean. In faith, hope, and love, believers approach God, Godself, by God's agency. The theological virtues provide the possibility of participation in the reality of Christ. Faith, hope, and love do not simply offer a glimpse of the truth about reality; they allow believers to receive the revelation of reality itself. According to Aquinas, some knowledge of God is possible for all humans within created nature, without the assistance of grace, but humans frequently do not make good use of this innate ability.⁶⁰ Through the gift of grace, God "imparts" reality to wayfarers turned toward God.⁶¹ In this way, a human "actually or habitually knows and loves God, though imperfectly; and this

55. II-II, q. 17, a. 1.
56. II-II, q. 17, a. 1, ad 2.
57. I-II, q. 62, a. 1, ad 1.
58. I-II, q. 55, a. 4
59. Pieper, *Faith*, 99.
60. II–II, q. 12, a. 11 ad 3.
61. II–II, q. 93, a. 4.

image consists in the conformity of grace."[62] Faith, hope, and love help humans participate in God's procession of Word and Love to the extent that the object of human knowing and loving is the same as the object of God's knowing and loving: God. In this life, human participation is still imperfect, manifested as conformation and as analogy. In beatitude, the blessed attain the image of God in the "likeness of glory."[63] In faith, hope, and love, believing wayfarers participate in the reality of Creator and creation, while they are still on the way to the perfection of creatureliness in the beatific vision. The theological virtue of hope provides the wayfarer with a foretaste of beatitude and guidance for this life. These virtues, which flow out of habitual grace and perfect (at least inchoately) the powers of the soul not only orient the justified to God as end but also provide a foretaste of the enjoyment of God that will have come for others in the next life. One walks by faith now; in the next life, one will have the direct vision of God. One hopes now for union with God; in the next life, the beatified partake of that union. And one loves now, aspiring to the fullness of love's expression that will come in the immediate presence of God, the ultimate good.[64] Hope thus witnesses to beatitude through creaturely participation in the reality of God.

The Theological Virtue of Faith

> I'm comin' up on the rough side of the mountain,
> I must hold to God, His powerful hand.[65]

Faith, hope, and love mutually support and build up each other, such that it is difficult to determine which comes first. Aquinas begins with faith, because faith provides the foundation for hope. Faith precedes hope, because in order to hope, one needs to know for what to hope. "Now the primary subjection of man to God is by faith, according to Heb. xi. 6: He that cometh to God, must believe that He is."[66] The act of faith, then, means to accept someone else's witness, to trust, and to participate in someone else's knowledge. A believer retains some uncertainty, because the believer does not see or know for him/herself; "rather, the mind, insofar as it believes, is

---

62. Ibid.
63. Pieper, *Faith*, 113.
64. See also Jordan, *Rewritten*, 162–63.
65. Barnes, "Rough."
66. II-II, q. 16, a. 1.

operating not on its own but on alien soil."[67] Faith pertains to participation in the testimony of a witness, by identifying with the witness and seeing the witness's reality as if it were one's own. The theological virtue of faith pertains to belief in the reality whose witness and content is God.[68] Theological faith asserts the certainty of God's identity, guaranteed by the testimony of God. God moves people inwardly, by grace, such that they can rise above that which is possible to human nature alone and then think and assent to the reality of God. In this way, the true end of humans in God resides first in the intellect, by faith. Once the end is present in the intellect by faith, the end can be present to the will, which "has no inclination for anything except in so far as it is apprehended by the intellect."[69] Yet, even though an act of faith comes from the intellect and the will, the virtue of faith resides in the intellect, because of the object of faith, "the true, which pertains properly to the intellect."[70] Faith establishes the possibility for hope and love which uphold and sustain faith.[71] Faith adheres to God as the source of the knowledge of truth.

The infusion of grace moves faith to this knowledge of God's truth, and faith claims certainty of this knowledge about God, because of the witness, who is God. Faith is certain of the Trinity and the incarnation, and of God's omnipotence and mercy, even though the wayfarer does not know the fullness of God's truth.[72] The certainty of faith grounds hope and love and continues to build until the fulfillment of faith in beatitude, at which point faith is no longer necessary, since the object of faith—God—stands eternally present. Certainty pertains to the faith in God that sustains a wayfarer not yet in the presence of God. Certain faith no longer applies to those who have reached the beatific vision, who have attained the completion of createdness and no longer reside in a state of "not yet." Faith is fulfilled and therefore voided in, or subsumed in the love of, beatitude. Aquinas interprets Hebrews 11:1: "Faith is the substance of things to be hoped for, the evidence of things that appear not"; or, in the form of a definition: "faith is a habit of the mind, whereby eternal life is begun in us, making the intellect assent to what is nonapparent."[73] He explains that the

67. Pieper, *Faith*, 116.
68. II–II, q. 4, a. 8.
69. II–II, q. 4, a, 7.
70. II–II, q. 4, a. 2.
71. II–II, q. 4, a. 7.
72. II–II, q. 4, a. 8.
73. II–II, q. 4, a. 1.

object of faith is the First Truth, which is as yet unseen and unattained, and therefore hoped for. The substance, the assent of faith, contains what is to be hoped for, and the evidence, or conviction, commits the intellect to the truth.

The Theological Virtue of Hope

> But the hope of life eternal
> Makes all old hopes brand new.[74]

Aquinas explains that the theological virtue of hope anticipates the fulfillment of creatureliness in God that faith proposes as a certainty: "... the act of hope presupposes the act of faith ... Hence an act of faith is experienced in an act of hope."[75] Natural hope (hope as a passion) aims toward a future good that is difficult to obtain.[76] The theological virtue of hope (hope as a grace-infused habit of the mind) aims toward eternal happiness in God, and it enjoys divine assistance in obtaining that eternal happiness. In other words, the object of hope is God, and the means of obtaining the object is God's assistance.[77] Natural hope reaches toward goods in general, "toward the arduous 'not yet' of fulfillment."[78] The theological virtue of hope reaches toward the Good, which is God, toward the arduous not yet of fulfillment, which has already been inaugurated by Jesus Christ. This hope is "a steadfast turning toward the fulfillment of man's nature, that is, toward good, ... it has its source in the reality of grace in man and is directed toward supernatural happiness in God."[79] The impossibly arduous goal of human perfection in God has become possible through Christ's suffering, death, and resurrection, and has been rendered attainable through the graced infusion of hope.

Aquinas teaches that the reality of grace which supplies the virtue of hope in humans also reveals the reality of Creator and creature. Hope reflects the true identity of humanity as wayfarers, creatures directed toward, drawn toward, and eager for the rest that will only come in beatitude. Pieper explains: "In the virtue of hope more than in any other, man

74. Massengale, "Adjusted."
75. II–II, q. 17, a. 6, ad 2.
76. II–II, q. 17, a. 1.
77. Ibid.
78. II–II, q. 23, a. 1.
79. Pieper, *Faith*, 236; I–II, 2, 7 ad 2.

understands that he is a creature, that he has been created by God."[80] Hope both accepts the reality of the incompleteness that accompanies the creature's wayfarer status and expects the resolution of wayfaring, the completion of creation in the eternal enjoyment of God. This expectation does not suggest divine delay or lack for not yet having effected perfection.[81] Hope's expectation refers to the necessity of divine assistance, and therefore points toward the additional dimension of the supernatural, rather than simply to a chronological timeline. Similarly, the image of wayfarer suggests less a sense of geographic travel and more the true character of created nature in itself.[82] The reality revealed in hope, and in all three of the infused virtues, far exceeds the limitations of finite existence; through hope that reality reorders the lives of believers toward God. Hope orders the lives of believers radically differently from the familiar priorities of daily life. Hope claims eternal happiness in God as its primary object, instead of physical comfort, gratification of all desires, or financial success. "For we should hope from Him for nothing less than Himself, since His goodness, whereby he imparts good things to His creature, is no less than His Essence. Therefore the proper and principal object of hope is eternal happiness."[83] God's assistance provides theological hope, and appropriately proportioned hope must aim toward the infinite good of enjoyment in God.

Aquinas allows that the virtue of hope also extends to that which contributes to those goods that contribute to the creature's end in the Creator; these constitute the secondary object of hope.[84] No person or creature can replace God as the first cause of happiness, and hope should not be directed to a person or creature as if to God; still, others can hope for and help to provide those things that support wayfarers along the way to happiness in God. Aquinas argues that it is "lawful to hope in a man or a creature as being the secondary and instrumental agent, through whom one is helped to obtain any goods that are ordained to happiness. It is in this way that we turn to the saints, and that we ask men also for certain things."[85] Cessario elaborates on the secondary objects of hope that are important to the aquisition and sustenance of theological hope:

80. Pieper, *Faith*, 98.
81. II-II, q. 17, a.5, ad 4.
82. II-II, q. 18, a. 4.
83. II-II, q. 17, a. 2.
84. II-II, q. 17, a. 4.
85. Ibid.

> Theological hope relates the Christian directly to God, so it includes among its material objects all of the good things that the Christian believer lovingly looks forward to receiving: the vision of God, the accompanying bliss, the resurrection of the body and its glorification, and fellowship with the blessed. Theological hope also entitles the Christian to expect the secondary objects, that is, created instruments of hope that form part of the Christian dispensation for salvation. This means above all the instrumental causality of Christ's humanity; however, it also includes spiritual goods, such as grace, the infused virtues, the gift of the Holy Spirit, the maternal mediation of the Blessed Virgin Mary, the intercession of the saints, and the forgiveness of sins (especially mediated through the sacraments of Penance and Holy Anointing). Furthermore, one can rely on theological hope for temporal goods, such as holy friends, good health, psychological equilibrium, at least to the extent that these things conduce toward beatitude.[86]

Thus, hope recasts every relationship in terms of the end revealed by grace, and hope ranks all goods in relation to the one true good in God. A multiplicity of secondary goods assist the goods of hope of eternal life with God. These secondary goods indicate some of the ways that Christians can facilitate and support hope in those who are hopeless.

The Theological Virtue of Love

> Take my love; my Lord, I pour
> At Thy feet its treasure store.
> Take myself, and I will be
> Ever, only, all for Thee.[87]

The theological virtue of love[88] is generally listed after faith and hope, but it holds first place as "that which attains God most."[89] Aquinas explains that faith and hope adhere to God for the sake of the one who believes and

---

86. Cessario, "Theological," 276.

87. Havergal, "Take."

88. *Caritas* has often been translated as charity. The connotations of charity are currently so connected to a particular response to needy people, that I use love here, alongside the citations which use the translation of charity. There are ample problems with various connotations of love, as well, but my intent is to underscore that God is the source and primary subject of all rightly ordered love.

89. II–II, q. 26, a. 6.

hopes, and faith and hope find their completion when in eternal happiness with God. Faith, the assertion and assurance of the reality of God, no longer pertains once fulfilled in the presence of God. Hope, the anticipation and expectation in the "not yet" of the "already" accomplished redemption, through Christ and in the Holy Spirit, no longer applies once perfected in beatitude. Therefore, faith and hope do not perdure in beatitude. Love, however, adheres to God for God's sake, unifying human minds to God by the emotion of love. When the union of lover and beloved is effected in beatitude, love then perdures for ever.[90] In this life, love manifests itself most fully in friendship between humans on the way to friendship with God; in such friendships, enabled by the infusion of the Holy Spirit ("who is the love of the Father and the Son"[91]), humans anticipate participation in divine love.[92] Love affirms the reality of God and God's good creation that faith asserts and hope anticipates, by moving toward union with God according to the example of Jesus Christ. Jesus Christ models love through friendship with all sorts and conditions of people. By imitating Christ's friendships recorded in scripture and the friendships of those saints who are exemplary imitators of Christ, believers can learn to participate in divine love. "Thus, in the order of generation, love follows faith and hope, which proclaim and point toward the love of God. In the order of perfection, however, love is the most excellent of virtues, and without love, neither faith nor hope can be perfected."[93] Love affirms the goodness of God's creation, by loving the other for being. Aquinas observes that what believers should love in their neighbors is precisely that their neighbors might "be in God."[94]

Creation-affirming love includes self-love, which, as a theological virtue, loves oneself as a form of loving God.[95] As the source of and reason for love, and as the entirety of good, God leads believers to love themselves: "in the order of love man should love himself more than all else after God."[96] God also leads believers to love others and God in friendship

---

90. I–II, q. 67, a. 6.

91. II–II, q. 24, a. 2.

92. II–II, q. 23, a. 5.

93. II–II, q. 23, a. 6.

94. II–II, q. 25, a. 1.

95. The inclusion of self-love in the theological virtue of love opens the possibility of distortion and delusion, which underscores the importance of keeping love closely tied to faith and hope, as well as the importance of other supporting moral virtues (including humility and prudence).

96. II–II, q. 26, a. 13 ad 3.

that participates in God's love. Charitable friendship communicates mutual love shaped by and toward God's love.[97] Love that communicates God's love for those of Christ's body constitutes friendship with God. "Accordingly, since there is a communication between man and God, in as much as He communicates His happiness to us, some kind of friendship must needs be based on this same communication, of which it is written (1 Cor. i.9): God is faithful: by Whom you are called unto the fellowship of His Son. The love which is based on this communication, is charity: wherefore it is evident that charity is the friendship of man for God."[98] Love guides hope in friendships toward hope in friendships in Christ.

Here, the goal of friendship with God does not refer to the contemporary notion of egalitarian friendship on human terms. Mutual love between God and humans is not a matter of equality between creator and creature, in this life or eternal life. Friendship with God, which is eternal happiness with God, entails the fullness of God's love and the fullness of human love, drawn together as one love in God. Jesus Christ manifests this love and demonstrates the love of God in friendships now through presence, constancy, companionship, humble service, poverty, shared resources, and guidance toward life in God. The eucharistic sacrament effects this friendship, as Wadell notes: "We become God's friends by eating Christ. We grow in charity by feeding on the one who is perfect friendship with God. 'So it is that we were reborn in Christ through baptism,' Aquinas writes, 'we eat Christ through the Eucharist.' . . . To feed on Christ is to take Christ to heart, it is to allow Christ to affect every dimension of who we are."[99] Friendship with Jesus Christ builds friendships with others that approach eternal friendship with God.

Love turned toward friendship with God requires faith and hope until that friendship is complete.

> Charity signifies not only the love of God, but also a certain friendship with Him; which implies, besides love, a certain mutual return of love, together with a mutual communion . . . Now this friendship of man with God, which consists in a certain familiar colloquy with Him, is begun here, in this life, by grace, but will be perfected in the future life, by glory; each of which things we hold by faith and hope. Wherefore just as friendship with a person would be impossible, if one disbelieved in, or despaired

---

97. II–II, q. 23, a. 1.
98. Ibid.
99. Wadell, "Growing," 162.

of, the possibility of their fellowship or familiar colloquy; so too, friendship with God, which is charity, is impossible without faith, so as to believe in this fellowship and colloquy with God, and to hope to attain to this fellowship. Therefore charity [as the theological virtue of love not yet complete in beatitude] is quite impossible without faith and hope.[100]

Aquinas's theological virtues depend on the connection between God's knowledge and human knowledge, assisted by grace. Present-day understandings of people who do not possess the cognitive capacities to participate in that knowledge challenge the necessity of cognitive knowledge for theological hope. This concern pertains to the hope the church might have *for* the very young, the very old, and those who have cognitive disabilities; and it pertains to the hope *of* the very young, the very old, and those who have cognitive disabilities. These questions deserve ongoing work, some of which has been begun in the work of Miguel Romero, who engages with Aquinas's account of the *amens*, one afflicted with *amentia*: "a person who is congenitally unable to communicate, who manifests no capacity for discursive reasoning or intentional acts, and is entirely dependent upon others for her proximate wellbeing."[101] Romero presents a basis for ongoing consideration of eschatological hope for those who cannot participate in the rational thought and expression we recognize as indicative of mental fitness. He notes that, "for Aquinas, what is 'rational' about the rational soul is the image of God in the human creature—insofar as the rational creature is always capable of knowledge and love, and cannot be rendered incapable of knowing and loving. Moreover, this capacity for 'rationality' does not originate from an instrumental faculty belonging to some bodily organ, i.e., the brain . . . Aquinas vehemently rejects all attempts to reduce human nature to a corporeal operation, while affirming the goodness and beauty of human existence as an embodied creature . . ."[102] Baptism in Christ, not human intellect, provides the restoration of grace[103] and the "infusion of faith, hope, and love."[104] Aquinas's conviction that the theological virtues can be inhabited even by those who cannot act independently or responsibly underscores the character of faith, hope, and love as gift rather than sheer human will.

100. I–II, q. 66, a. 1.
101. Romero, "Aquinas," 112.
102. Ibid., 105.
103. Ibid., 112.
104. Ibid., 121.

The Beatitude of Heaven, the End of Hope

Heaven

> When the gates swing wide on the other side...
> On the right hand and on the left hand
> Fifty miles of elbow room[105]

All language about the end of theological hope depends on analogy. Efforts to avoid images of heaven, so as not to be distracted from the here and now, fail to recognize that the Christian hope of resurrection life cannot be expressed without analogy. Since humans have no access to direct or indirect knowledge or experience of life that is not this life, we are left with silence, language of what God (and life with God) is not, and language that suggests something more, better, and beyond human thought and expression. Ample images from scripture and the lives of the people of God feed our imaginations with ways to point beyond what we know.

Gregory of Nyssa speaks of this world and the world of beatitude with the analogy of a city: "Let us take as head not the Jerusalem below, but the mother City above; not the one that at this very hour armies are trampling underfoot, but that which the angels glorify."[106] Benedict cites Augustine, who wrote to the widow Proba that the end of prayer is "the blessed life," the life of "happiness."[107] Benedict describes this blessed happiness as joy beyond measure: "This is how Jesus expresses it in Saint John's Gospel: 'I will see you again and your hearts will rejoice, and no one will take your joy from you' (16:22)."[108] On the one hand, endless joy sounds wonderful; on the other hand, endlessness distresses our familiarity and comfort within time. Benedict notes that the phrase "eternal life" stretches our imaginations beyond capacity, since we are so bound by and reassured by the frame of time.

> To imagine ourselves outside the temporality that imprisons us and in some way to sense that eternity is not an unending succession of days in the calendar, but something more like the supreme moment of satisfaction, in which totality embraces us and we embrace totality—this we can only attempt. It would be like plunging into the ocean of infinite love, a moment in which

---

105. Buffum, "Fifty Miles."
106. Lubac, *Medieval*, 185.
107. Benedict XVI, *Spe salvi*, §11.
108. Ibid., §12.

time—the before and after—no longer exists. We can only attempt to grasp the idea that such a moment is life in the full sense, a plunging ever anew into the vastness of being, in which we are simply overwhelmed with joy. [109]

Benedict argues that the many attempts by the people of God to describe the indescribable end of hope have given to the people of God the gift of perseverance in faithful hope.[110]

Aquinas sketches a grammar of what can be said about the divine beatitude that cannot be known except by God and the blessed, "who are called blessed by reason of the assimilation to His beatitude."[111] He determines that beatitude belongs to God, because it is "perfect good of an intellectual nature,"[112] beatitude belongs to God as also to the blessed who are assimilated to God's beatitude; beatitude is God and therefore uncreated, while it is a created thing in creatures[113]; and the beatitude of God includes all other beatitudes.[114] In keeping with his recognition of the ontological distinction between God's knowledge and human knowledge, Aquinas does not attempt to solve the mystery of beatitude; however, within the guidelines he presents, we might imagine that there is an existence, outside the time and place we now understand, that participates as fully as creatures can participate in the perfect goodness that is the knowledge of God. The object of this theological hope pertains to body and soul, exceeds and absorbs all other partial beatitudes we might hope for, and assimilates the blessed to God's own beatitude.

Gregory of Nyssa describes the means of assimilaton to God's beatitude with an image of bubbles of air in water: "For as air is not retained in water when it is dragged down by some weighty body and left in the depth of the water, but rises quickly to its kindred element, while the water is often raised up together with the air its upward rush, being moulded by the circle of air into a convex shape with a slight and membrane-like surface, so too, when the true life that underlay the flesh sped up, after the Passion, to itself, the flesh was also raised up with it, being forced upwards from corruption to incorruptibility by the Divine immortality."[115] Tanner proposes

---

109. Ibid.
110. Ibid., §13.
111. I, q. 26, a. 2.
112. I, q. 26, a. 1.
113. I, q. 26, a. 3.
114. I, q. 26, a. 4.
115. Tanner, *Jesus*, 117, citing Gregory of Nyssa.

that eternal life consists of existence in a new identity, in an inseparable relation to God, as modeled by the incarnate Jesus Christ.[116] "The very meaning of this new identity is that our dependence upon God for our existence is now complete: in Christ we essentially *are* that relationship to God in a way that simply being creatures of God does not entail."[117] Hope that anticipates this relationship with God that we are in Christ might manifest in human relationships that look toward radically irresponsible, economically impractical, communally ordered friendships, modeled on the friendships of those whose lives illustrate the imitation of Christ.

Certainty

> Standing on the promises of Christ my King,
> Through eternal ages let His praises ring,
> Glory in the highest, I will shout and sing,
> Standing on the promises of God.
>
> Standing, standing,
> Standing on the promises of God my Savior;
> Standing, standing,
> I'm standing on the promises of God.[118]

The theology of hope explored in this chapter claims a certainty based on God's work in history and the unknowable reality of beatitude. The focus of Moltmannian hope has developed from an exciting, open and somewhat uncertain future, to a certain future salvation, imagined as the transformation of this known life with God's arrival. Moltmannian hope prioritizes care for the people, systems, and condition of the earth now; and it secondarily prioritizes the future new creation which determines and supports present hopes and actions. Moltmannian hope rests not on God's fulfilled promises of the past, nor on an unknowable other-wordly eternal life, but on the future of the earth, which future gathers God's future into the knowable and imaginable prospects for this earth. The importance of human efforts to sustain the creation for God's coming is certain, despite the sinful limitations of humans. In contrast, the hope Aquinas describes relies on God's constant and eternal certainty, despite the uncertain present and future of this life.

116. Tanner, *Jesus*, 110.
117. Ibid.
118. Carter, "Standing."

Aquinas assumes the primary priority of eternal happiness in God and the concurrent secondary priority of those earthly goods that support that end, because they support the end of eternal happiness in God. Through faith, God provides knowledge that extends beyond current conditions and offers a faint glimpse of God's reality, which far exceeds current human experience. Through hope, God provides a confident—but not fully understood—expectation of the fulfillment of that which is known by faith and accessed through participation in Christ in love. Through love, God provides friendships that anticipate friendship with God and that exercise care for the current conditions of others, that friendships now may become eternal friendship. In this context, hope addresses the approach to eternal beatitude *and* the earthly conditions that support that approach. These two concerns are distinct and inseparable (analogically just as the two natures of Christ are distinct and inseparable).

The goods of creation are not radically opposed to the infinite good of enjoyment with God; rather, in hope, one can participate in a taste of God's goodness to come, through those material goods which help to lead toward beatitude. Hope calls believers not to withdraw from the world, but to so direct their lives toward the ultimate enjoyment of God's reality that they might be sustained in anticipation of that fulfillment by the spiritual and temporal goods God provides along the way. At the same time, Aquinas reminds believers that hope rests in God's reality. Temptations abound to confuse natural ends with supernatural ends, to rest one's hopes on the more readily attainable and imaginable goods of human capacity. The continuity of goods does not mean that the ultimate goals of hope are those goods of earthly life, only bigger and better. As soon as the goods of health, friendship, or even the sacraments, become ends in and of themselves, they no longer support the true end of beatitude, and they no longer manifest the virtue of hope or its foundation in faith. Christians continually struggle to discern the legitimate goods of hope, in faith and love, through Christ and the Holy Spirit. The apparent goods of independence, wealth, control, and comfort all compete powerfully for positioning as primary objects of hope. The goods of liberation, justice, and improving the lives of the oppressed—the secondary goods of Aquinas's language—vie for position as primary goods, especially given the urgent needs of those in unbearable suffering. Aquinas argues that the natural passion of hope looks toward future, difficult-to-attain goods which might—but do not necessarily—support and sustain perseverance in the theological hope that looks toward the fulfillment of God's reality revealed in faith.

A Thomistic Grammar of Hope

The anticipatory, not-yet aspect of the wayfarer's hope might suggest heightened uncertainty about the attainment of the goods hoped for, both temporal and spiritual, but Aquinas explains that certainty is indeed found in hope, both essentially and by participation. Hope draws its certainty essentially from faith, which is located in the intellect, and the gift of divine grace provides human intellect with a glimpse of God's intellect. This cognitive certainty adheres to the truth of God incarnate by grace and presents that truth to theological hope as solid and unshakable. The affective certitude particular to hope is "a form of practical knowledge that directs any operation to its proper end, viz, either as realized or as tending toward an end."[119] This means that faith's cognitive power moves the will toward the attainment of its end; and in the process, the intellective certitude of faith becomes the willed, affective certitude of hope, the domain of the tending-toward God. The divine intellect moves nature to its end with divine certainty, and therefore the divine intellect moves human creatures to their end in beatitude with divine certainty.[120] Reason moves the moral virtues, as a kind of second nature, to their end with certainty. Faith moves hope to its end in eternal happiness with certainty, by sharing its cognitive certainty and by prompting its affective certainty[121]: "Hope does not trust chiefly in grace already received, but on God's omnipotence and mercy, whereby even he that has not grace, can obtain it, so as to come to eternal life. Now whoever has faith is certain of God's omnipotence and mercy."[122] The secondary goods of hope remain essential, but their value is not assessed in degrees of visible improvement, because the certainty rests in God's certain ends for creation.

Individual effort and accomplishment do not affirm the virtue of hope, but the knowledge of faith undergirds hope to its certain end, as designed and moved by the divine intellect. The certainty of theological hope that Thomas presents pertains to God's sure, true, unchanging, and omnipotent nature, rather than to the hopeful believer, the particulars of the believer's life, or the social programs developed to relieve and then eliminate hopelessness. Contemporary versions of hope frequently look to human knowledge, effort, or accomplishment as the basis for the certainty of their hope. Thomas (with the the Council of Trent) places the certainty of hope in God, and not in those who hope. Some politial agendas stir

---

119. Cessario, *Virtues*, 47.
120. II–II, q. 18, a. 4.
121. Ibid.
122. Ibid.

up and confirm hope when their policies seem possible and effective. Upstanding Christian community leaders inspire hope when their acts of generosity and dedication improve the quality of impoverished lives. Christian lives of unselfish service seem bound for the fulfillment of hopes in eternal life. "Even though all should place a most firm hope in God's help and rest in it, let no one promise himself with absolute certainty any definite outcome."[123] The exemplary figures of Christian hope place their confidence in God, without personal knowledge of God's plans for the future and without expectations that their own agency will determine particular outcomes. Faithful hope does not presume to know what will happen, but only that God is good and that the fulfillment of hope rests in God. Theological hope participates partially in the certainty of God, while living the life of the created, finite, limited, uncertain human, and while moving toward beatitude; but the imperfection of humanity in no way lessens the certainty that is of God.

Benedict affirms the certainty of hope that stands strong in the face of human failure to make the world better. The hope that is redemption in Christ does not diminish in the face of disappointment or falter in the face of disaster. Christ has redeemed us by his love, and "through him we have become certain of God."[124] He continues: "Man's great, true hope which holds firm in spite of all disappointment can only be God—God who has loved us and who continues to love us 'to the end,' until all 'is accomplished' (cr. Jn 13:1 and 19:30)."[125] The certitude of this hope rests entirely in God, who has shared God's love with us through Jesus Christ, and who provides "the great hope that sustains the whole of life (cf. Eph 2:12)."[126]

The saints and martyrs and the models of faith in Hebrews lead lives of hope characterized by *hypomonē* (10:36): patience, perseverance, constancy. "Knowing how to wait, while patiently enduring trials, is necessary for the believer to be able to 'receive what is promised' (10:36).[127] Benedict argues that *hypomonē* reflects Israel's persevering faithfulness to God on the basis of the certainty of the covenant in a world which contradicts God. Thus the word indicates a lived hope, a life based on the certainty of hope.[128] In the New Testament, this life of certain hope in God focuses

123 Cessario, *Virtues*, 47, citing Council of Trent, "Decree on Justification," chapter 13.

124. Benedict XVI, *Spe salvi*, §26.

125. Ibid., §27.

126. Ibid.

127. Ibid., §9.

128. Ibid.

on Christ: "in Christ, God has revealed himself. He has already communicated to us the 'substance' of things to come, and thus the expectation of God acquires a new certainty."[129] Hope is "the expectation of things to come from the perspective of a present that is already given. It is a looking-forward in Christ's presence, with Christ who is present, to the perfecting of his body, to his definitive coming."[130] Hope gains certainty because it is grounded in the certain faith granted by Christ's already/not yet presence.

In contemporary culture, Benedict claims, faith and hope are widely understood to be tentative and provisional when they refer to matters spiritual, and certain only when supported by material, tangible, provable facts. His presentation of Christian hope claims certainty based on faith in Christ's presence, which cannot be proven except by the gift and witness of faith and hope. The hope that Benedict describes looks to both an eschatological end and to the ends of improved lives now. He declines to endorse disputes that posit two opposing ends. He declines to accept that hope in the Kingdom of God in heaven and hope in God's peace and justice effected in practical reality here on earth are mutually exclusive options. Benedict's account reflects his embrace of paradox, and it features a sacramental connection between present life and eternal life: life transformed by baptism in Christ through the Holy Spirit and sustained through the eucharist.

Continuity

> Are you ready for the great atomic power?
> Will you rise and meet your saviour in the air?[131]

While Moltmannian hope envisions a continuity of this creation into the new creation that preserves the goods of this creation in God's future coming, a more Thomistic hope claims continuity of God's relationship with creation, such that the creature/creator difference remains even through the assimilation into beatitude. Humans may obtain their perfection through Christ, as creatures in the presence of God, regardless of the condition of the known world. At the same time, continuity may be described by means of an analogy of being that enables speech about God and life with God, drawn from the knowable and pointing toward the unknowable.

129. Ibid.
130. Ibid.
131. Louvin Brothers, "Atomic."

Our Only Hope

This certainty of hope does not provide a certain knowledge of the location, content, or time of beatitude. Descriptions of beatitude, at their best, suggest the beyond-imagination character of recognizable and impossible goods of heaven: a city floating above the sky, wild creatures coexisting peaceably, poverty becoming true wealth. Imaginative use of known images to point toward the unknown suppose some sort of continuity between present knowable life and the unknowable life eternal, while acknowledging the ultimate distinction between this life and that life, a gap which humanity can never bridge on its own. Benedict argues that "the term 'eternal life' is intended to give a name to this known 'unknown' that cannot accurately be expressed. Inevitably it is an inadequate term that creates confusion. 'Eternal,' in fact, suggests to us the idea of something interminable, and this frightens us; 'life' makes of think of the life that we know and love and do not want to lose, even though very often it brings more toil than satisfaction, so that while on the one hand we desire it, on the other hand, we do not want it."[132] Instead of an interminable extension of the life and time we know, the "eternal life with God" for which we hope indicates something greater than this life, set somehow outside the boundaries of time we currently rely on to make sense of our lives. Although we cannot grasp what this might be like, we can catch small glimpses that hint at the character of this "known unknown."[133] The joy of this life with God is thus not the exhausting continuation of calendar days, nor the endless "do-overs" of a *Groundhog Day* existence, but a joy that overwhelms, beyond the limitations of capacity, quantity, quality, and duration that define our current lives.

Tanner points toward the continuity of this life and eternal life with a focus on the transformed identities and relationships of creatures who share in Christ's resurrection life: "So for us, life in Christ brings not just created goods but divine attributes such as imperishability and immortality, which are ours only through the grace of Christ in the resurrection of our bodies. When the fire of our own lives grows cold, we come to burn with God's own flame.[134] Tanner's understanding allows for "a more spatialized than temporalized eschatology."[135] She highlights the paradoxical already/not yet character of life that participates in Jesus' incarnation and

---

132. Benedict XVI, *Spe salvi*, #12.
133. Ibid., §14.
134. Tanner, *Jesus*, 101.
135. Ibid.

Christ's bodily resurrection. The end of hope is not over, and it is not in the future as a promise as yet unfulfilled.

> The future-oriented eschatology of a future-oriented society here gives way to an eschatology in keeping with the present epoch, which, as Michel Foucault describes it, is "the epoch of space. We are in the epoch of simultaneity; we are in the epoch of juxtaposition . . . of the side by side, of the dispersed . . . Our experience of the world is less that of a long life developing through time than that of a network that connects points and intersects with its own skein." Eternal life is not the endless extension of present existence into an endless future, but a matter of a new quality of life in God, at the ready, even now infiltrating, seeping into the whole. Eternal life is less a matter of duration than a matter of the mode of one's existence in relation to God, as that caliber of relation shows itself in a new pattern for the whole of life.[136]

The pattern for the whole of life is Jesus Christ; the end of hope, eternal life, is life in Christ, now *and* outside time.

Moltmannian hope argues against apocalyptic visions of in which God dramatically sweeps away this world, in order to establish a new kingdom of the just. Moltmannian hope advocates confidence that this world will not end, but God's future will bring a new beginning here: continuity rests on God's creation, and the condition of this creation determines the possibilities for God's new creation. Tanner supplies an alternative to the end of the world vs. new beginning of the world dichotomy with a continuity that depends on creation's relationship with God. If relationship, rather than beginnings or endings, defines salvation, then eschatological hope looks to "a new level of relationship with God" as the "consummation of the good"[137]; and that relationship with God in no way depends on the destruction or preservation of the world we know. This continuity releases us from concerns about the effectiveness of our efforts to solve the problems of corruption, suffering, and environmental collapse; while at

---

136. Ibid., 101–2. When he wrote the essay from which Tanner draws, in 1986, Foucault could not yet have experienced the possibilities for transformed relationships among people with access to the communication technologies of texting, twittering, internet chatting, and skyping. Much analysis of recent communication possibilities underscores the risks of technological relationships. Additional analysis may well indicate the ways that these new patterns of communication add possibilities for strong, sustained, faithful relationships in hope.

137. Ibid., 104.

the same time it requires immediate and unceasing action that addresses the problems of corruption, suffering, and environmental collapse. Hope thus responds with affirmation, witness, and thanksgiving to the resurrection life already accomplished in Christ and to full participation in the perfection of creation in Christ.

People of Hope

Theocentric Anthropology

> Blessèd assurance, Jesus is mine!
> O what a foretaste of glory divine!
> Heir of salvation, purchase of God,
> Born of His Spirit, washed in His blood.
>
> This is my story, this is my song,
> Praising my Savior, all the day long;
> This is my story, this is my song,
> Praising my Savior, all the day long.[138]

Thomas names the people of hope as wayfarers, who will not rest until in death they find themselves completely in the presence of God. Pieper writes: "It would be difficult to conceive of another statement that penetrates as deeply into the innermost core of creaturely existence as does the statement that man finds himself, even until the moment of his death, in the *status viatoris*, in the state of being on the way."[139] Thomas narrates the hope of the wayfarer in the context of God's providence and predestination. God's providence includes God's predestination of all humans toward their eternal and natural ends. God, in God's abundant goodness, draws creatures to their end in God. God's providence grants hope to humans and supplies the way toward hope's fulfillment. God predestines both the grace that humans receive in this life and the glory hoped for in the future life.[140] A creature can only attain naturally what is proportionate to its cre-

---

138. Crosby, "Blessed."

139. Pieper, *Faith*, 102; II–II, q. 161, a. 1.

140. I, q. 23, a. 4 ad 2. Providence and predestination have been understood in a wide variety of ways over time, before and after the Reformation, and I am not here offering a history of the relevant doctrines. I introduce the Thomistic connections between hope and prayer, providence and predestination, in order to illustrate a less familiar way to imagine the relation between God, creation, and theological hope. Contemporary constructions of theological hope that narrate this connection

ated nature. Humans, as rational creatures, are created for an end beyond natural life, the end of eternal life, which is beyond its own power to attain and is dependent upon God's direction.[141] Thomas explains:

> Now if a thing cannot attain to something by the power of its nature, it must be directed thereto by another; thus, an arrow is directed by the archer towards as mark. Hence, properly speaking, a rational creature, capable of eternal life, is led towards it, directed, as it were, by God. The reason of that direction preexists in God; as in Him is the type of the order of all things towards an end, which we proved above to be providence. Now the type in the mind of the doer of something to be done, is a kind of pre-existence in him of the thing to be done. Hence the type of the aforesaid direction of a rational creature towards the end of life eternal is called predestination. For to destine, is to direct or send.[142]

Hope looks to God not only for certainty and support on the way to fulfillment; hope also looks to God to propel and to aim the arrow toward its mark.

Just as Hebrews urges believers to "seize the hope set before us" (6:18) and to "cling to the confession of our hope without wavering" (10:23), Thomas's imagery suggests that believers must cling to the hope that is an arrow, shot toward its end by God on its path of predestination. Sure hope flies toward the target with the arrow, following the path predestined by God's love, to God. Predestination indicates God's will to love and elect God's people to eternal happiness. As God's will, predestination resides within God rather than in the creature predestined by God. Humans do not contain programs of destiny, installed by God, that move them through motions automatically. God contains predestination in God's mind, and God actively executes the ordering of humans towards eternal salvation by calling the elect and by magnifying the responses of the elect to that call.

---

differently might consider the questions that Aquinas's theology of providence and predestination asks and answers and consider which questions newer constructions answer, and how.

141. This project touches on the rich and controverted discussion of the theology of natural and supernatural grace, the interpretation and authority of Aquinas, and sacramentality. A further consideration of theological hope might begin from within this discourse. For an introduction to manifestations of this debate, see Healy, "de Lubac," and Oakes, "Surnaturel." Also see Mansini, "Abiding," and Hütter, "Natural."

142. I, q. 23, a. 1.

Thus, hope can be seen as cooperative anticipation of the predestined to their target of eternal happiness.

An emphasis on creaturely dependence on God acknowledges God's all encompassing care while accounting for free will and free hope. This gift of freedom is not freedom from God, and God does not release those who turn away from God to a life in some part of creation outside God's purview; there is no such place. The freedom of hope in God needs God's direction and design; God determines how and when God's goods are granted and received. Thomas reminds his readers that God's reasons are God's alone, and he adds Augustine's reminder, "Why He draws one, and another He draws not, seek not to judge, if thou dost not wish to err."[143] If one names humans as the primary agent of hope, then it might seem pointless for anyone to hope if God has already predestined some to eternal happiness and some to reprobation and eternal punishment; however, Thomas is not talking about or to *anyone* in the *Summa*. The *Summa* is a primer for Christian believers: those who hope, the faithful who do not wish to err, and those who have already received sufficient grace to posit some faith, claim some hope, participate in some love. Thomas's is, at least in part, a circular argument; there is no one, identifiable, point in time at which the theological virtue of hope begins, and there is no way to discover the line between God's will and the will of the believer infused with theological hope.

Thomas does point toward scripture's encouragements to hope within the divine promises, "for he who promises rewards to them that obey him, by that very fact, urges them to hope: hence all the promises contained in the law are incitements to hope."[144] Beyond the Law itself, scripture offers additional encouragements, by way of promise, warning, and command, as evidenced especially in the Psalms. Thomas notes that natural hope inclines humans toward the goods proportionate to the possibilities of human nature. In order for humans to become hopeful wayfarers, in order for humans to hope for the supernatural goods of the eternal life for which they are created, they need divine inducements, and the first inducements are provided by the promises, admonitions, and commands of the divine law.[145] Precepts of scripture induce the faithful to hope, since scripture names it the duty of the faithful to hope in God in order to be saved.[146]

143. I, q. 23, a. 5 ad 3.
144. II–II, q. 22, a. 1 ad 1.
145. Ibid.
146. II–II, q. 22, a. 1 ad 3.

Hope directed toward eternal, transformed, life with God does not explain the ways of God or reveal a blueprint for earthly life, but when the faithful are turned toward beatitude, they are blessed with ample assistance to live rightly in this world. Hopes directed toward new life beyond this world shape just hopes and acts in this world.

The preceding account of the people of hope presumes an anthropology of dependent creatures in God's providential care. In this context, human creatures are stewards of hope given by God, and the fulfillment of hope is effected in Jesus Christ. In contrast, Moltmannian hope risks placing so much responsibility for achieving the goods of hope on human shoulders that the impossibility of the task can either cripple hope or limit it to smaller-scale, practical goods. Moltmannian theology rests so much on God's suffering with creation that human experience and desires may seem more important than hope ordered to God's will and God's ends. The practices of virtue and prayer, as set out by Thomas, offer contemporary theology examples of the formation of God's people into members of Christ's body whose hope is ordered by God.

Discipleship: Practicing the Theological Virtue of Hope

> To the work! To the work! We are servants of God;
> Let us follow the path that our Master has trod;
> With the balm of His counsel our strength to renew,
> Let us do with our might what our hands find to do.
>
> Toiling on, toiling on,
> Toiling on, toiling on;
> Let us hope, let us watch,
> And labor till the Master comes.
>
> To the work! To the work! Let the hungry be fed;
> To the fountain of life let the weary be led;
> In the cross and its banner our glory shall be,
> While we herald the tidings, "Salvation is free!"
>
> To the work! To the work! There is labor for all;
> For the kingdom of darkness and error shall fall;
> And the love of our Father exalted shall be,
> In the loud swelling chorus, "Salvation is free!"
>
> To the work! To the work! In the strength of the Lord,
> And a robe and a crown shall our labor reward,

> When the home of the faithful our dwelling shall be,
> And we shout with the ransomed, "Salvation is free!"[147]

The theological virtue of hope depends on the grace of God and the perfection of humanity through Christ, but it still calls for particular human activity along with the divine infusion of grace that enables the virtue of hope. The practice of natural virtues nurtures readiness to receive grace; and the practice of theological hope, once received, sustains its presence and growth. Natural hope grows in relation to the natural virtues of magnanimity and humility, whereby acceptance of the limitations of created finitude tempers openness to the breadth of wonderful possibilities to produce properly ordered hope and its true realization.[148] Magnanimity aspires to greatness with confidence, through difficulty.[149] Humility accepts the dependence of creation and faces the effects of sin, as a human facing God.[150] Together, humility and magnanimity order natural hope toward the possibility of godly hope, and together they function as "the most essential prerequisites for the preservation and unfolding of supernatural hope—insofar as this depends on man. Together they represent the most complete preparedness of the natural man, whose existence is 'postulated' by grace."[151]

Once received, theological hope requires fear for perfection. Thomas articulates four forms of fear, only one of which supports hope: filial, or chaste, fear. The Holy Spirit grants the gift of filial fear, which fears separation from God and therefore eschews sin and the possibility of turning away from God. Filial fear reflects the reality of human imperfection, and acknowledges that the certainty of God's omnipotence and mercy does not change the uncertainty of human action. Filial fear binds to the wayfarer's hope, encouraging hope's perfection toward God.

The second fear, worldly fear, loves worldly goods and fears their loss by way of punishment from God or God's enemies. Such a fear is evil, since it is directed away from God.[152] In the twenty-first century, this fear might manifest as love of a comfortable—ever improving—standard of living and the accompanying panic that any decline in that position might remove prospects for hope. The third, servile fear, turns to and adheres

---

147. Crosby, "Work."
148. Pieper, *Faith*, 101–2.
149. II–II, q. 129, a. 6.
150. Pieper, *Faith*, 102; II–II, q. 161, a. 1.
151. Pieper, *Faith*, 102.
152. II–II, q. 19, a. 3.

to God out of the fear of punishment and eternal damnation; this fear can move one toward the good, but because the motion is from without, instead of from within, as a work of love in freedom, servile fear is evil precisely in its servility.[153] The fourth, initial fear, turns to and adheres to God out of the fear of committing a fault and then being punished. The fear of punishment, although secondary, diminishes the good of initial fear, but the concern about committing a fault marks it as a potential beginning to filial fear, an imperfect filial fear.

The filial fear that Thomas describes is moved by love, from within, and fears committing a fault, as a child fears offending a parent. Filial fear turns toward God in love and fears God, out of a recognition of the reality of God's perfection and power. Filial fear sustains and perfects theological hope, because it upholds the reality of God to which faith witnesses and hope aspires. Today, the recognition of abuse and neglect at the hands of parents and others in power renders Thomas's filial fear suspect or even complicit in harmful human relationships. It is possible, however, that theological hope might be strengthened by a renewed consideration of the fear characterized by awe of God whose goodness and sovereignty far exceeds capacities of human parents and sinful systems of torture and oppression. When the people of God were enslaved by the Egyptians and could see no way out, God rescued them from Egypt and challenged them with many demonstrations of God's awe-fulness, so that their hope might reach beyond immediate comfort. Jesus' demonstrations of God's power in healings and the removal of demons helped prepare his followers toward a hope that could persevere beyond his death. Today, images of God as infinitely more powerful than the economic and military powers that govern global society might offer those suffering pain and death at their hands a more certain hope for release than that offered by the image of a more vulnerable companion God.

Thomas continues his description of theological hope with two primary dangers to hope: despair and presumption. These gravely misconstrue God's mercy and judgment by underestimating God and disordering anticipation: "against all reality, they transform the 'not yet' of hope into either the 'not' or the 'already' of fulfillment."[154] In despair, one assumes that God cannot effect his/her salvation and thereby gives up hoping to participate in divine goodness. One might despair because lust has rendered spiritual goods no longer appealing, or because sloth has

---

153. II–II, q. 19, a. 4.
154. Pieper, *Faith*, 113.

diminished one's spirit so that the attainment of spiritual goods appears impossible.[155] Either way, according to Thomas, despair entails claiming an untruth about God: "Now the true opinion of the intellect about God is that from Him comes salvation to mankind, and pardon to sinners, according to Ezech. xviii. 23, I desire not the death of the sinner, but that he should be converted, and live... Therefore, just as the movement of hope, which is in conformity with the true opinion, is praiseworthy and virtuous, so the contrary movement of despair, which is in conformity with the false opinion about God, is vicious and sinful."[156] Pieper observes that Thomas's understanding of despair addresses an intellectual act of the will, in which one actively decides for a disordered determination about God.[157] Thomas speaks of "the despairing" as those who can see what God offers but deliberately turn away from God as their hope, having decided that "there is no hope of Divine mercy."[158] This decision denies both God and the longing for God granted all creatures. "In despair man actually denies his own desire, which is as indestructible as himself."[159] Those in despair turn to goods which have no capacity to save them, thereby inhibiting their ability to receive the grace that supplies hope.

At present, it is clear that an additional form of despair inhibits theological hope for those who suffer debilitating mental illness or impaired cognitive and physical capacity to the extent that they cannot on their own know of hope; they cannot deliberately turn toward or away from hope. Others have never known the unconditional love of parents and caregivers that allows hope to grow. Still others face constant threats to their survival, with no conceivable relief except death and no opportunity to receive any exposure to eschatological hope in God they might receive. In these circumstances, other members of the body of Christ need to help with the physical, emotional, and spiritual healing necessary for participation in hope. Friends might also be called to hope for and with those who cannot know God even enough to reject God.

In Thomas's narration, despair's partner in pride, presumption, also resists reality by claiming a disordered and unbecoming truth about God's power to remit sin, either by relying on human power apart from God or by relying on God's mercy without any repentance assisted by the Holy

---

155. II–II, q. 20, a. 4.
156. II–II, q. 20, a. 1.
157. Pieper, *Faith*, 114.
158. II–II, q. 20, a. 2 ad 2.
159. Pieper, *Faith*, 116.

Spirit. Both forms of presumption demonstrate an appetitive movement conformed to a false intellect,[160] as does despair; both presumptive independence and presumptive reliance willfully adhere to hope in what God is not. Thomas explains, "for just as it is false that God does not pardon the repentant, or that He does not turn sinners to repentance, so is it false that He grants forgiveness to those who persevere in their sins, and that He gives glory to those who cease from good works."[161] Presumption leans too heavily on the "already" and not enough on the "not yet" of salvation. It rejects the role of wayfarer and downplays the arduous character of hope, settling instead for false comfort in personal merit and a merciful and nonjudging God. "In other words, presumption destroys supernatural hope by failing to recognize it for what it is; by not acknowledging that earthly existence in the *status viatoris* is, in a precise and proper sense, the 'way' to ultimate fulfillment, and by regarding eternal life as something that is 'basically' already achieved, as something that is 'in principle' already given."[162] The danger of presumption for Moltmannian hope is the risk that confidence in the "not yet" of salvation might downplay both the "already" effects of divinely fulfilled promises and Christ's death and resurrection and the need for divine grace to navigate the arduous, (humanly) impossible character of hope on the way toward salvation. This presumptive confidence risks limiting the scope of hope to mercy without judgment, forgiveness without repentance, and good works over systemic sin. It further risks losing the necessity of Christ's redemption, in the face of non-judgmental universal salvation.

Prayer

> As I went down in the river to pray
> Studying about that good old way
> And who shall wear the starry crown
> Good Lord, show me the way!
>
> O sinners let's go down,
> Let's go down, come on down,
> O sinners let's go down,

---

160. II–II, q. 21, a. 2.
161. Ibid.
162. Pieper, *Faith*, 125.

> Down in the river to pray.[163]

Prayer is the primary action of the theological hope that Thomas presents. Prayer is the expression of hope and the shaping of desire toward God. Prayer names hope for the known/unknown end of life with God, and, in prayer, one receives the formation necessary to live all of one's life in that hope.

Thomas's account of prayer coheres with his account of hope. Hope moves toward God: it is eternal happiness in God, and God's assistance provides the means of obtaining that end. Prayer's object is God, and God's grace instigates prayer. Faith establishes the basis for hope and its articulation in prayer. Love moves the faithful toward God in hope and prayer, and love motivates hopes and prayers for others in godly friendship, that they too may be drawn toward God. Hope reflects and shares in God's reality through anticipatory readiness for fulfillment and the divine assistance that will bring it. Prayer reflects and shares in God's reality by asking for fulfillment and for the divine assistance that will bring it. Humans, as rational creatures, receive grace to pray to God as rational creatures. As an act of reason, prayer participates imperfectly in the intellect of God, from which it receives by faith knowledge of God's reality.[164]

Grace-infused love moves hope to its end in beatitude; likewise, grace-infused love moves reasoned prayer to its end in the divine intellect. Prayer, like hope, accepts, with humility, the incomplete and transitional state of the wayfarer, while directing, with magnanimity, all desire toward the already (but not yet perfected) state of beatitude disposed by divine providence. Prayer does not presume to impose on God or to direct God according to human interests. "For we pray, not that we may change the Divine disposition, but that we may impetrate that which God has disposed to be fulfilled by our prayers, in other words *that by asking, men may deserve to receive what Almighty God from eternity has disposed to give*, as Gregory says (Dial. i.8)."[165] The claim that prayer does not change God contradicts current understandings of cause and effect, and of economies of time and energy. Contemporary common sense dictates that in order to improve an untenable condition, God must change from not-changing it to changing it. On those terms, prayer must change God's mind and actions; if it does not seem to, then God is unmoved and insufficiently compassionate. Tanner addresses this sense that there ought to be some

---

163. "Down."
164. See I, q. 79, a. 8.
165. II–II, q. 83, a. 2.

extreme circumstances in which God must be changed by prayer, with a Thomistic grammar of God and God's creatures: "Christians do say... that God responds to the prayers of the faithful. Are there not, then, exceptional cases where God's agency for created effects is determined by what the creature does? We have to say that a statement like 'God grants petitions' holds, not because God's agency is itself altered by prayer, but because prayer is according to God's will a necessary created condition in particular cases for a created effect or for the alteration of the usual order of created cause and effect."[166] Prayer performs hope by turning those who pray toward to God in anticipation, and by asking God for assistance in attaining the end God has prepared. Aquinas notes that "our motive in praying is, not that we may change the Divine disposition, but that, by our prayers we may obtain what God has appointed."[167]

Hope reorders the desire and purpose of the faithful, first toward God and eternal life with God, and second toward those people and temporal goods that will contribute to beatitude. Prayer reorders the lives of the faithful by first asking for eternal happiness, and then asking for those temporal things that assist in tending towards beatitude.[168] Prayers concerning salvation conform the lives of the faithful to God's will, thereby exercising hope for the approach to God. The reordering role of prayer operates from within a realistic context of human capacities and tendencies: the reality of human creatureliness includes an inability to sustain prayerful attentiveness indefinitely.[169] Jesus Christ provides the proper content and order of prayer in the Lord's Prayer, which "teaches us to ask and directs our affections."[170] Prayer interprets human desires before God,[171] and the Lord's Prayer demonstrates how to pray for those desires.

The Lord's Prayer begins with the end of human desire, God, and continues by ordering everything else in relation to God and the enjoyment of God's glory. The first two petitions name the love of God in Godself (hallowed be your name) and then the love of creatures in God (your kingdom come). In this way, those who pray focus their attention on the one, supreme good who is God, first as Creator alone and then as the one in whom creatures find their end of eternal happiness. The next

166. Tanner, *God and Creation*, 97–98.
167. II–II, q. 83, a. 2, ad 2.
168. II–II, q. 83, a. 6.
169. II–II, q. 83, a. 9.
170. II–II, q. 83, a. 14 ad 2 and 3.
171. II–II, q. 83, a. 9.

two petitions ask for God's direct assistance in obtaining beatitude (your will be done on earth as it is in heaven) and then the secondary goods which contribute to the attainment of beatitude (Give us this day our daily bread). Thomas notes here that "daily bread" can apply to sacramental bread and/or bread as the chief food of sustenance. The temporal things for which it is lawful to pray (which Thomas mentions earlier) apply here as well: the things that are "the means of supporting the life of the body, and are of service to us as instruments in performing acts of virtue"; and (citing Augustine), that which is enough for a livelihood, for the sake of the body, and clothing befitting one's station.[172] The church today might continue with attention to all that needs to be done to share the nourishing provisions of daily bread—and health, shelter, and friendship—so that these secondary goods might support the lives of the whole body of the church.[173] The last three petitions ask for the removal of the three obstacles to the attainment of beatitude: sin (trespasses), distractions from God's will (temptation), and all that inhibits the sufficiency of life (evil). The exercise of presenting these seven petitions to God inspires and shapes human imaginations and wills to align with the will of God. Thomas adds: "Prayer is offered up to God, not that we may bend Him, but that we may excite in ourselves the confidence to ask: which confidence is excited in us chiefly by the consideration of His charity in our regard, whereby He wills our good—wherefore we say: Our Father; and of His excellence, whereby He is able to fulfill it—wherefore we say: Who art in heaven."[174]

God can and does answer prayers to encourage faith, and God's grace can and does use natural happiness to awaken awareness of possibilities beyond, but the faith and love which ground hope exceed the range of natural hope. Confusion about the ends of hope and prayer can lead to the perception of a sharp distinction between the eternal and earthly end of creatures: a pious, personal orientation vs. a political, social orientation. This distinction fuels belief in an apparent conflict between the two positions, despite the fact that each is incoherent without the other. On the one hand, there is no access to beatitude except as creatures, through created nature, with the divine assistance of grace. On the other hand, the goods of natural life are not an end in themselves, since all material goods particular to natural life are given by God. Accordingly, a Thomistic hope

---

172. II-II, q. 83, a. 6.

173. Yoder notes the radical social and economic changes necessary for the possibility of sharing bread in community in *Body Politics*, 14–27.

174. II-II, q. 83, a. 9, ad 5.

expects that, as the body of Christ in the world and for the world, the church should look to beatitude for all as the primary aim of its hopes and prayers. The church should hope and pray that all might be released from suffering and that all might receive health, food, clothing, and shelter, in order that all might have the inhibitions to faith, hope, and love removed. The church should tend to the oppressed and depressed in mind, spirit, and body, in order that they might be free to receive the grace necessary for approaching eternal happiness in God. Sharing the body of Christ in the eucharist should lead the church to care for the needy, in order that the needy may come to hope and pray for beatitude. The false division between spiritual and physical needs rejects the reality of the creation, incarnation, and resurrection, by denying the divine truth that precedes, sustains, exceeds the natural capacity of human hopes. The theological virtue of hope steadfastly turns toward the fulfillment of human nature, eternal happiness in God, which has been perfected in Christ. Grace provides the assistance necessary to participate in Christ's perfection and to attain beatitude, through the gifts of infused faith, hope, love; through the revelation of scripture and the witness of the saints; and through friendships which model God's love and sustain the hopes and prayers of the faithful.

One criticism of an emphasis on prayer as a discipleship of hope observes that prayer does not seem to do anything; lives spent in prayer are not lives spent doing the important tasks that need to be done now, in a broken and wounded world.[175] Two responses illustrate the argument of this section. First, prayer is a good in and of itself, as an expression of hope and as an action of hope. Prayer asks God's help to shape desires and behaviors into hope aligned with God's end for creation. The practice of prayer names God as the object of hope, directs hope to the primary and secondary goods of hope, and informs relationships with others based on God's relationship with humans, established in Jesus Christ. Second, prayer and servant ministry are not mutually exclusive, just as hopes in eternal life with God and hopes for justice now are not mutually exclusive. The argument that one necessarily depletes the other is defied by the lives of countless faithful people of God. Each informs the other, and the Spirit of God inspires and sustains both.

175. Here one might think of Reinhold Niebuhr, who appreciated the potential goods of individuals living lives of piety and devotion, but argued that social change could only come about through the actions of communities, despite their selfish impiety. Thus, hope is best invested in the best that groups can manage, in the midst of their agonism and defensiveness. See *Moral Man*.

Our Only Hope

Theological hope is performed in the practices of prayer and action. Prayer helps keep lives of hope in balance and full of discernment about what to hope for and how to exercise that hope in our world. Prayer helps order and direct hopes for the goods we know and the goods to come. Care for neighbors, the needy, and the world informs prayer and the hope that prayer expresses; prayer shapes and orders actions, relationships, and the hope that they express. Rowan Williams observes that "we can never use the Last Judgement as an alibi for not doing what is good in itself—caring for each other, making peace, above all, caring for our environment. It is one of the silliest and most unchristian things imaginable to say that we should not care for our material environment.[176]" At the same time, he adds, care for creation should not distort the true end of hope and prayer or distort our role in achieving God's will:

> St Paul reminds us that we need to do what is required of us here and now; but he also reminds us that if we live in the light of the imminent coming of Christ, we need a profound detachment from the pressures of the here and now; we need a sense of what does matter and what doesn't in our lives and a freedom from loading all our expectations on the success of our projects and the degree of comfort and stability we can attain. We take our responsibilities with deep seriousness and then we must learn to say, "If we don't succeed in the way we wanted, so be it; God is still God."[177]

The inseparability of eternal and immediate concerns does not mean that the connections are necessarily visible to humans. In Hebrews, the exemplars of faith prior to the coming of Christ did not necessarily receive visible benefits in their lifetimes. Some saw fruits of their faithfulness, some didn't, and none of them attained the perfection not available until now, through Christ (11:1—12:2.) The letter calls for those who know Christ to imitate faithful leaders, and to remember that "Jesus Christ is the same yesterday and today" (13:7–8). Hence, the faithful should persevere in the imitation of the righteous, regardless of the apparent results of their efforts, because the truly effective agent of divine purpose is Jesus Christ, the same yesterday and today. Thomas likewise emphasizes that

---

176. Williams, *Tokens*, 98. He continues: "That is exactly like the people Paul is so cross about who refuse to work because the end is nigh.... Martin Luther apparently said that if he knew the world would end tomorrow, he would plant a tree—meaning that what is good today is just good: and it doesn't become somehow unimportant because the time frame is too short" (98–99).

177. Ibid., 99.

the efficacy of hope and prayer depends on God's grace, mercy, and justice. Efficacy in prayer comes from the grace of God to whom we pray and who instigates us to pray. Prayer (and all virtuous acts) is meritorious because of sanctifying grace, not human will or intention; even prayer for sanctifying grace proceeds from grace. Prayers themselves do not remove suffering or institute the kingdom of God, any more than soup kitchens eliminate poverty on a neighborhood or global scale. The importance of praying and sharing lies not in any human capacity to change the world but in the graced opportunity to participate in God's work in the world.

Thomas urges the faithful with that capacity to hope and pray to do so for themselves and for others, including the just and sinners. Love leads to the desire for good things, for oneself and for others. "Therefore charity requires us to pray for others. Hence, Chrysostom says (Hom. xiv, in Matth.): Necessity binds us to pray for ourselves, fraternal charity urges us to pray for others: and the prayer that fraternal charity proffers is sweeter to God than that which is the outcome of necessity."[178] The effects of hopes and prayers for others will depend on factors outside the knowledge of those who hope and pray. The faithful should hope and pray for themselves and others, not based on visible results or reasonable prospects for success, but because they hope for the salvation of all in Jesus Christ, which salvation is ultimately fulfilled through God's agency, on God's terms.[179]

THE HOPE OF FRIENDSHIP

> When I must cross that rolling tide,
> There'll be someone on the other side
> Welcoming me to that fair land, made perfect by love
> When I walk up the milky white way,
> I'll see that homecoming in array
> How great it must be for angels to see
> A pilgrim reach home
>
> Just singing His praise through endless days

---

178. II–II, q. 87, a. 7.

179. Even the eternally blessed play a role in the dynamics of divine providence and human hopes. The eternally blessed have no hope for their own happiness, because happiness is a present—not a future—good for them. Nothing, not death or space or time, can separate God's people from God's love, or the wayfarers from the blessed.

Our Only Hope

> On Heaven's bright shore [180]

Contemporary Christians may observe that participation in the theological virtue of hope seems far more difficult and far more unreasonable than most humans can manage. Many Christians find it hard to accept that a hope that cannot be mustered by individuals can really be the best hope. The account of Thomistic hope described here may well seem inadequately attentive to the fact that some people have hope and others do not. Clearly, the *Summa* does not represent recent psychological, psychiatric, socio-economic and –political understandings of what is and what should be available to everyone. While the general knowledge and expectations of Thomas's life in the twelfth century do not readily fit with those of the twenty-first, there are resources in Thomas's theology worth investigating toward a richer present-day theology of hope. Among these, the theology of friendship offers the means to perform, assist, and witness to eschatological hope.

In the *Summa*, Thomas recognizes that the goods ordained to happiness include sufficient health and well-being so that the intellect and will can function freely and hope is possible. God's assistance in the fulfillment of theological hope can take the shape of material goods, physical bodies, social structures, and relationships, as well as the spiritual goods of grace. In this context, holy friendship is one of the goods of the theological virtue of hope. Friendship builds and sustains hope; hope grants friendship toward the end of beatitude. Formed by grace, virtue, and prayer to be Christ-like, Christians can demonstrate their hope in the lives they lead and in the friendships they keep. And yet, friendships are hard to keep: injury, dishonesty, and unfaithfulness all contribute to broken friendships and broken hopes. Friendships provide the opportunity for forgiveness and reconciliation. Shared lives between humans in human (imperfect) constancy requires humility, confession, forgiveness, and change, on the part of both friends.

Friendships often seem impossible when there is no chance of communication, reciprocity or mutual support; but equality is not an essential component of friendship, and the success of friendships cannot be determined by what is possible to attain in this life. Hope made possible in friendship nurtures theological hope in beatitude, as friends hope for eternal happiness with God for their friends. Hope in the eschatological reconciliation of the sinner with God is manifested in the reconciliation between friends, through penitence and forgiveness. Friendships that aim

---

180. "Heaven's Bright."

for constancy of presence and that work toward reconciliation illustrate hope in the eschatological perfection of friendship.

The possibilities for friendship extend beyond one's neighborhood. Injustice may be a global, systemic disorder, but it is also a matter of broken friendships. Christians moved to provide hope to victims of oppression might add to strategies for large-scale reform by reaching out in friendship to one person at a time. An attempted friendship between people otherwise divided by neighborhood, class, war, or health might open possibilities for hope otherwise unimaginable. As Wadell observes, "friendships give us space to rethink our lives. They offer us a context for reflecting on the habits and paterns of our lives and what they are making of us. They offer us the security we need to risk asking why we really are not happy and to inquire about what might be missing from our lives. Best of all, they invite us to imagine much more promising ways of life and give us the courage we need to embrace them."[181] Together, hope might be more possible than apart.

Christians who live in friendships with each other cannot avoid the need for reconciliation when those friendships reflect hope for eschatological life with God. Even when conflicts seem impossible to resolve, and even when the renewal of a broken friendship seems unimaginable, friendships in God cannot pretend to stand outside hope for reconciliation. There may be no greater mark of theological hope than the attempt to be a friend, through brokenness and in the hope of eschatological reconciliation.

Friends who share the desire to turn toward God in hope, faith, and love can support each other, hold each other accountable, challenge and encourage each other to claim citizenship in heaven as their primary identity and as the basis for the shape of their lives. Friends can also carry hope for and with those who cannot sustain it themselves. People captured by depression, delusions, or dementia need friends who can hold onto hope for eventual relief, when they cannot approach it themselves; sometimes, the hope of a trusted friend can stand in for one's own hope. When someone is suffering severe pain or facing certain death a friend can provide companionship, prayer, and hope by witnessing to the presence of God through and after life and death. Those who are victims of war, oppression, abuse, and deprivation may be assisted toward hope by ceasefires, revolutions, reform, and food. They will also be assisted in hope by those friends who stand by them in their misery, confident that there is comfort beyond

---

181. Wadell, *Becoming*, 74.

what this world can supply. Friends who are not daunted by circumstances demonstrate hope that devastation, division, and death are not final.

Conclusion

> Shall we gather at the river,
> Where bright angel feet have trod,
> With its crystal tide forever
> Flowing by the throne of God?
> Yes, we'll gather at the river,
> The beautiful, the beautiful river;
> Gather with the saints at the river
> That flows by the throne of God.
>
> On the margin of the river,
> Washing up its silver spray,
> We will talk and worship ever,
> All the happy golden day.[182]

Thomistic theological hope fits within a theological grammar of God, beatitude, humans, and their friendships. God's passibility that does not diminish divine impassibility provides hope in God who is mightier than death and perfect in compassion. Christ's full divinity and full humanity draws humans in hope toward creaturely perfection and beatitude, through lives of theological virtue and prayer. Theological hope is not bound by what humans can imagine for this world, nor by modernity's expectations of responsibly productive lives. Thomistic hope claims an anthropology of creatures dependent on their creator and formed by prayer, the gift of grace, and virtuous discipleship. In hope, people can live into friendships intimate enough to be broken, but not defined solely by that brokenness. Friends in hope can witness to the possibility of reconciliation. These witnesses demonstrate their hope through lives and deaths marked by citizenship in heaven and the performances of that citizenship in their relationships with others. The theological virtue of hope described by Thomas and demonstrated by multitudes of witnesses grows in the midst of communal worship. There, Christians can learn the practices of faithful obedience, loving constancy, and hope that, through the grace of God, they might participate in the reconciling and reordering of all things to God.

182. Lowry, "Shall We."

A Thomistic Grammar of Hope

This sounds absurdly naïve and embarrassingly outdated to most twenty-first century Christians. It might be a lovely idea, but there seem to be no churches or Christians who recognize, identify, and nurture such virtues and practices: in fact, the opposite seems far more common. This has always been the case. When Thomas wrote the *Summa* in the thirteenth century, Christians did not find it easy to accept and participate in the gifts of grace. The quality and character of daily life did not facilitate the reflection of eschatological hope in the midst of dire circumstances. A multitude of events of devastation and despair raised questions about the presence of God in the midst of human suffering. The theology of hope that Thomas presents in the *Summa* sets out a way of addressing perennial Christian concerns from within the core of a large body of theological teaching. The point of this investigation of a Thomistic theology of hope is not to suggest that twenty-first century Christians reverse the clock and change social, geographical locations, but to retrieve some resources lost when the framework for hope is narrowly conscribed.

Christian hope need not be confined to the teachings, imaginations, and particulars of any one country in any one epoch. The circumstances and experiences of hope in Thomistic twelfth-century Europe should not dictate the particulars of contemporary hope. Similarly, hope need not be confined to twentieth/twenty-first century Moltmannian theology. A theology of hope today that embraces exclusively either construction risks denying God who is I AM, God the creator of all, "Jesus Christ, the same yesterday, today, and forever" (Heb. 13:8); the ever present Holy Spirit; the one Trinity. Theological hope bound to one time, place, and set of images risks dismissing God's transcendence; hope detached from its physical context risks dismissing God's immanence in history, God's direct relation to God's creation.

Without explicit connections to long-term Christian doctrine, theology risks losing track of any differences between popular understandings of hope and particular markers and ramifications of Christian theological hope. When contemporary theology adopts the modern assumption that older, so-called traditional language and teaching is simply no longer intelligible or relevant today, it rules out any possibility of learning from and in conversation with the wisdom of the church that precedes this moment. Tanner addresses common criticisms of older theology, with a reminder of the ideological presumption of exclusive normativity that grounds contemporary dismissals of past theology: "From a modern standpoint, it is traditional Christian accounts of God and creation that seem recondite and unfamiliar, disquieting in their attempts to bring together obvious incompatibles. This very charge of unintelligibility will become for us an odd fact to be accounted for, when that modern standpoint loses its fixity as a 'natural' given for thought."[183] A theology of hope today cannot exit its modern roots and ties, but it can sustain a discerning connection with previous iterations of Christian hope and remain open to insights to come. Chapter 4 considers five discourses that might provoke Christians to continue considering the distinctive character of theological hope.

---

183. Tanner, *God and Creation*, 6.

4

Provocative Hope

RESOURCES FOR A CONTEMPORARY Christian theology of hope extend far beyond the narratives discussed in the previous three chapters. This chapter considers five discourses that are not conventionally consulted for input on theological hope: nihilism, lament, disability, feminist theory, and feminist theology. The philosophical and critical theory conversation of nihilism and its relative, indeterminism or undecidability, suggests a kind of hope without over-confident claims of knowable hopes for the future. Scriptural and extra-scriptural lament demonstrates a persistent and apparently futile hope that continues into and through death with no sign of God's response or rescue. Disability theology challenges hopes about the continuity and difference of resurrected bodies. Feminist theorists and philosophers Luce Irigaray and Judith Butler examine autonomy, divinity, and dependence in ways that might prompt rejuvenated Christian imaginations of the subjectivity of the body of Christ and its eschatological hope. Feminist theologians who revisit practices of humility, agency, and piety recast the character and agency of Christian disciples and their theological hope. This preliminary exploration illustrates how additional discourses can provoke theologians of hope to reconsider classical teaching in relation to contemporary ideologies.

No Hope and Not (Yet) Hope: Nihilism and Indeterminacy

The realm of nihilism and indeterminacy may seem the least likely discourse to consult on theological hope, and yet that realm suggests both cautions and proposals for Christian considerations of hope. Some accounts of nihilism charge that over-confident, positivist hope in absolute truth is itself a nihilism. Discussions of indeterminacy/undecidability leave open a space for possibility in the "perhaps" moment of not quite despair, not quite hope. These philosophical narratives challenge theological hope to resist dismissing or glossing over painful moments—or lifetimes—of no apparent hope.

"Nihilism stands as the opposite of hope and presents the greatest threat (along with postmodernism) to truth, God, the church, the nation, and life as we know it." This (imagined) statement represents the dominant impressions of nihilism held by Christians. Such a casual dismissal fails to represent the many definitions of nihilism, the varied relationships between hope and nothingness within nihilisms, and the possibility that some uncritical claims to theological hope may have more in common with nihilism than might seem obvious. Nihilism is indeed a term that can be used to designate that which is bad and offensive to truth, but there is not much agreement about the nature of truth or nihilism. Friedrich Nietzsche adopted the term from its use in Russian politics to describe those who worked to demolish social structures and governmental authority in order that new, improved living conditions for all might grow from the rubble. In that context, nihilism reflects a hope in what might be, what should be, and it somewhat resembles contemporary political anarchism. Theodor Adorno describes how Nietzsche built a philosophical critique of those who perceived themselves to be the defenders of the good from the evils of nihilism: Nietzsche aimed "to denounce Christianity as the institutionalized negation of the will to live."[1] As Nietzsche's description of Christianity became more widely known—and misunderstood—the backlash of anti-nihilism reasserted precisely the absolute, self-duplicating, and self-authorizing will to defeat the will to live that Nietzsche had been criticizing, and his point has not since been generally absorbed into popular consciousness or much of theology. Instead, the charge of nihilism has become a means of derogatory dismissal: now, it "is simply moral defamation—by mobilizing a word generally loathed and incompatible with universal good cheer—of the man who refuses to accept the Western legacy of positivity and to subscribe to any meaning of things as they exist."[2] Those who profess to be nihilist philosophers or activists today claim varying degrees of connection to the Russian Nihilist Movement, Nietzsche, and the Frankfurt School, but the facile critique of

1. Adorno, *Negative*, 379.
2. Ibid.

nihilism as a threat to all that is good and true remains problematic at the very least.

Adorno charges that the assertion of positivity that frequently claims to be a bulwark against nihilism is itself nihilism. He argues that the Western legacy of positivity believes that an (*the*) absolute, universal truth must be accepted in order for the goods of civil society to be maintained. The uncritical embrace and vigorous defence of self-serving goods diminishes the possibility for criticism, nuance, or outright difference, and it constrains hope to more of the same. Adorno unseats such absolutist positivity by naming it as the real nihilism: "The true nihilists are the ones who oppose nihilism with their more and more faded positivities, the ones who are thus conspiring with all extant malice, and eventually with the destructive principle itself. Thought honors itself by defending what is damned as nihilism."[3]

Adorno argues that absolutism claims a fullness of life that actually reflects nihilism and hopelessness, because there is no possibility of difference, and therefore no possibility of hope[4]: the defenders of good from nihilism themselves promote nihilism and hopelessness. Accordingly, those who are conventionally declared and condemned as nihilists are, instead, the truth-tellers. They unmask the nothingness of the absolute, allow for the possibility of alternative thoughts and actions, and try to make space for an object, instead of asserting the one subject alone.

Christians who promote absolute truth might understand themselves to be positive, forward thinkers, supporters of progress, facilitators of unending possibilities; and yet the positive, progressive, possibilities they promote perpetuate the easily imaginable same. They might scorn those they call nihilists, because anyone who does not endorse the one true position must be an enemy of all that is. Absolutism that occupies the subject position, acknowledging only those subservient to the subject, sees all difference as a threat to that subject position; the claim to absolute truth leads to death. Adorno names Auschwitz as the confirmation of this connection between absolutism and death, noting that efforts to overcome

---

3. Ibid., 381.

4. Moltmann, in his early writings, appreciates Adorno's contributions along these lines, and he tries to escape the absolutism trap by naming the open future possibilities as a hope freed from the perpetuation of the same. However, his dialectical subsumption of already into the not-yet and the coming future into the imaginable next; his commitment to universal salvation (on God's part anyway); his rejection of apocalyptic; and his confidence about the coming of God here to this earth all compromise eschatological hope that allows for radically new resurrection life.

and defeat difference are always worse than whatever those efforts seek to overcome.

The current war against terror illustrates Adorno's account of nihlism, because the universal good of US safety and stability authorizes any and all means to eradicate terrorism. Any questions about the aims or methods of anti-terrorism are seen as threats, as are all allegiances, actions, and potential actions that threaten national security. The costs, in lives and integrity, do not factor into the economy of this war, because the positivism accepts no resistance. One cause of death necessitates another cause of death, and there is no end, because there is no way to eliminate the possibility of threat.

Adorno's response to absolutist nihilism arises from his negative dialectics, a system which does not find its rest in itself, but outside itself, in thought outside the system's thought. The concept of universalism does not tolerate contradiction, but even naming this state of affairs can begin the first stop out of the circle of identity. Negative dialectics opens up the possibility of something which is not yet, of hope in potential change and in something other than the non-identical.

In Adorno's political-philosophical context, idealism constitutes the antimony of bourgeois society, whose very existence depends on that which it cannot accept. In order to survive, society must expand, grow, change; and yet anything new or different, anything that does not reproduce the recognizable sameness on which the society's identity is based, must be eliminated, often by way of violence. Unity means unity over and against something different, and it suppresses division and particularity. Dedication to the protection and perpetuation of variations on the same blocks from view those who lack comfort, food, and peace, because the unified, closed, society only has limited resources of material, energy, and imagination. Hunger, suffering, and death cannot be addressed within a closed system of resources. Confident affirmations of closed unity eliminate hope.

Christian theological hope risks collapse into nihilism when it places too much confidence in the present and in the present's re-presentation as new and improved. When Christians proclaim eschatological hope with certainty based on an expectation of more of the same (only better), they reveal the closed system that constrains and strands them. Within the affirmation of the same, there is no need for dependence on God, except to the extent that God sustains and supports the known and knowable. There is no room for hope for a relationship with God in which God's power and love for creation surpasses human forecasts and conceivable futures. The affirmation of the same that Adorno casts as nihilism resembles the presumption that Thomas presents as a danger to hope. Presumption excludes the possibility of eschatological transformation at the same time that it shores up its defenses against perceived threats of doubt and change. When theological hope is chastened by this critique of nihilism, Christians might revisit the benefits of a more apophatic grammar for God and hope in God, such that proclamations of certain salvation (identified as the comfortable continuity of the same) would be checked by acknowledgments of what God and God's salvation are not. For example: the unity of eschatological salvation is not the unity knowable now; theological hope in reconciling unity might look toward a unity unlimited by human frailty and error. Chastened theological hope might also reconsider its dismissal of hopes in an other-worldly heaven as escapist avoidance of reality. At the very least, hope that stretches past responsible projections within a closed system of imagination opens up possibilities to receive God's radical transformation. Visions of soft clouds and haloes can certainly distract people from faithful practices, but the greatest threat of a so-called escapist eschatology may be its challenge to positivity that God is not limited to human imagination.

Many a church reform movement is based on either a desire to keep things the way they used to be, as a defense against encroaching difference, or a desire to change things within the church to align with the way things are outside the church. Both positions frequently carry much merit; but when these are the only recognized positions, the church risks suppressing gifts and activities of the spirit in the community that reach toward hope through and beyond that which is most familiar. The church has succumbed to this approach to unity far too often, rejecting difference (from the past or in the present) in the name of inclusive unity. This imposed unity has manifested as physical violence, ideological suppression, and schism. Unity through rejection is as ineffective as peace through violence. Fading hopes and efforts for reconciliation *now* diminish hopes for eschatological reconciliation.

Another account of nihilism describes a spiraling increase of will against will that has grown out of Christianity: humans project upon God a superhuman amount of their own will and then fight against it by ever more forceful assertions of human will.[5] A Feuerbachian projec-

---

5. Gillespie, *Nihilism Before Nietzsche*. Gillespie narrates the historical development of nihilism as the result of and the primary characteristic of Christianity's obsession

tion of humanity's desire for power creates an omnipotent God, against whom humanity competes for more and more power. In the reversal of a comfortable Christian narrative against nihilism, this account would mean that Nietzsche's proclamation of will is not the alternative to Christianity, but the epitome of Christian will to power.[6]

The critique of Christianity's over-willing nihilism might serve as a corrective to some effort- and works-based versions of Christian hopefulness. Christianity has its own critiques of attempts to will the fulfillments of hope through human accomplishment, but those critiques can be hard to hear over the loud cultural cries for effectiveness. The loss of a real difference between God and creation presents an even more pressing challenge to hope that depends on or rejects God's omnipotence. If God's power is of the same order as human power, such that competition or sharing is possible, then belief in a super-human God who does power or weakness the way humans can (only better), confines theological hope to what humans can effect (only better). This scenario sets God up as a competitor in the production and sustenance of hope.

Kathryn Tanner's account of the non-competitive relation between God and creatures offers one manifestation of a Christian narrative that resists the nihilism of sameness by underscoring the divine-human difference. She argues against both comparisons between humans and God and conflicts between humans and God. These comparisons and conflicts are incoherent, because they assume a single plane of existence. "A non-competitive relation between creatures and God means that the creature does not decrease so that God may increase. The glorification of God does not come at the expense of creatures."[7] Because God creates the creature, "the creature in its giftedness, in its goodness, does not compete with God's gift-fullness and goodness because God is the giver of all that the creature is for the good. This relationship of total giver to total gift is possible, in turn, only if God and creatures are, so to speak, on different levels of being, and different planes of causality—something that God's tran-

---

with will. He ascribes to William of Ockham a prioritization of God's omnipotence, which, in turn, leads to the human defensive response of increased will.

6. One might use this model to describe the powerful—if futile—desire of a (Christian) democratic nation to transform the countries of the world into dependent, controllable democracies, through violence (directly imposed by U.S. military and indirectly facilitated by U.S. weapons). Hopes for individual and national safety and development then rest on the larger nation's capacity to protect and dominate international and terrorist threats.

7. Tanner, *Jesus*, 2.

scendence implies."[8] This non-competitive relation rules out a spiraling battle of will between humans and God and human claims of absolutism that contain God within creation. It also rules out the shared experiences of a weakened God in mutual relations with creatures. The hope of the creature who is the gift of the giver relies on the utter transcendence of God, and issues in a divine-human relationship of closeness that can only come from difference.[9] A contemporary theology of hope that relies on a non-competitive account of God and creation avoids positivistic absolutist nihilism and resists deflating God into humanity or inflating humanity into God.

Undecidability, or indeterminism, shares with nihilism a resistance to positivist closure and to an over-confidence in more of the same. Undecidability can remind Christians of the hope that hope *might* be possible, even when it is not now.[10] One version of postructuralist indeterminacy, narrated by Shane Weller's analysis of Beckett's plays, declines to settle with either the ultimate abyss, on the one hand, or the vanquishing of nihilism, on the other. This indeterminacy resists resolution and fulfills no promises; even a broken promise, by virtue of its repeatability, includes the possibility of its fulfillment, alongside the absence of fulfillment. The moment of neither possibility nor impossibility is difficult to sit with. The abyss of nothingness, of no possibility for hope ever, can seem preferable to an interminable *perhaps*.

Elizabeth Grosz points toward possibility outside the possible when she argues that Jacques Derrida "seems to suggest an alternative economy [than that of violence], which exceeds the very notion of economy," an alternative he calls "the Other," or "the gift, hospitality, donation, generosity, or ethics."[11] The gift gives time, and therefore a future distinct from the present, "a temporality in excess of the present and never contained within its horizon."[12] There is no assurance of a positive or negative resolution, and there is no assurance that the moment of indeterminism will end. The condition of being "in no position to know" can be characterized as the ultimate (or nadir) of nihilism, in perpetuating a nothingness that cannot even be claimed. Contrariwise, indeterminism suggests a possibility for theological hope when the possibility of hope cannot be found.

8. Ibid., 3.
9. Ibid.
10. Weller, *Negative*.
11. Grosz, "Time," 143.
12. Ibid., 244.

Our Only Hope

Christians often wonder what hope there might be for those trying to survive in the midst of unspeakable suffering in uninterrupted cycles of abuse, murder, and global devastation. Christians of privilege and distance who send much needed money, food, medical supplies can be tempted to identify their efforts as gifts of hope. It is much more difficult to accept that the shipments of first world aid may or may not reach the neediest, they may not effect the desired improvements in life, and they may not carry the intended hope. Instead, desperate efforts to survive may well require the exquisite agony of seeing no grounds for hope and yet recognizing that freedom from suffering has not been ruled out by the fact of its absence so far. Hopes for survival may need to extend through *and* beyond the possibilities of this life. Christians, who understand themselves to have a connection with or responsibility for those in dire need, might send aid *and* sit in indeterminacy with those whose hope is not, cannot be, dependent on the attainment of material goods. Christian theologians trying to make sense of unspeakable devastation might sit longer with the painfully uncomfortable condition of being in no position to speak and in no position to assert either the affirmation nor the negation of hope.

Theological hope that accepts the seemingly unending moments of radical indeterminacy might then find itself in a position to recognize when hope comes from that moment of impossible possibility. Christian hope rests in Jesus Christ, whose death and resurrection opens the unprecedented possibility of eternal resurrected life, a survival that embraces and exceeds the inability to survive. In a hope that recognizes both indeterminacy and the promise of an entirely *different* life, Christians might see opportunities for creative and compassionate demonstrations of their hope in ministry to and in company with those trying to survive.

Indeterminacy and undecidability remind theological hope not to close off space and time for the real difference of God's space and time. We have seen that Adorno's negative dialectics looks for the possibility of difference and hope in the breaks in structure. Weller notes the position of *perhaps* in Beckett that does not preclude or posit an unforeseen difference. Grosz sees in Derrida's undecidable, the creation of time for an uncertain addition or gift. Conor Cunningham, a Christian theologian and philosopher, argues that nihilism promotes dualisms that turn out to be an ontic monism, grounded on the univocity of being.[13] Instead, he sees difference and hope in the analogy of being. Cunningham grants that nihilism does involve provenance and, therefore, a kind of hope, promise, and

---

13. Cunningham, *Genealogy*.

expectation, but it issues only in nothing. His account of Christianity and its hope posits difference as prior to change, so that creation is not simply a change, but a real difference. Nihilism provides nothing (as something) out of nothing; in *creatio ex nihilo*, the unity-in-difference Trinity creates substantial something, that remains different from its creator.

The creator God has created all that is, in a creation that illustrates likeness and not-likeness simultaneously: likeness in that creation is of the abundance of God's goodness; unlikeness because creation is not God, or on a plane of existence with God, or competitive with God. All that is, therefore, *is* only analogically. Claims about God can only be made analogically, pointing toward God's unimaginably perfect difference with words from human knowledge. Even the idea of analogy is analogical itself. This means that while Adorno's negative dialectics assumes a non-closed system, with space for difference, and therefore hope, Cunningham's Christian account of creation assumes a non-closeable *real* difference of Creator and creation. The openness does not extend into a space beyond or other than God, and God is not finite. Creation is not God, created from nothing other than God. The analogy of being is a human strategy for trying to narrate this paradox in a grammar which resists collapsing God into human imagination. The analogy of being sustains hope, in faith and love, until the perfection of creatures—the beatitude—which places humans eternally face-to-face with God (while eternally remaining creatures). Theological hope thus affirms what it cannot know, through analogies it can imagine, looking toward an unimaginable fulfillment in real difference.

Moltmann is not interested in debating real difference or analogy of being; although he sometimes argues for the possibility of real difference in creation, in the new creation, his emphases on eschatological panentheism and human participation in the relationships of the Trinity render real difference and the analogy of being unnecessary. Michael Scott Horton observes that "despite his intentions, real difference is surrendered to a final synthesis in Moltmann's account."[14] Moltmann's priority is "relationality," and by that he means a very specific kind of relations, that excludes any God-creation relations that seem hierarchical, uneven, unequal. Relationality trancends the absolutism of a single identity and the totality aspect of relativism. God shares with creation an open future, that God, as well as humans, hopes for. Although Moltmann's future claims a new openness, his reduction of the difference between God and creation suggests

---

14. Horton, *Lord and Servant*, 85.

the univocity of being, the nihilism of the same. Moltmannian theological hope looks toward full human participation in perichoretic relations of the Trinity and to full divine participation in new creation. Resting in the shared identity of God and humans, Moltmannian theological hope has little use for *perhaps* moments, for being in no position to say, or for an unimaginable eschatological future.

Jesus' disciples often find themselves in no position to know or state what is going on. Not long after witnessing two occasions when Jesus produced ample food for the crowds from meager supplies, the disciples talk amongst themselves in confusion about Jesus' words about the dangerous leaven of the Pharisees and the Saducees. They wonder if he meant that they forgot to bring bread on the boat trip (Mark 8:4–21; Matt 16:5–12). After witnessing the Transfiguration, the disciples talk amongst themselves, bewildered about what Jesus could possibly have meant when he talked about the Son of Man being being raised from the dead (Mark 9:9–10). While sharing their last Passover meal with Jesus, the disciples argue amongst themselves about which of them is greatest (Luke 22:24). And on the road to Emmaus, a disciple and his companion talk about what has happened in Jerusalem, not able to make sense of anything at all. In each of these cases, the disciples stand in a space where they can neither reject nor affirm that Jesus truly is radically other than what they think they already know. And, in each of these cases, they remain in no position to state anything coherent, until clarification comes from God. Divine clarification might come by way of the resurrected presence of Jesus Christ, the presence of the Holy Spirit among them, the conversion of Cornelius's household, or the still-to-come-resurrection of all the members of the body of Christ. Their hopes for understanding and their hopes for participation in that which they do not understand are partially resolved in their lifetimes, with the promise of perfect fulfillment still open to a future outside of time. And the disciples themselves are not the resolvers.

Theological hope that looks to God's transcendent difference as the source and end of creation's possibilities is bound neither to a closed system of the same nor to an imaginable future that extends the same. The eschatological identity of humans who are "citizens of heaven" even while citizens of earth makes possible a life of witness to an unknowable but nonetheless hoped for eternal life transformed by Christ. Graham Ward notes that Christians in hope can "practice an art of living in the name of a transcendental hope which breaks free of the vicious circularities of the same."[15] Christians who practice this art of living in broken-free hope

---

15. Ward, "Suffering."

may encounter a space of no hope or not (yet) hope; in facing that space, Christians can witness to the improbable and possibility of hope in the already/not yet eschatological resurrection.

Devastation Hope: Lament

Biblical lament similarly leaves open a space for hope in improbable rescue from suffering. The not-yet-answered cries to God express unresolved despair to God, carried on through generations of inconsolable loss, anger, and grief. The survival and repetition (albeit not identical repetition) of these cries over time sustains the particularity of bodies lost and mourned, in an unhopeful hope that resists closure and refuses to stop lamenting until God responds.

The genre of biblical lament challenges the account of God's constancy and responsiveness to the creatures made in God's image by highlighting what appears to be a gap between human suffering and God's mercy. One engagement with biblical lament focuses on repentance: people accept their suffering as God's punishment as a step toward reconciliation with God. Hope rests in God who provides, guides, and maintains the covenantal relationship through and beyond human failure. Another approach encourages contemporary participation in scriptural lament in order to express and work through present-day crises in relationship with God. There is hope in the process of progressing through anger, grief, and moving forward. A third interprets the biblical and extra-biblical traditions of lament as a persevering refusal to accept that God will not restore the dead to their loved ones. This lament narrates the absence of any basis for hope, holds God responsible, and carries the lament through and beyond the possibility of resolution. Lament voices the grief, pain, loss, and death that are too overwhelming to understand, bear, or survive. Lament demonstrates a hope often overlooked in favor of optimistic confidence. Participation in lament can take the form of a repentant reliance on God's judgment and mercy; a process of working through the pain of (temporarily) inaccessible hope; an undaunted cry to God that accepts nothing less than restoration.

Jože Krašovec illustrates the first interpretation of lament with his account of Lamentations as God's call to conversion through punishment.[16] He argues that the great suffering should turn God's people to repentance: "Everything comes from God; the present situation cannot be an excep-

---

16. Krašovec, "Source."

tion. And yet the covenanted people have no right to complain against the Almighty."[17] The fact of God's covenant relationship should reestablish right relations with God and underscore the true foundation for hope in God's constancy; but first, the people need stern reminders of their relationship to God. Relief comes with repentance and a recommitment to their one God. Krašovec explains that "the consciousness of their election and the superiority of God's benevolence and mercy provides a basis of the hope that God had not rejected them for ever. This hope is, of course, inseparably linked to the desire for conversion."[18] Krašovec's interpretation leans heavily on divine justice through the punishment of injustice. At the same time, he reinforces the covenant relationship between God and God's people that cannot be broken by turning away from God; no sin or devastation separates people from their ever merciful God. Lament thus demonstrates God's steadfastness, even when humans cannot detect it, and grounds hope in God's restoration of broken relationships that humans cannot mend.

Another reading of lament downplays any punitive aspects of God's justice by highlighting the therapeutic possibilities of lament for congregational worship to provide comforting hope in desperate circumstances. While lamenting may be seen by some as inappropriate behavior in church (expectation of emotional expressions vary among denominational, racial, social, and ethnic traditions), a therapeutic understanding of lament encourages congregants to express their emotions and be open to the hope available in practices of lament. Shortly after September 11, 2001, Dr. David A. Davis preached to the congregation of First Presbyterian Church in Princeton, NJ, a community that lost friends and family in the fall of the twin towers. Davis drew the congregation into Psalm 137, to help them express and narrate their feelings into a form of biblical lament. He affirmed their anger and grief and encouraged them to direct those feelings to God:

> Guided by a profoundly pastoral purpose on the one hand and the raw out-cry of Psalm 137 on the other, Davis entered with his congregation into the welter of soul-shredding emotion precipitated by the events of September 11, allowing the biblical lament to mirror and articulate inchoate anger and grief through the images of tears and displacement. Yet, guided hermeneutically by biblical lament, Davis allowed the psalm not only to give grief a voice, but to invoke a boundary on the human impulse

17. Ibid., 232.
18. Ibid., 233.

to multiply evils in the face of evil. Like sufferers of old, we trust our broken, angry hearts to the God who weeps with us and will not abandon us or the world.[19]

Biblical lament offered the worshipping community the beginnings of hope through grief and anger shared with God.

Peter Paris describes the ways that songs of lament sustained generations of African slaves with fortitude and hope in the face of suffering and oppression. He notes that the slaves shaped their experiences into lament songs as a way of narrating their circumstances in light of God, resurrection, and heaven.

> Singing about sadness helps one overcome the loneliness of suffering. Consequently, enslaved Africans composed and sang countless songs celebrating God's liberating presence in the midst of suffering, for the purpose of strengthening a people to keep hope alive when it is threatened by terrible circumstances in life. The songs that have enduring value in such situations are those that tell the truth by critiquing their situation in light of a transcendent theological principle. African slaves equated that principle with God, the resurrected Jesus, and heaven. All three symbols constituted injustices to endure.[20]

In this way, lament both expresses and feeds hope in divine freedom from suffering in the eschatological inclusion of their bodies into Christ's resurrected body. Lament performs eschatological hope in the ultimate transformation of abused bodies into Christ's resurrected bodies. The slaves' songs of lament sustained their hope in a heaven constructed entirely of God's justice, completely free from the oppression that fills every moment with suffering.

While Davis leads the people of First Presbyterian through lament toward the faint hope of recovery, and the slaves Paris describes sustain each other with laments that look to hope in heaven, Kathleen O'Connor claims the Book of Lamentations as Zion's explicit "act of hope," subsequently fulfilled in Second Isaiah.[21] In O'Connor's account, Zion finds comfort in the narrator of Lamentations,[22] and the contrasting male voice (whom O'Connor identifies as "the strongman") receives a hope in God

---

19. Brown, "Sermon," 34.
20. Paris, "Motherless Child," 120.
21. O'Connor, *Lamentations*, 127.
22. Ibid., 43.

when he least expects it, and then clings to it.²³ O'Connor sees hardy hope in the characters of Lamentations, hope that stands up to their suffering and to God. "Speakers in Lamentations tenaciously persist in trying to engage God. They make claims on God, demand attention, and beg for a future. They do this even as God walks away and silently closes the door on them. God may be unfaithful, but they are faithful. God may hide, but they stand in plain view. They berate God, protest God's work, and dare to ask for more than patent cruelty. Lamentations is a bare act of hope and a plea for life."²⁴

Lamentations ends without a response from God to Zion's hope and plea for life. O'Connor finds the response in Second Isaiah, where, through a variation of the account in Lamentations, God relieves and restores Zion, fulfilling the hopes she expressed in lament. "Second Isaiah's sequel to Lamentations revivifies Daughter Zion on her hill of weeping and changes God's character from abuser to comforter. In Second Isaiah God is present, vocal, and repentant."²⁵ In this way, Zion, the city and the woman, represents the results of persevering lament and unflagging hope, and her example encourages those in exile to return to her and find their hopeful lament fulfilled as well. "God acknowledges, addresses, and reverses her sufferings. Her guilt virtually disappears, and God, not she, is on the defensive. She has named her world in Lamentations, and now God responds on her terms, using her language, and giving her what she needs and more."²⁶ God's compassionate response to lament does come, after a painfully long wait.

A third contribution to theological hope emphasizes the lack of resolution when persistent, desperate cries for help continue across lifetimes of impenetrable loss and pain, without releasing God from responsibility. There is a faint hope here, but it is a hope without optimism or prospect. The confidence of hope is that God *should* be listening, but that confidence is almost drowned out by the reality that God seems not to be listening. The hope survives as long as the lament survives, and the lament is passed

---

23. Ibid., 57, 113.

24. Ibid., 127. She continues: "even in the face of God's silence, the speakers persevere. Their hope resides in the strongman's words for whom, at least briefly, God's mercies are 'new every morning' (3:22–23). Hope resides in the broken, desperate pleas of Daughter Zion, who begs God to see (19c, 11c, 20; 2:20); in the urgings of the narrator, who tells her to weep day and night (2:18–10); and in the voices of the community, who plead with God to 'return us to yourself' (5:21)" (ibid.).

25. Ibid., 140.

26. Ibid., 147.

Provocative Hope

on after death to be picked up and continued by subsequent generations.[27] As long as the lament continues, however hopeless it is, the *possibility* for hope remains.

Tod Linafelt posits that God, in Lamentations, does not save Zion's children despite her explicit narration of God's accountability. In the last three lines of chapter 2, she names the horrific state of affairs in which mothers eat their children, the Lord has killed everyone, and the Lord invites the enemies to celebrate. Zion's declaration that "none survived or escaped," illustrates Linafelt's claim that the question of the survival of the children is the key theme of Lamentations.[28] He finds the survival of this lament for the lost children in Elleazar ben Kallir's Middle Ages liturgical poems: "By gathering together the fragments of these previous responses to the accusations of Zion and using them to construct new responses, Kallir calls attention to the fact that these erstwhile answers were finally inadequate."[29] Linafelt sees another continuation of lament through a short story by Cynthia Ozick. "The Shawl" tells the story of a mother who imprisoned in a Polish concentration camp with her two daughters, one a teenager and one an infant. The mother has no more milk for her baby, who sucks on the shawl which hides her and gives her comfort. The story cries of loss—of food, warmth, kindness, voice, and life—even as the mother must keep silent when her baby is discovered and murdered. Again, a story reflects and participates in Zion's loss of her children, with echoed phrases that repeat the absence of God and resist closure.[30]

These Jewish laments will survive until the messiah comes, returning the children to their mothers. For Christians, the adopted members of the community of lament, hope for the survival of children lost through hunger, war, abuse, and disaster extends through the ongoing expectation that God should be caring for these children. The rehearsal of Jesus' death and resurrection in scripture and the participation in that death

27. Linafelt, *Surviving*. Linafelt draws on the work of Walter Benjamin, Jacques Derrida, and Francois Lyotard, to argue that the survival of the texts of the Book of Lamentations, through translations, creates a space for the possibility of the survival of the dead children. He argues that Lamentations is written by and for survivors, in an attempt to persuade God to allow for the survival of Zion's children. He focuses on chapters 1 and 2, which begin with a sense of dirge/elegy and move toward lament and survival, from the (paradoxically) easier interpretation of pain and death as punishment for sin to the presentation of pain as (also) the inexplicable and unreasonable act of God.

28. Ibid., 58.

29. Ibid., 130.

30. Ibid., 133–42.

and resurrection in liturgy extends the survival of loss toward the rescue of salvation which is not yet experienced in full. The faithful who have died still wait for the resurrection of all. Christians can learn from those who lament the indefatigable conviction that God can and must rescue the suffering and restore the dead. Lament as the survival of an impossible hope in God underscores the inadequacy of this world as the source of present or eschatological hope. Surviving lament presses Christians to guard against both premature acceptance of suffering and death and blind confidence that human efforts alone can recover life.

The survival of lament depends in part on practices of remembering. The violent forces of nationalism, capitalism, oppression, and war establish and sustain their positions by renarrating the lives of those they seek to control. Murder becomes collateral damage or peace keeping; torture becomes a penal system or intelligence gathering; degradation and expulsion become homeland security; greed becomes market revitalization. Each of these changes threatens to erase the memories of those who are suffering and dying at the hands of the narrators; and each renarration increases the powers of domination while diminishing the power of alternative narratives. When the people of God remember suffering, and when they narrate those memories in the particular narratives of God's relationship with God's people, they are exercising a theological hope in God's narrative. Johann Baptist Metz articulates the memory of God's people as "dangerous memory" that tells history from the side of the people who are suffering at the hands of the those who benefit from their suffering.[31] "In this perception, history—as the remembered history of suffering—has the form of a dangerous tradition."[32] The hope of dangerous memory, like that of lament, asserts that those who suffer and die outside the history of heroes remain God's people. The forgettable will not be forgotten while their history—even when still unresolved—is claimed by the story of God's redemption of each and every one.

Flora Keshgegian builds (critically) on Metz's account of hope with an exploration of alternate narratives of time.[33] She reverses the future-determined Moltmannian hope by giving time to memories and by carrying forward memories of joy, promise, grief, and trauma. She argues that true hope does not come from leaping ahead to a tidy resolution of these memories; rather, hope comes when we take time to remember, recognize,

---

31. Metz, *Faith*, 105.
32. Ibid., 196.
33. Keshgegian, *Time*, 188–89, 213.

and share the messiness of loss and celebration. Like lament, Keshgegian's time for remembering trusts that even the worst experiences possible are included in God's life for creation. She suggests that "the prescription for hope is living," and that taking time for remembering strengthens hope.[34]

Lament that extends into the future affirms faith in the impassibility of God who responds, by presuming God's unchanging compassion and memory when it cannot be perceived. Lament performs the hope that trusts that God can, should, and will sometime accomplish the unimaginable; God will restore and return the dead children. The hope of lament sustains without resolving hopes for reconciliation and transcendent human thriving, from the midst of unabating suffering. Lament that persists and sustains the fragile possibility of hope in despair challenges Christian theological hope to embrace lament and lamenters without presuming to diminish either the reality lamented or the hope maintained. Desires to fight injustice and desires to discount the hopes of people who have no reason to hope exclude both the people who lament and their distinctive hopes. Christians who attend to this distinctive hope might attend to Old Testament and Jewish lament and claim it within a Christian eschatological hope as well, along with lives of saints and martyrs. Lament that survives beyond death and suffering demonstrates a theological hope that trusts in God to remember and respond.

BODYBUILDING HOPE: DISABILITY THEOLOGY

Theological hope pertains to real, specific bodies; but confusion abounds about which bodies participate in hope and in what ways. Disability theology often seeks to include people with disabilities in the lives and hopes of less-disabled people. This concern about including the particularities of all bodies challenges Christians to consider all sorts and conditions of bodies in hopes for bodily resurrection.

Recent disability theology shares with disability studies the goal of including people with disabilities in the full range of life's opportunities. Social historians explain that the people of scripture and of many centuries since have viewed people with disabilities in prejudiced and misinformed ways, based on medical misinformation, fear, and the perceived connection between sin and physical brokenness and demon possession. Disability studies scholars argue that contemporary ideals of athletic, youthful, and beautiful bodies discount the bodies and minds that do not meet that

34. Ibid., 213.

ideal now and those that do not have the potential to strive for it. International, national, and local communities work to make buildings, education, jobs, and activities accessible to all, regardless of capacity. Medical research and practice strive to detect potential disabilities and diminish their handicapping effects. Church teachers and preachers place biblical, traditional, and contemporary fears about disability in perspective, emphasizing the inclusion of all in the body of Christ, through attempts to include variously-abled people within the life of the church. All of these efforts demonstrate familiar markers of life lived to the fullest: access, independence, opportunity, productivity, and participation.

A human rights approach aims to include people with disabilities into the larger set of people who have been deprived of the rights understood to be due all people. Christian support for this movement adds its narrative of humanity created in the image of God: hope looks to full participation in created life. Christian efforts to gather all bodies into the body of Christ can overlap with international efforts to extend human rights to people with disabilities.[35] The human rights model of disability theology urges local and international action now, to improve and save lives now. Working toward the goal of equal opportunity for those with disabilities can redirect the attention of less disabled people from self-comfort to the needs of others easily forgotten, and it can hold Christians accountable to Jesus' call to continue his work with the people in need. A human rights model of disability hopes for full inclusion of all people in this life and the next, although it does not necessarily examine how hopes for this life might differ from hopes after the life we now know.

Another approach to inclusion notes that disability is a characteristic of all people. Some disabilities may be more obvious than others, but all humans share them. This model asks all Christians to be mindful of their imperfections and vulnerabilities. No one can claim superiority based on a lack of disability, and everyone shares in the human condition, which is flawed and yet still created in God's image. Present theological hopes pertain to fuller lives for everyone; eschatological hopes look to freedom from limitations and accompanying suffering. Thomas E. Reynolds argues that "disability is part of the fragile character of human existence in general,

---

35. Moltmann illustrates this approach through his involvement with international human rights work. In "The Theological Basis of Human Rights," Moltmann asserts that "the inalienable and irrelinquishable dignity of all human beings is rooted in their creation in the divine image. Irrespective of sex, race, age, health, abilities or disabilities, all human beings have the same dignity and share the same hope: having been created in the image of God, they all are destined for the kingdom of God."

wherein we can find genuine good in relationships of mutual vulnerability. Wholeness comes through mutual dependency; and dependency marks vulnerability, which involves disability. Our weaknesses open us to each other."[36]

Deborah Beth Creamer expands on the idea of shared vulnerability and varying disabilities with a model of "limits."[37] She critiques the themes in disability studies that she names as medical and minority models. The former, medical, model identifies disabilities in terms of bodies that cannot do everything "normal" bodies can do. "This model is closest to the commonsense idea that a disability is what someone has when his or her body or mind does not work properly."[38] The latter, minority, model identifies disability as exclusion based on socially dominant prejudices about difference and worth: "Under the minority group model, ableism, rather than any physical impairment, becomes the cause and the problem of disability."[39] Instead of these models, Creamer proposes a model of limits that acknowledges that all creatures are limited. God pronounces the limited creation good[40]; limitations are not confined to people customarily identified as disabled.

Some disability theology extends limitation and disability beyond creation, arguing for a disabled God: since humans are created in God's image, and since humans are limited, then God must be limited, even disabled, as well. Nancy Eiesland shows God's disability through Jesus' crucifixion wounds and in God's experience of the pain and rejection people with disabilities experience.[41] Wayne Morris recounts the way that God is understood to be culturally deaf by many deaf people.[42] These constructions of God who shares disabilities with people with disabilities offer an affirmation of inclusion in God's arms that can counter the feelings of exclusion caused when apparently-abled people claim the image of God.

Disabled God theology has yet to engage extensively with hopes beyond present survival, comfort, and social inclusion. While hopes for resurrection transformation frequently include the healing of all disability and infirmity, the eternal condition of the disabled God has yet to be

36. Reynolds, *Vulnerable Communion*, 118.
37. Creamer, *Disability*.
38. Ibid., 31.
39. Ibid., 26.
40. Ibid., 94–95.
41. Eiesland, *Disabled God*.
42. Morris, *Without Words*.

narrated. Humans and God could share disabilities eternally, but that scenario does not relieve resurrected people of their disabilities. One might speculate that God needs the transformed presence of people in order to be healed, a proposal that needs additional narration to account for the agency of healing. Or, the healing transformation of disabled people and God might rely on an as yet unidentified force, a suggestion that also needs radical reordering of theological grammar.

I propose a third way toward inclusion that calls on less-disabled people to ask, humbly, for inclusion in the lives of people with disabilities. This approach recognizes differences—physical, cognitive, emotional, social—without investing in normalcy, equality, or limitation; and it challenges common presuppositions about that in which one might want to be included. Disability theology that hopes for the inclusion of disabled people in a society shaped by the ideology of autonomy reinforces, without questioning, the value of autonomy. William Gaventa observes some of the problems with the ideal of including people with disabilities in normal, autonomous life:

> It is often said that persons with intellectual disabilities should live "as autonomously as possible" or "as normally as possible" or "as much included in the community as possible." This way of putting things clearly exposes a normative anthropology that, in confrontation with persons with severe intellectual disabilities, sees itself more and more pushed back. Eventually, this anthropology cannot explain in a positive sense that the value of life with intellectual disabilities—or even human life in general—can be based on other human characteristics than the ones that are highly appreciated within the framework of the dominant concept of individual autonomy.[43]

When the value of autonomy is called into question, additional possibilities of shared identities open up, in dependence and in dis/ability.

The limitations of cognitive disabilities present distinct challenges to discourses of theological hope. The Thomistic hope discussed above assumes the importance of the knowlege of God to feed hope and to draw those who hope closer to God's knowledge. Current understandings of physical, psychological, and psychiatric disabilities (and the ways they interconnect) afford richer theological possibilies for considering a hope of and for people that exceeds the limits of particular cognitive standards; and yet, if hope is not reserved only for those with excellent intellectual

43. Gaventa and Coulter, *Spirituality*, 17–18.

capacities, then the church is challenged to address concerns about what hope it might have *for* the very young, the very old, and those who have cognitive disabilities; the church is also challenged to addresses concerns about the hope *of* the very young, very old, and those who have cognitive disabilities. The church already has locations for the inclusion, formation, and appreciation of hope not reliant on particular standards of cognition. Perhaps Christians can look again at the spaces and times of church life open to sharing non-cognitively-specific theological hope. One such place is communal worship, where participation in the hope of the Christ includes sight, sound, taste, smell, and touch, and the simple presence of bodies. James K. A. Smith argues that capacities for conceptual and abstract thought do not determine hope for participation in Christ. He considers the limited cognitive capacities of children and mentally challenged adults in relation to Christian worship: "Does [the fact of such cognitive limitations] mean that they cannot achieve fullness in Christ? Do the limits of their cognitive abilities impair the hope of their ever 'growing up' *into* Christ (Eph 4:15)? Does their inability to traffic in concepts preclude them from being educated? . . . Because we are more fundamentally creatures of love and desire than knowledge and beliefs, our discipleship—our formation in Christ—is more fundamentally a matter of precognitive education of the heart. And Christian worship that is full-bodied reaches, touches, and transforms even those who cannot grasp theological abstractions."[44]

If the subject/object relation of inclusion were shifted away from the abled inclusion of disability, those who are not primarily identified as people with disabilities might present themselves as available for possible inclusion in the lives of people who understand themselves to be people with disabilities. Perceptions of normalcy and priorities of autonomy would not disappear, but the chief end of inclusion would be relationships not governed by dominant expectations of individual capacity. These relationships, however awkward and fragile, might perform a theological hope in the perfected *relationships* of the eschaton, rather than in confused and disordered ideas about perfected *bodies*.

Mary McClintock Fulkerson describes her experiences as a participant in the worship and fellowship of Good Samaritan, an United Methodist Church, whose members are female, male, black, white, richer, poorer, and differently-abled.[45] Good Samaritan stands out among Chris-

---

44. Smith, *Desiring*, 136.

45. Fulkerson, *Places*. At their best, the leaders and congregants of Good Samaritan witness to the possibility of shared community in difference, without trying to erase

tian communities because it tries to be a community of integration, of resistance to the segregation that marks the vast majority of congregations.[46] Fulkerson's work stands out in the discourses of disability and theology, because she approaches Good Samaritan as a white, socially-advantaged, and not-disabled woman, prepared to be received on the terms of the congregation. She attends some of the special needs worship services, noting that although a wide range of participation is accepted, she feels awkward and uncomfortable. In one service, the sermon took the shape of an interactive engagement with the 10 Commandments. The minister drew two tablets on the board and asked if anyone knew any of the commandments, but the numbers soon became the focus of excitement. "A couple of the participants look at their Bibles, but it is the job of enumerating the commandments that is taken most seriously. Several hands shoot up with fingers raised triumphantly in the air. 'First!' then 'Two!' 'Second,' call out several of the men. Getting the 'next number' seems more important than getting the content of the commandment."[47] Several of those who were not able to participate in the sermon join in the singing that follows, by singing, clapping, or moving their bodies. Some do not appear to be participating, but sit still or rock and squeal. Worship for and with those who do not fit traditionally familiar forms of worship shows that participation in the body of Christ does not depend on a minimum threshold of capacity. Theological hope can be experienced and expressed at the far edges of recognizable liturgy. Those who are more-abled can share in eschatological hope with and for those whose participation in hope is difficult to perceive.

L'Arche communities create communal homes for people with disabilities and those who care for them and are their friends. The members of a L'Arche community eat together, pray together, share their lives—with celebration.[48] Unlike many institutions that provide care for people with

---

difference through equality of class, capacity, or theology. In times of struggle, Good Samaritan demonstrates the difficulties of establishing and sustaining relationships in a community not primarily identified by similarities of appearance, preference, or social location outside of the Good Samaritan community. People argue and leave, accept and disapprove. Shared worship among people with profound disabilities and those without has not yet seemed possible. Fulkerson joins in with Good Samaritan, and she is included in the sharing of struggles and joys.

46. Good Samaritan's history includes divisions and departures from the church in the midst of conflicts over race and shifting leadership.

47. Fulkerson, *Places*, 111.

48. Hauerwas and Vanier, *Living*, 37.

disabilities, L'Arche prioritizes friendship over a care-giver/care-receiver relationship. Live-in and Live-out Assistants are paid to be part of L'Arche communities, to support and attend to the residents with disabilities; but L'Arche encourages friendships among the community, and the friendships define the character of the communities. Jean Vanier, the founder of L'Arche, explains that, "the heart of L'Arche is to say to people 'I am glad you exist.' And the proof that we are glad that they exist is that we stay with them for a long time. We are together, we can have fun together. 'I am glad you exist' is translated into physical presence."[49]

L'Arche community members are caregivers and care receivers who nurture and sustain each other. These relationships embrace particularity and help those with disabilities to grow, thrive, and participate in the community according to their capacities. Vanier corrects those assumptions about people with disabilities that consider them to be partial, incomplete, or less than human subjects; he explains that human identity does not depend on a particular degree of strength or autonomy. "The weaker members of the society are total human persons, children of God. They are not misfits or objects of charity. Their weaknesses and special needs demand deep attention, real concern and support. If we listen to their call and to their needs, they will flourish and grow. If we do not, they will sink in depression, sadness, interior revolt and a form of spiritual suicide. And we who carry responsibilities will have closed our beings to love and to strength, which comes from God and which is hidden in the smallest and the weakest."[50] Vanier's account can remind Christians that relationships between differently-abled people are relationships between people, not between a "total human person" and a not quite human person.

Good Samaritan and L'Arche communities suggest a hope for this-worldly relationships that reflects hopes for the eschatological reconciliation of people currently divided by dis/ability. In small-scale, partial ways, these communities illustrate the possibility of a radically transformed, shared life which is not yet possible, not quite imaginable.

The possibility that these communities illustrate might challenge a theology of hope to consider disabilities and resurrection hope. Since New Tesament scripture, Christians have talked about and hoped for bodily resurrection. Throughout many centuries and many disagreements, the church has repeatedly affirmed that bodies—not just souls, minds, spirits, or Platonic forms—persist in the resurrected life, albeit transformed.

---

49. Ibid., 69.
50. Vanier, "Spiritual Needs," 98–99.

Our Only Hope

While no definitive explanations of how bodily resurrection works are available, the content and context for such questions continue to reveal Christianity's hopes. Within a discourse of disability theology, questions include: Does resurrection remove all suffering, weakness, handicaps, and limitations? Does the resurrection retain the personality and particularity of transformed bodies? What difference does it make to our lives now which sort of resurrection bodies we imagine and hope for?

As we have seen, some might argue that engaging in eschatological speculation distracts Christians from the very urgent practical theology of improving the lives of needy people now: people with disabilities require care and respect; and the systemic problems of human rights, economic disparity, social ignorance, and segregation can only be improved through persistent effort. However, Christian hopes for this life and the next cannot be separated. Eschatological hopes shape and order present identities and practices; hopeful practices today expand possibilities and imaginations beyond limitations of current existence.

The church ancient and modern wonders about the particularity of resurrected bodies. Recent accomplishments of medical science and social anti-discrimination movements encourage the idea that people might be freed from disabilities, physically and/or socially, if not in this life, perhaps in the next. This increased confidence about ultimate healing intensifies the risks of imagining heaven without the particularity of bodies. If disabilities are removed, particularity is removed. If handicaps are sustained through the bodily resurrection, then suffering and the hierarchies of difference will persist as well.

People who care for family members and friends with severe disabilities often find comfort in eschatological hopes of relief, for the afflicted person and for themselves. Amos Yong notes the relationship among images of heaven as free of disabilities, images of heaven as free of *people* with disabilities, and images of churches as free of people with disabilities.[51] Hopes for resurrected bodies shape, and are shaped by, hopes for bodies now. Yong participates in a discourse of bodily resurrection that claims the continuity of particularity through the transformation of resurrection. Physical disabilities cannot be deleted from a subject without radically changing the subject; likewise, cognitive disabilities cannot be removed from a subject, as if they are an unfortunate add-on to an otherwise fully functioning subject. Eschatological hope in the erasure of disability particularity risks hoping that someone will be someone else altogether.

---

51. Yong, *Down Syndrome*.

Transformation might then become the replacement of one subject with another. Frances Young speaks of her son with severe cognitive disabilities: "There is no 'ideal Arthur' somehow trapped in this damaged physical casing. . . . I find it impossible to envisage what it would mean for him to be 'healed' because what personality there is is so much part of him *as he is*, with all his limitations. 'Healed' he would be a different person."[52] Yong argues that life in heaven will not be governed by the exclusion of differences but will display the perfection of the embrace of differences.[53]

Objections to Yong's arguments about the resurrection of bodies include concerns that an emphasis on continued particularity means an insufficient appreciation of the difficulties and pains of disabilities now and an insufficient appreciation of the benefits of medical and, ultimately, divine healing. Ryan Mullins articulates three unfortunate misunderstandings of Yong's argument in a set of questions similar to the puzzles the teachers of the temple posed to Jesus: If Yong is right, 1) will surgery to correct disability erase subjectivity particularity?; 2) will pain continue along with disability through the transformation of resurrection?; 3) if an otherwise healthy adult is severely injured in an accident, will the healthy or the disabled person be resurrected?[54]

Eternal life with God in Christ remains beyond what we can imagine, and the specifics of how God heals, resurrects, preserves, and transforms bodies remain impossible for humans to imagine. Just as faithful speculation about heaven does not necessarily inhibit caring for creation, hope for some eschatological continuity of bodily particularity need not inhibit empathy for the pain of people with disabilities now. Small gestures and long-term commitments of friendship and care suggest and reflect a heavenly reconcilaition of difference, in hope. The ecclesial practices of Good Samaritan United Methodist Church, and the practices of daily life performed by members of L'Arche communities witness to ways that less-disabled people might be included into the lives and hopes of people with disabilities—in these bodies and in the transformed bodies of the resurrection.

---

52. Ibid., 269; Young, *Face*, 61–62.
53. Yong, *Down Syndrome*, 291.
54. Mullins, "Difficulties."

Hope in Difference and Dependence: Feminist Theory and Subjectivity

Some recent feminist theorists explore ramifications of dependent and transcendent relationships outside the canonical priorities of gender equality, self-knowledge, and the stability of identity. These explorations are as unsettling to twentieth and twenty-first century feminism as they are to contemporary Christianity; yet the same explorations that unsettle may also provoke Christian theology to reevaluate some of its foundations for hope. Theologians of hope might learn from these theorists by investigating the ways that hope is tied to ideological constructions of gender and identity, as well as the ways that Christian identity is defined as membership in the body of Christ. Attention to the fluidity and dependence of individuals may resonate with some pre-modern understandings of the transcendent human flourishing, discipleship, and reconciliation of theological hope.

Luce Irigaray and Judith Butler each examine the limitations for identity and self-knowledge, from within their (overlapping) psychoanalytic, philosophical, political, and feminist theory discourses. Their proposals about possibilities of self-narration, self-imagining, and relationships-in-difference feature the role of human and transcendent others/otherness. While Irigaray and Butler do not write from or for Christian theology, they present insights that challenge some presuppositions of contemporary theologies of hope and might remind Christians of traditions of theological hope that have faded from view. In particular, they offer analyses of the subject that could help Christian theologians recast the identity of the one who hopes and the character of hope in terms that both resonate with pre-modern understandings and suggest reconfigured embodiments of hope today.

Irigaray's writing did not make much of an impact in the United States until a significant portion of her work had been translated into English. Now that her previous work has been translated and her ongoing work is promptly available in English, Irigaray is classified in the subset of Continental, complicated, contrary feminist theory. Her earlier work is generally received as supporting constructions of the feminine that allow for lesbian love and for women's relationships outside of masculine subsumption. Her explorations of sexual difference that seem to essentialize sexual difference and undermine challenges to heterosexual normativity have met with a more mixed response. Even more unsettling are her writings that address sexual difference *and* the divine. Eizabeth Grosz, in 1993, observes that Irigaray's interest in the divine greatly frustrates those who have worked to free women from the oppression of religion. "Irigaray's recent writings on the divine have evoked shock, outrage, disappointment, and mystification in her readers. To many, she seems to have succumbed to the most naive essentialist reliance on religion to overcome or to provide solutions for women's socio-politial and psychical oppression."[55]

One defense of Irigaray could point to her life-long committment to European politics, which demonstrates no decline in her commitment to the social circumstances of women. Another might note that Irigaray has never shaped her work to cohere with the priorities and imaginations of American feminism. Grosz explains Irigaray's explorations of the transcendent as one strategy among many to open up space for women's autonomy, for women's identity not established as the other of the one, true, masculine, identity of man and God.[56] When Irigaray considers women's subjectivity and desire in connection with gender difference, she is not attempting to reinscribe first wave feminist essentialism. She makes no universal claims about biological or social difference. She is interested in difference and/in relation; relationships between men and women capture her attention because of the ways those relationships demonstrate both difference and relation. She recognizes the constructed nature of gender difference, yet she does not claim that that construction in any way diminishes or erases difference: gender difference is real. (One could argue that this claim also critiques the assumption that constructions are somehow not real.) Attempts to redress gender difference through inclusion or universalism tend to erase and deny real difference, and what remains is the primary—masculine—gender, leaving no possibility of feminine subjectivity. As the subject, men share their identity with the Subject, the divine, who is necessariliy masculine in the dominant system of identity relations. Women are defined as the other to men; there is no possiblity of woman except as a nurturer and shadow, except as not-man. Women are thus marked as objects, regardless of what they do. Women cannot obtain subjectivity (the one, masculine subjectivity) by grasping for it; women's own subjectivity becomes impossible to imagine; and there is no connection between women and the masculine divine Subject.

When Irigaray explores transcendence and God, she is not advocating a return to the patriarchal oppressions of Christian ideology and institution feminists have been resisting for decades. Nor does her return

---

55. Grosz, "Irigaray," 199.
56. Ibid., 214.

to the divine (much earlier than the much hailed recent turn to religion throughout a broader swath of philosphical and psychoanalytic theory) indicate an adoption of Christian identity.[57] Irigaray argues for the necessity of the divine feminine, the non-masculine Subject, in order to establish the possibility of a woman subject. Elizabeth Grosz explains that Irigaray is interested in the divine as part of her interest in creating an ideal self-image for women.[58] The God to which she refers is a vaguely Judeo-Christian God, as claimed in the symbolic and metaphorical grammar of her version of neo/post-Lacanian psychoanalytic theory.

In this exploration of bodies and difference, Irigaray notes that God provides the basis for identity; the type of God allows for the type of human, which to date has been masculine. "Man can exist because God helps him to define his *genre*, to situate himself as a finite being in relation to the infinite. . . . To set up a genre, a God is needed. . . . Man did not let himself be defined by another genre: feminine. His only God was to correspond to the human type which we know is not neutral as far as the difference of sex goes."[59] Without their own God to define the genre of their existence, women cannot exist, communicate, or become.[60] Irigaray's use of the language of God here reflects something of a merging of Feuerbachian and psychoanalytic understandings of the divine.[61] God provides the image for constructing a subjectivity of position, an identity not subsumed by another before it can be named. This God does not act in the lives of humans, but establishes the possibility of human existence. Grosz describes Irigaray's concept of God: "God represents being positioned in a place: social, natural, interpersonal. God, then, is not a personage regulating, governing, or judging these positions nor one's mode of occupying them. God is a name to describe the possibilities of awareness, and transcendence, of these positions."[62] Irigaray does not use a language of hope in this discussion of the divine, but she could be interpreted to be naming hope as the desire for subjectivity, for the possibility of identity in difference. Her account names God as the means of transcendence, the way to imagine—and therefore claim—subjectivity.

57. Ibid.
58. Ibid., 202.
59. Ibid., 208.
60. Ibid.
61. Ibid.
62. Ibid., 205.

Irigaray suggests that Christianity might be a model of human/divine identity worthy of attention. She sees in Christianity "the respect for the incarnation of all bodies (men's and women's) as potentially divine: nothing more or less than each man and each woman being virtually gods."[63] The virtual divinity of women with a feminine god establishes the possibility for truly autonomous subjectivity.[64] The fact that this presentation of divine incarnation overlaps little with most Christian theology of Jesus Christ—incarnate, wholly divine and wholly human—or of humans, sin, and the life of redemption and resurrection matters little for Irigaray's purposes. She is tapping into available symbols and using them to the end of creating space for women. The imaginary creates possibilities for change.

Irigaray often describes identity as fluid, unstable, touching itself. If these images seem contradicted by the real gender difference of divinely constructed subjects, that might be because Irigaray is not building a manifesto of the feminine. She is acutely aware of the power, limitations, and possibilities of language, and she stretches and disrupts images in order to imagine changes that otherwise seem impossible. The divine feminine is one strategy to empower women to find and claim subjectivity *outside* the power structures that determine and sustain dominant masculine subjectivity.

Whether or not Irigaray's strategy accomplishes the subjectivity she hopes for, a contemporary theology of hope might consider what power structures are determining and sustaining the subjectivities of those who hope and the content of their hopes.[65] Persuasive images of the person who hopes abound, and Christian theological discernment about which images reflect and support Christ-like identities may not be making such a strong impression. Variation and conflict within Christian theological discernment about the character and image of Christ-like identity

---

63. Ibid., 204.

64. Amy Hollywood critiques Irigaray's argument about the divine feminine and female subjectivity in *Sensible Ecstasy*, in particular, 217–19, on Irigaray's reliance on Feuerbach. While I agree with Hollywood on this point, I would also argue that Irigaray's heavy emphasis on autonomous subjectivity in this argument reflects her practice of strategic shifts in emphases for specific arguments. In this case, she is working to create a possibility for identity that otherwise appears impossible, by shifting one dependence (on a subjectivity-denying masculine identity) toward another, subjectivity-granting feminine divine identity).

65. This challenge to theology holds regardless of whether Irigaray's strategy will bring the escape from the gender structures she critiques, the projection of a god who can effect the subjectivity of the projectors, or whether her argument applies directly to Christianity.

complicate the topic further. In order to recognize and share distinctly Christian hope, subjects who hope need ways to imagine subjectivity in Christ differently from and in relation to subjectivity in civic responsibiity, patriotism, gender construction, and fiscal solvency. Subjects who hope in Christ through and beyond this life need ways to narrate a certainty and continuity of identity that engages with, without depending on, conflicting social, political, and economic constructions.

Irigaray finds the means for subjectivity freed from subjugation by looking to (constructing) a feminine divine. If divine identity provides hope for humans in need of liberating identities, in the narrative of a non-Christian theorist, how much more should Christians remember that liberating identity comes through the participation in and imitation of Jesus Christ. Subjectivity in Christ might embrace the radical particularity of unique individuals transformed in that particularity into members of Christ's body. Irigaray's strategy of creating the possibility of an evidently impossible, culture-resisting subjectivity challenges Christian theologies of hope to develop strategies for discerning and embodying the possibility of an evidently impossible, culture-resisting subjectivity of eschatological hope in Christ.

Butler has questioned norms of masculinity and heterosexuality, opening up possibilities for gendered identity much appreciated by feminists and non-heterosexually-identified women and men. She has also questioned the categories of gender itself, challenging the very identities she was perceived as having made possible earlier. Butler describes some of the shifts mentioned above in Irigaray's work, and how she understood and participated in the transitions of French feminist theory, as a young American scholar. She notes the thrill of discovering a discourse of gender that names the relationship between sexual difference and language. With the claim that sexual difference and its culture produce the conditions for language came with an awareness that "the possibility of communication itself" depends on the terms of the operating system of gender difference: "To understand the exhilaration of this theory for those who were working with in it, and for those who still do, one has to understand the sea-change that took place when feminist studies turned from being the analysis of 'images' of women in this or that discipline or sphere of life to being an analysis of sexual difference at the foundation of cultural and human communicability. Suddenly, we were fundamental. Suddenly, no human science could proceed without us."[66] As Butler participated in this

---

66. Butler, *Undoing*, 208.

Provocative Hope

sea-change, she began to ask questions that challenge both heterosexual normativity and the developing normativity of feminist claims about cultural production. In *Gender Trouble*, she considers whether butch and femme relationships simply reproduce heterosexual relationships in different bodies.[67] Does the symbolic inscribe an alternative, but equally restraining framework for identity? Butler looks at drag culture as a way to question assumptions about real and false gender performance.[68] She proposes that these questions about what can and cannot be imagined pertain directly to the pressing physical needs of real people for real survival. "There is a normative aspiration here, and it has to do with the ability to live and breathe and move and would no doubt belong somewhere in what is called a philosophy of freedom. The thought of a possible life is only an indulgence for those who already know themselves to be possible. For those who are still looking to become possible, possibility is a necessity."[69]

Butler's work since *Gender Trouble* continues to consider the necessity of possible life and the practices that fund possibility. Her book, *Undoing Gender*, is a collection of essays that follows *Gender Trouble* and continues her critical explorations of gender norms. In *Undoing Gender*, she wonders if the "I" comes before or after sexuality,[70] leading a discussion that affirms Foucault's claims about the inseparable relationship between knowledge and power. Any narrative of knowledge—including self-knowledge—depends on the systems of power that supply and constitute knowledge.[71] In the first essay, "Beyond Oneself: On the Limits of Sexual Autonomy," she argues that the "I" is more vulnerable, and less contained, than it is generally comfortable to imagine. These are the issues she focusses on in *Giving an Account of Oneself*,[72] in which she asserts the impossibility of complete self-knowledge and self-narration and how recognition of that human condition grounds the possibility of moral action.

Butler draws a picture of the "I" who comes to self-knowledge through self-narration. Contrary to common assumptions of subjectivity, the "I's" knowledge can only be partial, and it can only be narrated—incompletely—through interaction with others. One cannot access the

---

67. Butler, *Gender*, 209.
68. Butler, *Undoing*, 219; *Trouble*.
69. Butler, *Undoing*, 31.
70. Ibid., 16.
71. Ibid., 27.
72. Butler, *Account*. The book was originally the Spinoza Lectures that Butler gave for the Department of Philosophy at the University of Amsterdam, in 2002.

beginnings or endings of self-narration, and the process of narration only begins in response to another. An individual other who prompts one's narrating and one's context of social norms and regulations initiates and shapes one's narrative possibilities; one becomes a subject in the process of self-narrating.

One criticism of this theory of limited self-knowledge and dependent, partial self-narration charges that it embodies irresponsibility and inhibits moral action. Such a criticism makes sense within a construction of the "I" that assumes autonomy, self-awareness, and independent self-narration, in which the "I" decides who to be, what to do, and how to do it, based on individual (self-) determination. Accordingly, someone without access to autonomous individuality, knowledge, and narration, lacks the capacity for ethically choosing and willing right action. Butler names the challenge: "Does the postulation of a subject who is not self-grounding, that is, whose conditions of emergence can never fully be accounted for, undermine the possibility of responsibility and, in particular, of giving an account of oneself?"[73] Echoes of this question might arise in legal discussions about whether children and mentally handicapped persons are culpable for their actions. Similarly, murderers sometimes receive lessened sentences if they are determined to have committed the murder in a temporary state of diminished mental capacity. These legal scenarios illustrate the presuppositions Butler identifies: subjectivity precedes moral action; adequate self-knowledge and self-narration are prerequisites for responsible behavior. She continues: "If it is really true that we are, as it were, divided, ungrounded, or incoherent from the start, will it be impossible to ground a notion of personal or social responsibility?"[74]

Butler's answer to both questions is, "No," and she presents the reverse—the presence of a prior morality allows for the possibiltiy of the subject and agency—through an examination of the personal relationships and power systems that participate in the self-narration of the "I." The claim that full, autonomous, self-knowledge is possible and can be narrated in completion reflects a presumption of disembodiedness, or perhaps of identity not dependent on embodiedness. In order to give an account of one's own beginnings, one's boundaries and borders, and one's knowledge, one would need an eye-in-the sky view of one's own body—the capacity to be in and out of oneself at the same time. That multi-positioned identity is impossible and unnarratable (unless one has an infinite

73. Ibid., 19.
74. Ibid.

Provocative Hope

number of perspectives, each situated beyond the previous); but it is a familiar foundational myth of identity and agency. Butler argues for identities and narrations fully attached to bodies, and that means accepting the limitations of bodily capacities.[75]

Butler's reminder of the limitations of self knowledge and the necessity of interdependent and incompletable narratives of identity suggest possibilities for non-cognitive considerations of hope, as well as cognitive delusions of knowledge and hope. If no individual can fully know herself or narrate her identity, then the difference between the cognitive limitations to hope of people with mental handicaps and those of people who do not consider themselves to be mentally handicapped would be one of scale, rather than category. And no one would be able to claim for their own the fullness of the knowledge of hope. The theological hope of someone with severe cognitive limitations would be constructed by the shared presence, care, and friendship of others—as would be the case for those without severe cognitive limitations. The absence of theological hope in and for someone with severe cognitive limitations might be caused by abandonment and alienation, when no such friends are present. And contributions to the possiblity of theological hope where there seems to be none could take the shape of friendships between otherwise divided by cognitive capacity. Eschatological hope is for the reconciliation of God with creation, and creatures with each other. Christians who strive for reconciliation with each other in spite of capacity-difference witness to a hope greater than cognitive reasoning and broader than individual self-narration.

Irigaray and Butler explore possibilities for subjectivity beyond the familiar—if deceptive—comforts of individuality enmeshed in ideologies of autonomy. Irigaray imagines a feminine divine that might help women discover and claim an identity not defined by the masculine, the masculine God, and the perpetuation of both. The feminine divine offers a distinct identity that is inconceivable within the dualism of masculine and feminism, which is actually the same of the masculine. Butler discounts the knowability and narratability of the I, apart from relationships of self-narration, and even then, self-knowledge and self-narrative can never be fully attained. Both Irigaray and Butler look beyond the body while at the same time resisting the normative dismissal of (women's) bodily particularity and limitation.

This complex imagination of subjectivity might raise some questions for Christian theological hope about the subject who hopes and the

---

75. Ibid., 38ff., 81ff., 111.

subjectivity one hopes for. Neither Irigaray nor Butler asserts any commitment or investment in Christianity. In response to Irigaray's argument that the divine is necessary for human subjectivity, a Christian theology of hope might want to review what it claims is necessary for human subjectivity. Theological hope that focuses chiefly on the godlike character of being made in God's image risks leaning too heavily on the goodness of creation and too lightly on sin, brokenness, redemption, and resurrection. Humans might then settle for hope in an enhanced version of humans as created, without turning to the gift of Jesus Christ who, as wholly divine, demonstrates and effects the fulfillment of the wholly human subject.

Butler's reminder that individual bodies are not, by themselves, capable of knowing themselves or telling their own stories, challenges a theology of hope to remember that the fulfillment of eschatological hope is completed membership in the body of Christ, *with* all the other members of that body. Daily life that reflects that hope can acknowledge ultimate interdependence by accepting and embracing the limitations of human autonomy and the necessity of mutually dependent relationships for knowing and narrating any one particular life. Conventional constructions of identity can be freed from the singular assertions of external judgment or individual claims, such that discernment in relationship trumps inflexible subjectivity in terms of gender, sexuality, race, ethnicity, physical and cognitive capacity, social position, wealth, geographic location, or family history. The particularity of Christian life in hope is narrated in the scriptural and sacramental story of the body of Christ, through the work of the Holy Spirit in the members of that body.

Unorthodox Hope: Feminist Theology and Subjectivity

Feminist theology, like most schools of thought and actions, periodically settles into phases of generally-accepted presuppositions about the content and style of its discourse and practices. Some feminist theologians who appreciate the kind of work Irigaray and Butler engage in also share with Irigaray and Butler an interest in examining the structures that have been supporting their discourses. These feminist theologians consider contemporary feminist orthodoxies alongside reconsiderations of classical Christian doctrines. As Irigaray and Butler examine and reconsider the philosophical and psychoanalytic structures that have shaped their work, these feminist theologians examine and reconsider contemporary feminist orthodoxies alongside classical Christian doctrines. This method challenges theologies of hope to construct narratives and performances of hope from a broad range of theological resources, with sharpened discernment.

While feminist theology continues to call for renewed critical analysis of Christianity's well-established cultural assumptions and strategies, Susan Frank Parsons calls for feminist theology to reconsider its own commitments. She asks feminist theologians to "think anew in what is our hope,"[76] and to reconsider some of the tenets on which feminist theology has come to rely most comfortably. Parsons asks for this unsettling self-examination as a way of challenging that which has become orthodox to feminist theologians, and in an attempt to highlight grounds for hope. Feminists' reputation as revolutionary, disruptive, and creative does not free them from the risk of establishing their own orthodoxies, both implicit and explicit. Parsons reminds feminist theologians to attend to these orthodoxies with an ongoing readiness to revise and reclaim intentionally: "Challenging women's orthodoxies in the context of faith is a moment for such speaking in hope, for attending to the beginning and end of faith, a moment in which there is a turning to reflect upon the established orthodoxies of what have become feminisms and feminist theologies, and a turning into new forms of discourse that become challenging orthodoxies for our time."[77] Parsons embraces two senses of "challenging": she urges feminist theologians to challenge cultural orthodoxies with critical theological engagement; and she acknowledges that these revised orthodoxies will present challenges, requiring self-criticism, creativity, and patience.

The examination and clarification of orthodoxies matters, *not* because orthodoxies are inherently bad (they are necessary and potentially very good), but because *uncritical* reliance on orthodoxies, ideologies, and social structures encourages idolatry: disordered lives and misplaced hope. Theology reminds us that we are all prone to idolatry, and feminist theology consistently names the idolatries of patriarchy, racism, heterosexism, classism, and colonialism that permeate culture and the church. Through the identification of idolatry, feminist theologians work to redirect discourse, worship, and community life away from idolatrous orthodoxies and toward rightly ordered relationships with God and each other. Tanner notes that this process includes continually reconsidering that which appears to be normative. "In short, by doing what theologians

---

76. Parsons, "Accounting," 15.
77. Ibid., 4.

usually do—rethinking for themselves the meaning and organization of the cultural materials with which Christian theologians work—feminist theologians contest the cultural hegemony of patriarchal forms of theological discourse on the way to constructing new theologies for a new set of interpersonal relations, in which women are finally to be granted their full humanity."[78] Feminists are as subject to ideological blinders as anyone. While feminists' cultural and critical challenges to the oppressive orthodoxies of theology have certainly not yet transformed Christianity and the world, some of their arguments are gaining familiarity and credence outside self-defined feminist circles—while at the same time becoming orthodoxies within feminism. Parsons identifies the topic of "hope" as a touchstone for assessing the value of these feminist orthodoxies and the resources they offer feminist theology. Tanner aims to revise the particular forms of anthropology and Christianity that feminist theologians have come to lean on as orthodoxy; Parsons urges us to revise some of the secularly-informed orthodoxies of feminist theology.

Linda Woodhead goes so far as to suggest that there is little Christian hope to be found in feminism at all: "Feminists may indeed tell us new and important things about how religion has oppressed women, but their scattered attempts to tell us new and important things about God and about life lived in relation to God are rather less successful."[79] Woodhead criticizes feminist theology for "abandoning the central tenets of faith as the revelation of God in Christ."[80] Her corrective looks for balance by subjecting cultural claims to the authority of Christian tenets. Woodhead's critique lacks clarity, nuance (feminist discourses provide extensive and carefully constructed analyses of oppression, and much more), and perhaps charity. She does, however, hold feminist theology accountable to its relationship to broader discourses of theology; and she illustrates with her critique that the particulars of cultural embeddedness shape theology. It is not possible to shed that embeddedness, but attempts to clarify and claim location may help feminist theology to challenge theological orthodoxes, both long-standing and more recently established. That clarification may in turn challenge theologies of hope to notice and articulate some of their own orthodoxies.[81]

78. Tanner, "Social," 186–87.
79. Ramsey, "Losing," 128.
80. Ibid.
81. Of course, there are feminists who find that all of Christianity's orthodoxies are in need of correction or dismissal, but I assume that they are not interested in this conversation.

For most of its existence as a recognized field of study, feminism has tended to focus on the needs and desires of individuals, as defined in terms consonant with secular culture accounts of identity. Christian feminist theologians have drawn connections between these aims and scriptural texts and themes, focusing especially on the deprivation of freedom for those who are not independent, successful, effective men. Christian and secular feminists alike share the goals of listening to the voices of the silenced, relieving the suffering of the oppressed, and redistributing goods and power. Feminist theologians attend to the dispossessed and to restructuring societies with a view toward honoring the humanity of all people, in order to correct abusive practices and to bear hopeful witness to God's will for harmonious and liberative community life. At the same time, this focus reflects a construction of identity particular to one set of views about personhood, which set does not always connect with the sets of Christian teaching about personhood, or with the sets of ongoing analyses of subjectivity (illustrated by Irigaray and Butler). As feminist theologians continue to challenge the perversion of Christian subjectivity, evident in preferential and abusive ideologies of race, sexuality, class, and gender, they might also continue to examine theologies of personhood. For example, when feminist theologians espouse lifting individuals up to their full humanity, responding to natural needs and desires, and seeking universal and essential rights for all, they frequently rely on an understanding of identity as if it were a package, provided and communicated by God. Here, the ideal human identity of the enlightened, egalitarianly-directed, secular world appears to overlap with a vaguely Christian view that God wants the best for everybody and therefore creates for everyone a potentially free and liberated identity. According to this view, identities are divinely prearranged and one can receive them and live them out faithfully, or not, depending on social and individual particulars. The goal is to help others receive and fulfill their designated identities by redressing inhibiting institutional structures and by championing the virtue of non-idolatrous personhood, personhood that lives out its God-given identity.[82] Hope, then, rests on the removal of limitations and the freedom of the subject.

Such an account of identity rests on premises that feminist theorists and Christian theologians alike have questioned. The former critique calls attention to the social constructions of identity that cannot be put on or taken off, but which are embedded in systemic ideology. The latter highlights the distinctive character of freedom in Christ. Parsons notes that

82. Parsons, *Ethics*, 154–55.

gendered thinking does not begin at some point after having already received or developed a more generic sense of self; rather, what and how one thinks about oneself is already gendered thinking. One might pose a complementary christological critique, noting that people are not persons first and Christians later; rather, the very possibility of personhood is shaped in and through Christ. Gender is not something received at the beginning and then repeated through the expression of identity throughout life, but only one factor in the imagination and performance of beginnings, middles, and ends. There is no identity apart from that created by the triune God; no coexisting collection of "givens" alongside God and God's gifts. Freedom is then a matter of participating in identity and relationships as revealed by the ongoing work of the Holy Spirit, and as discerned in faithful community and in the midst of contemporary circumstances.

This understanding of identity in no way diminishes the urgent needs of those suffering from violence, marginalization, desperate poverty, and gender inequality. The challenge for feminist theology is to articulate what about its liberative efforts reflects a distinctly Christian identity. For example, one might ask about the relation between a Christ-shaped personhood, gender, and hopes for identities that embody both, without oppression, or, "What is the hope of Christian subjects, when subjectivity reflects some recent feminist theory and not so recent Christian doctrine?" In her discussion of a language for hope, Parsons connects a theology of grace with gender theory to suggest a subjectivity in Christ: "Being found in Christ opens up the subject to live in grace, to be revealed as the glory of one made to be godly in an utter generosity of spirit, that puts away the old ways of thinking and brings in the new. The possibility for grace, and thus the place in which hope for a turn from the old to the new, from death to life can be spoken, is what Christian ethics in every age must find a way of saying. Today that demand comes from within gender theory, as it uncovers the ways in which we are subjected and looks for the saying in which that condition is turned into hope."[83] The basis for personhood—and the basis for hope—rests on ongoing interpretations of life in Christ, interpretations that include constructions of subjectivity unimaginable in previous ages.

There is no pre-linguisic, no stable, universally-recognizable location of a subject. The experience of one's location depends on the narrative of the community, how it describes and performs what its locations mean. Similarly, the experience of oppression is not the same across the board;

83. Ibid., 164

careful attention to the identification of women's social locations and circumstances of oppression, can help keep focus on particular people. As Fulkerson points out, the positions of subjects are completely dependent on community relationships, and these relationships are not stable but always in flux. Likewise, the subjects who make up the body of Christ are destabilized subjects in flux. When feminist theology maps these destabilized subjects and relationships on a (likewise fluctuating) graph of life in the cross, hopes for subjectivity expand to include people otherwise dismissed because they do not fit on the conventional power grid.

Feminists know well the value of learning to become independent, self-possessed, and empowered agents in the world, taking on roles of public leadership previously denied to women, and casting aside assumptions about the natural weakness of women's bodies and minds. Christians know well that servanthood, obedience, and suffering characterize much of discipleship activity, as described throughout the life of the church. Ramsey takes up the challenge of holding canonically feminist activity accountable to theological authority when she asks if feminists might be able to reconstruct a theology of the cross. Feminist theologians have worked to undermine those traditional theologies of the cross which have perpetrated and perpetuated oppressive impositions of suffering in the name of Christ. Ramsey notes appreciatively how feminist theologians have criticized how the suffering servant is used to claim that suffering is good in and of itself, or that abused wives should submit to more abuse on the model of Christ's suffering.[84] Many perverted theological interpretations of suffering result in the perpetuation of women's suffering, often "seen to be supported and endorsed by a view of Christian love."[85] In response, feminist theologians have tended to support the elimination of all suffering, across the board; and yet, Christians continue to include Christ's suffering—and our participation within that suffering—as an entailment of their identity. Ramsey admits that it is risky for feminists to revisit suffering, when so many people still experience theological abuses of the concept and the physical ramifications of those abuses: asking that feminists reclaim suffering might well be asking that they lose their life in order to find it.[86] However, Ramsey takes up this risk, in part to reclaim, rather than avoid, some of the paradoxes of scripture. She affirms Sarah Coakley's clarification of differences between "abusive suffering and empower-

---

84. Ramsey, "Losing," 124.
85. Ibid., 128.
86. Ibid., 122.

ing pain,"[87] and she endorses Coakely's call for a reconsideration of Jesus' vulnerability in relation to gender and agency assumptions.[88] "In rejecting the outworn gender assumption that presumes power and the abuse of power to be a male problem, Coakley identifies the new task of feminist theology as one that is willing to construe forms of weakness or vulnerability as either normatively human or even revelatory of the divine."[89]

Ramsey is able to risk exploring these provocative claims in large part because of the risk-taking modeled for her by those who have suffered far more deeply than she. Ramsey is a white South African priest, now based in England, who cannot explain, but only marvel at, the response of a black woman in a township outside Natal to a lifetime of suffering. Ramsey visited the elderly woman to administer last rites, while she was working at the Cathedral of the Holy Nativity Pietermaritzburg, in the summer 1993.

> Together with an interpreter, a Mothers' Union worker and a clergyman, we drove twenty kilometers to the smouldering township and eventually abandoned the car on the unmanageable roads. Picking our way past burnt buildings and a police station hidden behind bullet-pierced sandbags, we found our way to the house—newly built. Blind, and in her nineties, the woman told of how she had rebuilt her home three times, buried all her sons and her husband in the struggle. On establishing that I was a white woman training to be a priest, her eyes filled with tears and she said in Zulu: "Now I know that my God and my Redeemer lives. He has saved me, for in my lifetime a white woman has come into my home to bring me healing.[90]

Ramsey does not claim the role of (white) savior for herself; nor does she presume to have effected liberation in this woman's life. Rather, Ramsey takes this unexpected expression of hope as a reminder of the importance of remaining open to scenarios outside familiar expectations—but not outside the Gospel witness to the power of the Cross. She continues: "Thinking about this experience and trying to come to terms with her willingness to conceive of herself as part of another generation's hope continues to challenge me. A victim of white racism greeted a perpetrator as a sign of hope, found hope at the end of a pain-filled life under the

87. Ibid., 129.
88. Ibid.
89. Ibid.
90. Ibid., 133.

banner of structural violence, and, in it all, identified such an experience with a redeeming God."[91] This dying woman who proclaims God's presence in an encounter with a perpetrator of her suffering might be modelling for feminist theology unanticipated variations on the feminist themes of active, empowered, independent agency.

With this witness in mind, Ramsey advocates taking up the cross and reclaiming Christ-like suffering. While Ramsey did not participate directly in the systemic persecutions and murders of Apartheid, she does not excuse herself from accountability.[92] She reconsiders the character of suffering, and she warns against the temptation to equate suffering with a privileging of victimization, drawing on Angela West's description of the romanticization of the scapegoat.[93] Ramsey proposes that we respond to others' suffering and work through our own suffering, while remembering that God worked through Christ's suffering in surprising ways. In the process, she provides a means for hope beyond cultural concerns about the glorification of suffering (without glorifying suffering herself) and suggests how feminist theology can engage in life lived in relation to God. "The question feminist theology faces in the task of this retrieval is whether we want a world with an essential incapacity for suffering or fateful subjection to suffering, or a willingness to open oneself to be touched, moved, affected by something other than oneself. Above all, we need to ask of ourselves if it is possible to *speak of suffering* without it leading to martyrdom, abuse, masochism, denigration or further justification for the trivialization of the oppression of women."[94] If the answer is no, if suffering's full potential is contained in abhorrent negative manifestations, then a Christian theology of the cross represents a perverted identity, clinging to a false hope. If the answer is yes, if there is something redemptive to the accounts of suffering throughout the Old Testament, to Christ's unique embodiment of suffering, and to the lives of the saints who have witnessed to that suffering—all of which include some degree of hope and trust in God along with their horrific suffering—then feminist theology must struggle with how to reclaim the cross.

---

91. Ibid.

92. Another discussion might address South African life after Apartheid and the extent to which it is not free of systemic violence, persecution, and murder, although some of the parties have changed. Those of us who rallied for peace and justice in South Africa in years past might well investigate the conditions and possibilities for hope there today, in the face of violence and murder throughout the country.

93. Ramsey, "Losing," 129–30.

94. Ibid., 132.

Feminist theology critiques the use of Christ's suffering as a justification for the abuse of women; and it challenges the ease with which those who are not suffering see hope in tragedy. Three discussions meet at the cross here: suffering, tragedy, and dependence. All three terms need complicating and nuance, in order to avoid painting them all with one brush, good or bad. "Suffering" can mean a wide variety of experiences and narrations of those experiences. Wendy Farley notes the importance of resisting with compassion the suffering of injustice and violence, and she counts as inappropriate narrations of suffering as divine punishment, penalty, and substitution.[95] Coakley describes the suffering of pain that led John of the Cross and Teresa of Avila nearer to God.[96] Edward Farley lists the sufferings of vulnerability, benign alienation, ontological alienation, and discontent.[97] The Archbishop's Council distinguishes between Christ's reconciling suffering of freedom and the suffering of domestic abuse, which is neither free nor redemptive.[98] Additional sufferings include solidarity with the oppressed, the model of Jesus the Suffering Servant, and suffering for justice. Theology that articulates its language of suffering and its assessment of different sorts of suffering creates possibilities for identifying narratives of suffering that participate in Christ's suffering on the cross without glorifying suffering in itself or imposing necessary suffering on some while protecting others from suffering.

Tragedy also needs careful narration, and Kathleen Sands challenges the orthodoxy of feminist theology that tragedy is simply a matter of bad winning over the good.[99] She critiques the approach that seeks to shift the good to the top by working against victimization, hierarchicalism, and all natural, divine, and social causes of tragedy. Sands argues for facing tragedy head on, for recognizing what has been lost and what needs to be recovered. In this context, suffering is neither dismissed, celebrated, nor unattended, but it is understood as a reminder of what to hope for. Tragedy both affects the loss of that memory and hope; and at the same time it enables the revitalization of hope. As a result, feminist theologians might find renewed horizons for hope in the midst of the onslaught of acute suffering in the world today.

95. W. Farley, *Tragic*; and *Wounding*.
96. Coakley, *Powers*.
97. E. Farley, *Good*, 122–24.
98. *Responding*, A1.5.
99. Sands, "Tragedy"; and *Escape*.

Suffering and tragedy are often narrated in feminist theology in relation to problematic understandings of dependence. Feminism often names dependence as a threat to the health, freedom, and subjectivity of women, especially as gendered dependence helps sustain perverse social systems. Feminist theology critiques in particular the endorsement of dependence as necessary (for those already oppressed) and redemptive and the ways that that endorsement draws on theological doctrines of submission, obedience, and service. Coakley helpfully articulates different sorts of dependence, bearing in mind the radical differences between the holy dependence of contemplation of God and the dependence of torture. She argues that conflicting sorts of dependences overlap in confusing configurations but that trying to distinguish among them is still important in order "to bring to consciousness how easily one fades into another, how the infinitely 'subtle' and 'obscure' operation of the divine on the dependent creature is entwined with the deepest hopes and fears about family relationships, about sexuality, power and death."[100] She names the "absolute dependence" of contemplation; the physical, emotional, and psychological dependences of children; the dependences of prisoners, the tortured, spouses, lovers, drug users, the sick and the handicapped. She notes the economic dependence within families and of families on the state or charities. She calls attention to the dependence of a "failure in critical thinking," of dealing with events beyond control, and the dependence of death.[101] By spelling out these distinctions, Coakley can then avoid the temptation to discount all dependence as unjust suffering and a tragedy of social malformation, while claiming a specifically Christian narrative of dependence. She explains that an "absolute dependence" is indeed at the heart of true human creatureliness and the contemplative quest. But such *right* dependence is an elusive goal: the entanglements with themes of power, hierarchy, sexuality and death are probably inevitable but also best brought to consciousness; they are an appropriate reminder that our prayer is enfleshed.[102]

The analysis and evaluation of suffering, tragedy, and dependence opens the door to a feminist reclaiming of the cross and its hope. Christ's Passion and death manifests exquisite suffering, tragedy, and dependence; and Christ's resurrection redeems through suffering, reverses—without avoiding—tragedy, and models the absolute dependence on God

---

100. Coakley, *Powers*, 57.
101. Ibid., 57–58.
102. Ibid., 68.

of created humanity. Coakley urges feminist theology to reconsider vulnerability in light of Jesus' vulnerability, which cannot simply be explained as weak.[103] It is at least possible that hope in suffering, tragedy, and dependence might be reconnected with Jesus' suffering and death, in ways that do not reinscribe the suppression of women's thriving, now and in the eschaton. Feminist theology that engages with this sort of reexamination of orthodoxies may create renewed narrations of traditional doctrines to contribute to a contemporary theology of hope.

Feminist theology critiques patriarchal structures that limit women's participation in the life of the church to private piety and supporting roles. The relatively recent acceptance of the ordination of women in most Protestant denominations demonstrates efforts to include women in leadership positions in the church. Preaching, presiding at worship, performing sacramental functions are all marks of visibly active and uncoerced agency—agency that for centuries has been chiefly excercised by men who hold social positions of power, even as they take on serving discipleship. Now, the church is beginning to recognize that the Holy Spirit's call to ordination, while not universally offered, can be given to and discerned by people of all sorts and conditions. At the same time, some of the lay practices of Christians may seem less important. Women who express an interest in more involvement in the life of the chuch are asked early on if they are interested in ordination. Previously common lay roles of ecclesial participation may be criticized as either gender-oppressing (expecting women to cook for a church celebration, or visit shut-ins) or unnecessary personal piety (attending church services every day, praying the Rosary, Bible study). Work against social barriers to ordination risks diminishing the appreciation and expansion of other ecclesial vocations and gifts. The result can be that ordained ministerial leadership trumps other serving and devotional practices, as though hopes for subjectivity in Christ are best fulfilled in one particular gift of the Spirit.

In the context of a productivity-based culture, in which professional recognition and income authorizes agency, hope for women focuses on access to leadership positions, and renewed attention to lay ecclesial and theological practices might seem outdated; yet such a narrowed account of hope risks dismissing the identity and possibilities for most women of faith. Saba Mahmood's anthropological study of the Islamic Piety Movement in Egypt[104] describes women seeking to find and excercise freedom to par-

103. Ramsey, "Losing," 129.
104. Mahmood, *Politics*.

ticipate more fully in the piety practices of their faith. Her observations of women in a geographically and ideologically different context might help Christian feminists gain some insights about its orthodoxies of agency and possible hope.

Mahmood challenges feminist presuppositions about agency in her study of a movement of women who want to know more about the texts and teachings of Islam in order to discern ways to continue piety practices in a secularly influenced world. These women—some of them young teenagers, some grandmothers, many in-between—are trying to negotiate their ways through the social forces that inhibit their Islamic identities and practices. "The piety activists seek to imbue each of the various spheres of contemporary life with a regulative sensibility that takes its cue from the Islamic theological corpus rather than from modern secular ethics."[105] However, they do not perceive or narrate their efforts in terms of patriarchally oppressive submission and the resistance thereof.[106] Rather, the women of Islamic reform in Egypt are working to express their faith in ever-shifting contexts. Mahmood explains that the women she studied do not desire to return to a previous era's interpretations of women's participation in faithful practices, but they want to practice piety in performances that cohere with teaching *and* can be practiced in the world outside the home. They seek variations in performance to continue their participation in secular society, despite the new challenges that such interactions present. Part of this process involves educating women about the virtues that piety practices reflect and encourage. She quotes a woman who has been giving classes at mosques for women for several years, in the midst of a lesson about what it means to wear a hijab: "You must remember that a lot of [women] wear it as a custom, rather than a religious duty that also entails other responsibilities.... What we have to do is to educate Moslem women that it is not enough to wear the veil, but that the veil must also lead us to behave in a truly modest manner in our daily lives, a challenge that far exceeds the simple act of donning the veil."[107] Wearing the veil as a practice of piety thus represents neither submission to men nor resistance to participation in the secular world, but the identity of women performing modesty as a crucial part of their Moslem identity. In order to pursue studies at university, for example, young women use their knowledge of

---

105. Ibid., 47.
106. Ibid., 15–16.
107. Ibid., 50–51.

the Quran and their time in discussion (and sometimes debate) with other women to develop strategies for practicing piety as university students.

Mahmood presents an account of women claiming agency and action defined radically differently from the definitions standard to western feminism. She critiques the notion that freedom, independence, and equality on western feminist's terms must be the norm by which women's agency is assessed. "Does a commitment to the ideal of equality in our own lives endow us with the capacity to know that this ideal captures what is or should be fulfilling for everyone else? If it does not, as is surely the case, then I think we need to rethink, with far more humility than we are accustomed to, what feminist politics really means."[108] She calls on western feminists to account for their ready dismissal of women whose desires for subjectivity agency do not support feminist orthodoxies of empowerment and freedom from doctrinal directives. "I hope to redress the profound inability within current feminist political thought to envision valuable forms of human flourishing outside the bounds of a liberal progressive imaginary."[109] Mahmood's challenge might encourage Christian feminist theologians to envision human flourishing for themselves and for their Egyptian sisters, with an eye to the limitations as well as benefits of various feminist imaginaries.

Fulkerson's work on subjectivity and agency shares some of Mahmood's focus. Fulkerson's work predates Mahmood's, but much room remains for subsequent development of her arguments.[110] Fulkerson observed the community of Presbyterian Women, an organization within the Presbyterian church, with members throughout the United States. The self-claimed roles of Presbyterian Women in church, domestic, and mission activity, are not those of feminist Christians. The Presbyterian Women she observed are white, middle-class, unemployed (they do not have jobs that pay), and decidedly not feminist. They attend to the care and support of their households, their families, and their churches, in ways that feminists have labeled submissive, passive, and patriarchially oppressed. However, Fulkerson argues that Presbyterian Women do not necessarily inhabit the subjection that feminists might assume; the practices of care and discipleship make spaces for subjects with agency and integrity.

> Presbyterian Women transgress the constraints that construct their subject positions. In these positions multiple discourses

---

108. Ibid., 38.
109. Ibid., 154.
110. Fulkerson, *Changing*.

converge—gender, class, race, consumer, nurturer, homemaker, Christian—that are undermined by the contemporary social formation. Presbyterian Women "remake" their subject positions for global accountability. Their indirect targets, in the social formation, are the discursive processes of patriarchal capitalism that trivialize the home and de-skill and undermine women. More specifically, even while participating in both, they counter the discourses of romantic feminism/"true womanhood" and the rationalist feminism. Their transgressions are not those of liberation feminists. But they are significant productions of pleasurable, agapic, as well as ambiguous places. The places they produce mark off refusals of the patriarchal capitalist negation of the skills of homemaking and world-making.[111]

Feminist theology could ask if there is any hope for women whose agency includes some form of service, humility, and submission in Christian discipleship. Rather than setting practices of piety completely aside because of the ways they have been used to suppress women's agency, feminist theology might continue to explore reconstructions of subjectivity and agency. Fulkerson demonstrates that Christian women can thrive as subjects of faith in relation to discipleship, scripture, teaching, without being wholly determined by corrupted, idolatrous systems of oppression. These women model faithful resistance in ways that might spark ongoing investigations and constructions of theological hope that shape subjects and their agency in the midst of shifting and multi-valent contemporary social contexts.

Such investigations of hope might lead to new ways to worship God in unimposed humility and obedience to Christ, without the distortions of violence and victimization. Feminist theologians might imagine practices of piety shaped more by their particularly located fluid subjectivities and by reconsiderations of pre-modern and as-yet-unarticulated performances of *imitatio Christi*. The challenges remain: how to embody an identity in flux, participating in the conflicting and overlapping practices of discipleship and feminism; how to witness to eschatological hope in the non-conflictual resurrected body while situated in social oppression and conflict; and how to narrate subjectivity difference in a world that cannot imagine that difference. The possibilities for present and transcendent human thriving in eschatological hope are great.

Fulkerson, Mahmood, and Parsons (et. al.), held together in conversation, offer rich opportunities to reconfigure eschatological hope,

111. Ibid., 237.

identity, and practices. Feminist theology reconsidered in light of women's unorthodox claims to subjectivity suggests the possibility of an eschatological hope that exceeds the ideological boundaries of feminism vs. fundamentalism or liberated vs. unliberated society. Concern about limitations to subjectivity can include the concerns about the limitations born of reactions to other, imposed limitations. And theologies of hope can reach toward subjectivies in Christ determined by ongoing discernments of the continuity and difference of Christian and feminist doctrines.

Conclusion

Every *body* lives in the midst of shifting, overlapping communities of space, time, practice, ideology, and narrative. Christian accounts of theological hope cannot stand apart from the accounts of hope in the overlapping communities that bodies simultaneously inhabit. At the same time, some hopes contradict others, and the particularity of hopes and the fort mation that supports them can fade so much that it is difficult to identify any specific hope at all. Discernments about theological hope, made in conversation with and in accountability to Christian community, can be sharpened and clarified with input from resources that challenge familiar assumptions.

Critical accounts of nihilism and indeterminacy remind theologies of hope not to rush to resolve paradox, impossibility, and moments of "perhaps." Claims about the certainty of hope's outcomes might be tempered by humility about the divine source of that certainty. Confidence in God's capacity and responsibility through lament, disability, tragedy, and death may remind Christianity of the perseverence, patience, and fortitude of hope exemplified in scripture and in faithful lives. Challenges to familiar constructions of subjectivity, self-knowledge, and agency might encourage theologians of hope to reconsider subjects who hope and their eschatological subjectivity. Attention to bodies might strengthen theological hope in and for all sorts of bodies and hope for resurrected bodies. And, finally, theologies of hope ready to gain from a variety of resources might begin to lose the embarrassment of Christian particularity and enter into direct dialogue with conversations like the five mentioned here, open to the possibility that Christian theological hope might have something to contribute.

5

Our Only Hope

CHAPTER 1 DESCRIBED JÜRGEN Moltmann's future-determined, creation-focused, ideologically-modern, hope in the passible God who has been brought to suffer with humanity by Jesus Christ's suffering and death. I followed the sketch of Moltmann's theological hope with examples of Moltmannian hope and its humanist, this-worldly hope in the changes that responsible, hopeful actions can make. In chapter 2, I noted what an exclusive reliance on Moltmannian hope loses: non-modern imagination, divine impassibility, Christ's two natures, heaven, transcendent human flourishing, and apparently irresponsible discipleship. Chapter 3 considered patristic and Thomistic presentations of theological hope and twenty-first-century treatments of hope from theologians appreciative of a Thomistic systematic theology, in order to call attention to some theological hope resources that have been set aside. In chapter 4, I briefly considered nihilism, lament, disability theology, feminist theory, and feminist theology, as possible resources for theological hope.

I propose that contemporary efforts to find and sustain eschatological hope draw from an ongoing stream of church teaching and from related considerations of hope to discern wisdom about hope in Christ and the performance of that hope. The church will always need to work at recognizing and sharing the distinctiveness of Christian hope for eternal life in God through Jesus Christ and how that hope can be lived in the church. Jesus Christ, the one hope of the church, demonstrates and effects the fulfillment of hope through death to eternal life. God, one and three, demonstrates perfect, impassible compassion in covenantal relationship with God's creatures and through the incarnation. Human creatures can receive and participate in the hope of the resurrection in Christ in part through friendships that try to witness to the perfection of all friendship in the company of God.

Friends who participate fully in the theological virtue of hope rely on mutual accountability as they look and wait for out-of-reach possibilities. They hope for and with the hopeless, they narrate the hope of the heroes of the faith, and they provide for each other the physical and emotional nurturing that helps make possible eschatological hope anchored by Jesus Christ and sustained by the Holy Spirit. As the secondary agents of hope, friends and the goods they offer do not effect christological hope or obtain the object of the theological virtue of hope; but friendship is the location for an ethics of eschatological hope, in the interest of the divinely assisted fulfillment of eternal happiness. Friends are not our only hope, but friendship well done can demonstrate hope in the certain, continuing, and yet unimaginably new life with God.

None of this is easy. Friendships of hope often seem impossible. In the Introduction, I described sitting in church with my baby, as I struggled with depression and a sermon about hope. I have heard many sermons since on the theme of hope, and I am still dubious about the pastoral and exhortative value of claims that "God never gives you more than you can handle," "you should resist the forces of negativity and be filled with hope," and "you/they are the hope of the future." I would now ask preachers to consider teaching the distinctively Christian eschatological hope, its primary and secondary causes, and the importance of friendships in hope. But I remind myself that no one sermon can in and of itself mend loss and despair. I try to let myself fully participate in the liturgy regardless of how I feel. And I am grateful for the friends who have led me to needed treatment for depression and anxiety, who have carried hope for me when I could not, and who sustain me in hope through their presence in my life.

I also shared, in the Introduction, my awareness that Charlotte was sitting near me in the back of the church. At the time, I thought of Charlotte as someone who was also struggling, but I was not able to see her as a friend. I was unclear what friendship might mean if it was not a matter of equal give and take. I did not have much to give, and I did not think she had much to give back. I would like to think that today I would sit closer to Charlotte, to be a little more present to her, as a marker of the possibility of friendship and as a small sign of hope that friendship is possible. I know that I would need friends to hold me accountable to that witness of hope. The fulfillment of hope does not rest in my hands or my good intentions.

Our Only Hope

Today, as I write, I am looking for hope to share with my friend Leona, who sits in the ICU at the side of her husband, Michael, as he weathers yet another round of chemotherapy for an incurable cancer. His prognosis is not good. Michael might be well enough to leave the hospital at some point, but he is not likely to see their three young children grow up. Leona is not likely to have the chance to grow old with the love of her life. I am too far away to visit, cook meals, or help with the children. Leona and Michael already have abundant friends and family nearby and online who are sustaining them with food, child care, financial assistance, and good cheer. I can only write words and pray. The words of this book are not the words Leona needs today. The words in my little notes to her are small. My prayers will not change God's lasting love and care for her family. My part feels inadequate, ineffective, and difficult. I need friends to help me pray in hope anyway and to remember that God's compassion is already perfect, infinite, eternal, and effective, through Jesus Christ, our only hope.

Our lives are not overflowing with visible examples of eschatological hope. I will close now with a small proposal for drawing Christian hope closer to the only hope of Christ. I suggest that church congregations look at some popular stories that present the need for hope. These stories might lack literary or cinematographic excellence, but they can provide an opportunity to consider how Christian theological hope might be added to the story line. I call particular attention to popular movies and novels about earth-shattering, universe-shifting catastrophes; for the purposes of this argument, I'll refer to them as *popapocalyptic*.[1] Popapocalyptic movies and novels present unbelievable disasters in which salvation from certain death depends on some kind of *our only hope*. Most stories in this genre contain one big *our only hope* and any number of smaller ones to move the plot along. In these stories, *our only hope* is never Jesus Christ. The smaller and larger *our only hope*s never involve Christian prayer, worship, or practice, although we might catch a glimpse of some apparently pious people in a church, and we know that they will be dying early. Generally speaking, popapocalyptic stories do not mention eschatological hope. Generally speaking, Christian readers and viewers do not find the lack of such hope

---

1. "Popapocalyptic" is a genre category of my own construction, and I am including within it only those stories that support my point. I suggest that another good discussion point might address how and why other categorizations might make sense. The apocalyptic aspect refers to the sense that impending disaster threatens to destroy (or disaster has just destroyed) the world we know and love; therefore something needs to be done about it. The pop aspect refers to the broad appeal of thrilling special effects and a reassuringly happy ending, at least for the main characters.

in the plot remarkable. One way to reintroduce christological, eschatological hope might be to look at the *our only hope*s of popapocalyptic, note what is missing, and then imagine what theological hope might look like if added into the characters and plots. If Christians cannot imagine such hope in fictional accounts of global collapse, the likelihood of sustaining hope in real-life challenging times seems dim.

The format of a popapocalyptic story usually involves worst-case scenarios of challenge, disruption, and change, followed by death, endurance, overcoming all odds, super heroism, survival, and triumphalism. There may be a degree of tragedy but only at a safe distance. There is always some kind of salvation through *our only hope*, as these movie examples illustrate. In *Meteor*, the threat is a huge meteor. *Our only hope* is for the U.S. and the U.S.S.R. to coordinate their nuclear missiles to redirect the meteor's path. *Volcano* presents Tommy Lee Jones as *our only hope*, along with concrete barriers to contain the lava. In *Independence Day*, aliens threaten life as we know it, and *our only hope* is a carefully planned combination of a nuclear bomb and a computer virus. *The Day After Tomorrow* features the ruination of the northern hemisphere by climate change. Two *only hope*s save the day: a meteorologist father rescues his son, and the U.S. government moves the surviving population into Central America. *The Core* shows what happens when the core of the earth stops turning. Moments before the end of the world, all is saved by *our only hope*, a band of quirky and good-looking scientists who tunnel through earth to jumpstart the core with a nuclear explosion. *2012* follows the myth of the Mayan calendar's prediction of global destruction and shows the earth falling apart and a flood of biblical proportions. *Our only hope* comes in the form of huge ships and John Cusack's quick-witted determination. In *World War Z* the threat is zombies, and Brad Pitt leads the *our only hope* brigade. All of these movies end with the sense that the survival hopes of the main characters have been fulfilled, and there is hope for their continued survival.

Stephen Baxter's books *Flood* and *Ark* chronicle the years between 2016 and 2058, during which time the waters of the earth rise unexpectedly and steadily around the entire world.[2] This is a near-future, science fiction, epic tale of catastrophe on top of catastrophe and dashed *only hope*s. No scientific theories or strategic defences stop the flooding. Political infighting keeps responsive and responsible leadership from action. As land shrinks around the world, countries are divided and washed away; governments and economies collapse; nationality no longer matters.

---

2. Baxter, *Flood* and *Ark*.

Higher-altitude land is quickly claimed by the wealthy and powerful and by peoples who have recovered their ancestors' skills for living on land and in water without first world resources. The rest keep moving on foot or by raft, with nowhere to settle. In one mountainous region, those who survive the initial stages of the flood call themselves New Covenanters, believing that

> if God had broken the Covenant He made with Noah after the Biblical flood . . . it could only be because humans had broken it first. But, perhaps God wasn't punishing everyone. Surely those who had been wise enough to move to higher ground early were a kind of elect, raised out of the herd of sinners, and had a duty to preserve themselves for a new post-flood age to come. And conversely those who had not been smart enough to prepare showed their weakness as well as their sinfulness. So the high-altitude elect therefore had a holy duty to stay alive and hold onto their ground.[3]

This pseudo-biblical narrative provides the New Covenanters with a moral justification for killing the increasing numbers of people in rafts trying to land on dry ground. It does not engage with hope beyond self-preservation or life in Christ through discipleship, death, and resurrection.

Baxter continues the story through decades of radical change. Long after the leaders of the nations lose their positions of power, long after all emergency plans have been exhausted, long after whole continents have disappeared and cities are marked only by the floating "scum of garbage and boated corpses,"[4] the exceptionally wealthy continue to build wealth and influence in the midst of the ever-changing world. But others survive as well, as the world as we *knew* it becomes a world of raft communities. Meanwhile, a space ship—The Ark—has been launched with a selection of promising young people, sent to find a planet that might become Earth 2. The physical and emotional limitations of many years of space travel parallel the increasing scarcity that defines life on earth as the land vanishes. As Baxter's narrative ends, a thin, grim, but continuous hope remains for the survival of the human race, in space and on the water.

In these popapocalyptic stories, the goal is to survive. Killing, hoarding, and protecting resources may once have been subject to limitations and rules, but they become necessary for survival. None of these stories mentions the particular challenges that Christians might face when the

---

3. Baxter, *Flood*, 281.
4. Ibid., 393.

goal of survival conflicts with the practices of Christ-like discipleship. The New Covenanters kill to sustain their identity as the new chosen few. The space ship project rejects as potential passengers any people who claim any religious or atheistic beliefs, in the interest of avoiding conflict on board. (That strategy proves unsuccessful.) It is hard to imagine that Christians would last very long *as Christians* in any of these stories. Neighbor-love, enemy-love, preferential treatment for the poor, and eschatological hope are all hard enough to sustain in current, familiar life; in unfamiliar life, they seem completely impossible. Survival in a world in which resources are limited by monumental disaster seems to rule out efforts to live communally so that no one is needy.

These stories fit the popapocalyptic genre because they narrate disasters of amazing proportions which disrupt not only our daily assumptions about who we are and what our world is like but also the possibility of sustaining a narrative at all. Perhaps the most realistic character of popapocalyptic movies and novels is their display of the experience of one catastrophe on top of another, each outdoing the previous in intensity, scope and ramifications, on an exponentially increasing scale of disaster. The future is reduced to moment-to-moment survival until life seems plausible again.

On and off the screen, we expect more from life than apocalyptic-feeling catastrophes one right after the other. These expectations may be unrealistic. This does not mean that we should *expect* unprecedented, unpredictable disaster. The concern is rather that we are all too ready to take the *feeling* that everything has changed to mean that who we are, who God is, and what we do has changed. Christians in the midst of the end of the world as we know it risk confusing a change in circumstances with a change in identity. It is difficult to remember that God remains in relationship with God's creation, Christians remain members of the body of Christ; friendship in hope is still possible.

If everything *has* changed, then raiding a neighbor's home for food, stealing an unattended car, and killing people who threaten us all seem more acceptable actions than they would if everything were normal. Those who hesitate, those who fail to grasp that catastrophe has changed everything, simply do not survive. Heroes and survivors do what has to be done, even if what has to be done might otherwise be abhorrent, illegal, dishonest, or violent. In a world in which the ends justify the means, there is not much sense in loving your enemy or your neighbor if it does not lead to your own survival. When Christians do not question this reasoning, when we accept that the challenges of life together in discipleship become irrelevant in the face of catastrophe, we reveal the misgivings we have had all along about caring for others first, and we demonstrate our doubt about eschatological hope. We reduce survival to the delay of death, and we recognize no continuity of God's relationship with creation through death and into new life.

It is hard to imagine that approaching asteroids, ice ages, plagues, or the sudden standstill of the earth's core won't change everything; but we do have witnesses to the perseverance in hope, throughout scripture and the church, whose lives demonstrate their hope in God who is constant and present, even and especially in the face of radical and unimagined change in our world. They show us their hope that God is still God no matter how high the waters rise, that God was God before the waters were there to rise. They hope in God's greatness, God's love, and God's compassion which pre-date and post-date our lives, and they trust that God does not retreat in the face of catastrophe, no matter what the scale, even when God's presence cannot be discerned. They hope in God's son who died a painful and humiliating death and did not strive for survival in this world at any cost. Their lives demonstrate that survival—of people and of the whole creation—is not the end of hope.

When catastrophe of any scale strikes us, we can try to respond with the hope of the faithful who precede us, prepared to die with Christ instead of clinging to survival through the rejection of Christ in those suffering around us. However, models of such faith are few and far between, and our track record for living in eschatological hope is not good. Most of us are ready to claim catastrophe status and then feel released from discipleship practices. When life gets tough, we are quick to forget the martyrs and eager to shift allegiance from the cross to the lifeboat. In the less-unprecedented crises of financial recession, unemployment, violence, despair, and weary disappointment, we can easily convince ourselves that sharing with the poor, visiting the sick and imprisoned, and living peaceably with our enemies sitting are all luxuries for other times when calm prevails and prospects once again look promising. We tend to reduce survival to the delay of death or hardship, and we are ready to set discipleship practices aside to support that delay. The scope of hope shrinks to an individual-size portion with a short shelf-life.

If eschatological hope matters at all, then presumably it matters when life is threatened by giant killer bees, robot aliens, and the sudden loss of polar glaciers. The popapocalyptic genre gives us a limited range of characters, circumstances, and plot development in which to experiment with imagining Christians in catastrophe; and the absurdity of the premises keeps the focus sufficiently detached from our own daily lives to draw us into what might become a challenging conversation. For a start, I suggest that theological hope undaunted by disaster and inserted into a popapocalyptic movie might look like friendship in Christ. It might play out as local, neighborhood, workplace, small-scale friendship that does not change when circumstances change, when prospects look dim, and when life as we know it is changing.

A persevering friendship in the hope of eternal life with God through Christ might prioritize companionship, honesty, and trust. When crowds are running away to escape the molten lava, an able-bodied friend might stay behind with someone who is housebound, because friends do not want friends to be alone and abandoned. When the friend with the broken leg asks the friend with a good view of the horizon, "are we going to make it?" the friend who is clinging to eschatological hope might say, "no, because the zombies are coming and there is no escape, but we can pray together." In a lifeboat, when all the food is gone, friends might trust each other not to murder and cannibalize each other in order to survive. In each case, these inserted characters try to witness to a hope that relationships turned toward citizenship in heaven still matter now. Friends might help each other to remember that the commitment to care for each other and all of creation does not mean that death is the end: eschatological hope can shape on-the-ground acts of hope.

Imagining theological hope additions to popapocalyptic dramas will likely lead a congregational conversation to two observations: friendships of eschatological hope do not keep the world safe from cataclysmic danger; and these friends added to movies look silly. These are undeniably true assessments. For those of us not in a movie or novel, the questions remain: How can Christians narrate life beyond the ultimate goal of earthly survival, without downplaying or dismissing suffering and death? When survival requires actions antithetical to the body of Christ, can Christians claim a different survival more urgent than murder, greed, or selfishness? What does it mean to persevere in the hope of a constant God, when everything we know about how to be full of hope, how to be alive, seems to shift far out of control? How can we face the painful death of the ones we love in hope? We will need friendships to face these questions as the familiar world falters. We need friends to hold open the possibility of hope when we can see no hope in untimely death or powerful injustice. We need friends to help us receive and turn toward our only hope in Christ.

Our Only Hope

If there is anything true about the witness of scripture, tradition, the saints, and faithful friends to the hope of life up to and after survival, then silly and ineffective hope might still have a place in Christian life. Their witnesses remind us that God is constant in catastrophe, unchanged by disaster, and perfectly compassionate. Christ, who did not survive the catastrophe of the cross, but died to live anew, draws us in hope through pain, suffering, and death to eternal life in the love of God. May our hope persevere through the end of the world as we know it, until the fulfillment of hope in beatitude.

Bibliography

Adam, A. K. M. *Faithful Interpretation: Reading the Bible in a Postmodern World.* Minneapolis: Fortress, 2006.

———. *Making Sense of New Testament Theology: Modern Problems and Prospects.* Studies in American Biblical Hermeneutics 11. Reprint, Eugene, OR: Wipf & Stock, 2005.

———. *What Is Postmodern Biblical Criticism?* Guides to Biblical Scholarship. Minneapolis: Fortress, 1995.

Adorno, Theodor. *Negative Dialectics.* Translated by E. B. Aston. New York: Continuum, 2004.

Aquinas, Thomas. *Summa theologica,* Complete English Edition in Five Volumes. Translated by Fathers of the English Dominican Province. Notre Dame: Christian Classics, 1981.

Augustine. *City of God.* Translated by Henry Bettenson. London: Penguin, 1972.

———. *Enchiridion on Faith, Love, and Hope.* Washington, DC: Regnery, 1996.

———. *A Treatise on Grace and Free Will.* Edited by Philip Schaff. New York: Christian Literature, 1886.

Barnes, Rev. F. C. "Rough Side of the Mountain." *Rough Side of the Mountain.* Atlanta International Records, 10059, 1983.

Barton, John. "Jürgen Moltmann: Trinity and Suffering." *Evangel* 3/2 (1985) 4–6.

Bauckham, Richard. *God Will Be All in All: The Eschatology of Jürgen Moltmann.* New York: Continuum, 2005.

———. "Jürgen Moltmann." In *The Modern Theologians: An Introduction to Christian Theology in the Twentieth Century,* 2nd ed., edited by David F. Ford, 209–24. Malden, MA: Blackwell, 1997.

———. *The Theology of Jürgen Moltmann.* New York: Continuum, 1995.

Baxter, Stephen. *Ark.* London: Golancz, 2009.

———. *Flood.* New York: Roc, 2008.

Beauley, Lucien, "Organically Grown Foods: Our Only Hope." November 16, 2009. Online: http://www.associatedcontent.com/article/2396566/organically_grown_foods_our_only_hope.

Bedford, Nancy Elizabeth. "'God's Power Is God's Goodness': Some Notes on the Sovereignty of God in Jürgen Moltmann's Theology." In *The Sovereignty of God Debate,* edited by D. Stephen Long & George Kalantzis, 97–110. Cambridge: T. & T. Clark, 2010.

Benedict XVI. *Encyclical letter: Spe salvi: On Christian Hope.* Online: http://www.vatican.va/holy_father/benedict_xvi/encyclicals/documents/hf_ben-xvi_enc_20071130_spe-salvi_en.html.

Bibliography

Bloch, Ernst. *The Principle of Hope, Vol. 1*. Edited by Neville Plaice, Stephen Plaice, and Paul Knight. Cambridge, MA: MIT, 1986.

Blunt, Martin. "Carbon Capture and Storage: Our Only Hope to Avoid Global Warming?" Lecture at the 2010 Shell London Lecture Series, The Geological Society of London. March 10, 2010. Online: http://www.geolsoc.org.uk/gsl/events/listings/page6434.

The Book of Common Prayer. New York: Church Hymnal, 1979.

Borsch, Frederick Houk. *Outrage and Hope: A Bishop's Reflections in Times of Change and Challenge*. Valley Forge, PA: Trinity, 1996.

Brown, Sally A. "When Lament Shapes the Sermon." In *Lament: Reclaiming Practices in Pulpit, Pew, and Public Square*, edited by Sally A. Brown and Patrick D. Miller, 27–37. Louisville: Westminster John Knox, 2005.

Brown, Sally A., and Patrick D. Miller, editors. *Lament: Reclaiming Practices in Pulpit, Pew, and Public Square*. Louisville: Westminster John Knox, 2005.

Buck-Moss, Susan. *The Origin of Negative Dialectics: Theodor W. Adorno, Walter Benjamin, and the Frankfurt Institute*. New York: Free, 1977.

Buckley, James Joseph, and L. Gregory Jones. *Theology and Eschatology at the Turn of the Millenium*. Malden, MA: Blackwell, 2002.

Buffum, Herbert. "Fifty Miles of Elbow Room." Early twentieth century. Recorded by The Carter Family. *The Carter Family*. Bluebird, 1941, 1-9026. Reissued on *The Best of the Carter Family*. Performance, 2005, 38726.

Burns, L. "'You are our only hope': trading metaphorical 'magic bullets' for stem cell 'superheroes.'" *Theoretical Medicine and Bioethics* 30 (2009) 427–42. Online: http://www.ncbi.nlm.nih.gov/pubmed/20035405.

Butler, Judith. *Bodies that Matter: On the Discursive Limits of Sex*. New York: Routledge, 1993.

———. *Gender Trouble: Feminism and the Subversion of Identity*. London: Routledge, 1990.

———. *Giving an Account of Oneself*. New York: Fordham University Press, 2005.

———. *Undoing Gender*. New York, NY: Routledge, 2004.

Caputo, John D. *The Weakness of God: A Theology of the Event*. Bloomington: Indiana University Press, 2006.

Carter, R. Kelso. "Standing on the Promises of God." In Sweney, John, and Carter, *Promises of Perfect Love*, n.p. Philadelphia: John J. Hood, 1886. Online: http://www.cyberhymnal.org/htm/s/o/sotpogod.htm.

Castelo, Daniel. *The Apathetic God: Exploring the Contemporary Relevance of Divine Impassibility*. Milton Keynes: Paternoster, 2009.

Cavanaugh, William T. *The Myth of Religious Violence: Secular Ideology and the Roots of Modern Conflict*. Oxford: Oxford University Press, 2009.

Cessario, Romanus. *The Moral Virtues and Theological Ethics*. Notre Dame: University of Notre Dame Press, 1991.

———. "The Theological Virtues of Hope (IIa IIae, qq. 17-22)." In *The Ethics of Aquinas*, edited by Stephen J. Pope, 232–44. Washington, DC: Georgetown University Press: 2002.

Chopp, Rebecca. *The Praxis of Suffering: An Interpretation of Liberation and Political Theologies*. Eugene, OR: Wipf & Stock, 1986.

Chrysostom, John. *The Homilies of S. John Chrysostom, Apostle of Constantinople, on the Epistle of S. Paul the Apostle to the Hebrews*. Oxford: Parker and Rivingtons, 1877.

Bibliography

Clark, Fred. Blog commentary on the *Left Behind* series by Tim LaHaye and Jerry B. Jenkins. Online: http://www.patheos.com/blogs/slacktivist/tag/left-behind/.

Coakley, Sarah. *Powers and Submissions: Spirituality, Philosophy and Gender*. Oxford: Blackwell, 2002.

Copjec, Joan, editor. *Supposing the Subject*. London: Verso, 1994.

Cousteau, Jacques-Yves. "The Ocean." *National Geographic*, December, 1981, 780–91.

Creamer, Deborah B. *Disability and Christian Theology: Embodied Limits and Constructive Possibilities*. New York: Oxford University Press, 2008.

Crosby, Fanny. "Blessed Assurance." 1873. Online: http://www.cyberhymnal.org/htm/b/l/e/blesseda.htm.

———. "Take The World But Give Me Jesus." 1879. Online: http://www.cyberhymnal.org/htm/t/t/ttwbgmej.htm.

———. "To the Work! To the Work!" 1869. Online: http://www.hymnary.org/text/to_the_work_to_the_work_we_are_servants_.

Cunningham, Conor. *Genealogy of Nihilism: Philosophies of Nothing and the Difference of Theology*. London: Routledge, 2002.

Cushman, Philip. *Constructing the Self, Constructing America: A Cultural History of Psychotherapy*. Cambridge, MA: DaCapo, 1995.

Daniel, Jamie O., and Tom Moylan, editors. *Not Yet: Reconsidering Ernst Bloch*. London: Verso, 1997.

de Lubac, Henri. *Medieval Exegesis: The Four Senses of Scripture, Volume 2*. Translated by E. M. Macierowski. Grand Rapids: Eerdmans, 2000.

Dhar, Sujoy. "Are charity hospitals the only hope for India's poor?" Online: http://www.reuters.com/article/2010/02/22/us-india-hospitals-idUSTRE61L0NC20100222.

"Down to the River to Pray," based on "The Good Old Way." In *Slave Songs of the United States*, edited by William Francis Allen et al., 85. New York: Simpson, 1867. Online: http://docsouth.unc.edu/church/allen/allen.html.

Eagleton, Terry. *Sweet Violence: The Idea of the Tragic*. Malden, MA: Blackwell, 2003.

Eiesland, Nancy L. *The Disabled God: Toward a Liberatory Theology of Disability*. Nashville: Abingdon, 1994.

Farley, Edward. *Ecclesial Reflection: An Anatomy of Theological Method*. Philadelphia: Fortress, 1982.

———. *Good and Evil: Interpreting a Human Condition*. Minneapolis: Fortress, 1990.

———. *Theologia: The Fragmentation and Unity of Theological Education*, Eugene, OR: Wipf & Stock, 2001.

Farley, Wendy. *Tragic Vision and Divine Compassion: A Contemporary Theodicy*. Louisville: Westminster John Knox, 1990.

———. *The Wounding and Healing of Desire: Weaving Heaven and Earth*. Louisville: Westminster John Knox, 2005.

Fergusson, David. "Eschatology," In *The Cambridge Companion to Christian Doctrine*, edited by Colin Gunton, 226–244. Cambridge: Cambridge University Press, 2007.

Fiddes, Paul S. *The Creative Suffering of God*. Oxford: Clarendon, 1988.

Fiorenza, Francis Schüssler. "Being, Subjectivity, Otherness: The Idols of God." In *Questioning God*, edited by John D. Caputo et al., 319–41. Bloomington: Indiana University Press, 2001.

Fulkerson, Mary M. *Changing the Subject: Women's Discourses and Feminist Theology*. Minneapolis: Fortress, 1994.

Bibliography

———. *Places of Redemption: Theology for a Worldly Church.* Oxford: Oxford University Press, 2007.

Garrigou-Lagrange, Reginald, OP. *Providence.* Rockford, IL: Tan, 1998.

———. *Predestination.* Rockford, IL: Tan, 1998.

Gaventa, William C., and David L. Coulter. *Spirituality and Intellectual Disability: International Perspectives on the Effect of Culture and Religion on Healing Body, Mind, and Soul.* London: Routledge, 2002.

Gavrilyuk, Paul L. "Select Quotations." Lecture Handout. "God's Impassible Suffering in the Flesh: The Coherence of Paradoxical Christology." Lecture, *A Providence College Symposium: Divine Impassibility and the Mystery of Human Suffering,* Providence, RI, March 30–31, 2007.

———. *The Suffering of the Impassible God: The Dialectics of Patristic Thought.* Oxford: Oxford University Press, 2004.

Genesis Wildlife Sanctuary. Online: http://www.ncssm.edu/service/genesis-wildlife-sanctuary/.

Gilbertson, Michael. *God and History in the Book of Revelation: New Testament Studies in Dialogue with Pannenberg and Moltmann.* Cambridge: Cambridge University Press, 2003.

Gillespie, Michael A. *Nihilism Before Nietzsche.* Chicago: University of Chicago Press, 1997.

Global Genes Project. "Hope—It's in our Genes." February 25, 2010. Online: http://www.news-medical.net/news/20100225/Hope-e28093-Its-In-Our-Genes-rare-disease-campaign-slogan-translated-into-multiple-international-languages-and-Braille.aspx.

God's Unfinished Future. A Trinity Institute Conference. New York: Trinity Television and New Media, 2007. 6 DVDs.

Goetz, Ronald. "The Suffering God: The Rise of a New Orthodoxy." *The Christian Century* 103 (1986) 385–89.

Goris, Harm J. M. J. *Free Creatures of an Eternal God: Thomas Aquinas on God's Infallible Foreknowledge and Irresistible Will.* Utrecht: Thomas Institute, 1996.

Greene-McCreight, Kathryn. *Darkness Is My Only Companion: A Christian Response to Mental Illness.* Grand Rapids, MI: Brazos, 2006.

Greer, Rowan. *Christian Hope and Christian Life: Raids on the Inarticulate.* New York: Crossroad, 2001.

Grenz, Stanley J., and Roger E. Olson. *20th Century Theology: God and the World In a Transitional Age.* Downers Grove, IL: InterVarsity, 1997.

Griffiths, Paul J. *Lying: An Augustinian Theology of Duplicity.* Eugene, OR: Wipf & Stock, 2010.

Griffiths, Paul J., and Reinhard Hütter, editors. *Reason and the Reasons of Faith.* London: T. & T. Clark, 2005.

Grosz, Elizabeth. "Irigaray and the Divine." In *Transfigurations: Theology and the French Feminists,* edited by C. W. Maggie Kim et al., 199–214. Minneapolis: Fortress, 1993.

———. "The Time of Violence: Deconstruction and Value." In *Violence and the Body: Race, Gender, and the State,* edited by Arturo J. Aldama, 134–47. Bloomington: Indiana University Press, 2003.

Gudorf, Christine E. "Feminism and Postmodernism in Susan Frank Parsons." *Journal of Religious Ethics* 32/3 (2004) 521–43.

Hanby, Michael. *Augustine and Modernity*. London: Routledge, 2003.
Hart, David B. *The Beauty of the Infinite: the Aesthetics of Christian Truth*. Grand Rapids: Eerdmans, 2003.
———. *The Doors of the Sea: Where was God in the Tsunami?* Grand Rapids: Eerdmans, 2005.
Hauerwas, Stanley. *Naming the Silences: God, Medicine, and the Problem of Suffering*. Grand Rapids: Eerdmans, 1990.
Hauerwas, Stanley, and Charles Pinches. *Christians Among the Virtues: Theological Conversations with Ancient and Modern Ethics*. Notre Dame: University of Notre Dame Press, 1997.
Hauerwas, Stanley, with Richard Bondi and David Burrell. *Truthfulness and Tragedy: Further Investigations into Christian Ethics*. Notre Dame: University of Notre Dame Press, 1977.
Hauerwas, Stanley, and Jean Vanier. *Living Gently in a Violent World: The Prophetic Witness of Weakness*. Downers Grove, IL: InterVarsity Press, 2008.
Havergal, Frances R. "Take My Life and Let It Be." 1874.
"He's My Lighthouse." Traditional Gospel. No Pages. Online: http://www.pine-net.com/~joanbab/lighthouse.htm.
Healy, Nicholas. "Henri de Lubac on Nature and Grace: A Note on Some Recent Contributions to the Debate." *Communio* 35 (2008) 536–64.
"Heaven's Bright Shore." Traditional. Online: http://www.leoslyrics.com/ralph-stanley/heaven-s-bright-shore-lyrics/.
Helms, Richard B. "The Health Cost Problem: Is Regulation Our Only Hope?" *Bulletin of the New York Academy of Medicine*. 56 (1980) 26–37.
Heschel, Susannah. "Configurations of Patriarchy." In *Gender and Judaism: The Transformation of Tradition*, edited by Tamar Rudavsky, 135–54. New York: NYU Press, 1995.
Hofheinz, Marco. *The Passionate God: Jürgen Moltmann's Trinitarian Theology as Contribution to Jewish-Christian Dialogue in Germany*. Munich: GRIN, 2010.
Hollywood, Amy. *Sensible Ecstasy: Mysticism, Sexual Difference, and the Demands of History*. Chicago: University of Chicago Press, 2002.
Horton, Michael Scott. *Lord and Servant: A Covenant Christology*. Louisville: Westminster John Knox, 2005.
Hütter, Reinhard. "The Natural Desire for the Vision of God: A Relecture of Summa contra Gentiles III, c. 25, après Henri de Lubac." *The Thomist* 73/4 (2009) 523–91.
———. *Suffering Divine Things: Theology as Church Practice*. Grand Rapids: Eerdmans, 1999.
Ignatius of Antioch. "Letter to the Smyrnaeans." In *The Apostolic Fathers: Greek texts and English translations*, updated ed., edited by M. W. Holmes. Grand Rapids: Baker, 1999.
Irigaray, Luce. *This Sex Which Is Not One*. Translated by Catherine Porter. Ithaca, NY: Cornell University Press, 1985.
Jennings, Willie James. *The Christian Imagination: Theology and the Origins of Race*. New Haven and London: Yale University Press, 2010.
Johnson, Blind Willie. "God Don't Never Change." c. 1920s. No Pages. Online: http://blueslyrics.tripod.com/artistswithsongs/blind_willie_johnson_1.htm.
Jones, Serene. *Feminist Theory and Christian Theology: Cartographies of Grace*. Minneapolis: Fortress, 2000.

Bibliography

———. *Trauma and Grace: Theology in a Ruptured World*. Louisville: Westminster John Knox, 2009.
Jordan, Mark. *Rewritten Theology: Aquinas after His Readers*. Oxford: Blackwell, 2006.
Keller, Catherine. *Apocalypse Now and Then: A Feminist Guide to the End of the World*. Minneapolis: Fortress, 2006.
———. *God and Power: Counter-Apocalyptic Journeys*. Minneapolis: Fortress, 2003.
Keshgegian, Flora A. *Redeeming Memories: A Theology of Healing and Transformation*. Nashville: Abingdon, 2000.
———. *Time for Hope*. New York: Continuum, 2006.
Kim, C. W., et al. *Transfigurations: Theology and The French Feminists*. Minneapolis: Fortress, 1993.
King, Martin Luther, Jr. "Why I Am Opposed to the War in Vietnam," Sermon at Ebenezer Baptist Church, Atlanta, GA, April 16, 1967. Cited in James Cone: "Martin Luther King Jr. and the Third World." *The Journal of American History* 74 (1987) 455–67.
Kitamori, Kazoh. *Theology of the Pain of God*. Translated 1946. London: SCM, 1966.
Krašovec, Jože. "The Source of Hope in the Book of Lamentations." *Vetus Testamentum* 42/2 (1992) 223–233.
Jervey, Ben. "Seawater: Our Only Hope for a Drink." *Good Environment*. March 28, 2009. Online: http://www.good.is/post/seawater-our-only-hope-for-a-drink.
Legit, Carlo. "Eschatology." In *The Theology of Thomas Aquinas*, edited by Rik Van Nieuwenhove and Joseph Wawrykow, 365–85. Notre Dame: University of Notre Dame Press, 2005.
Linafelt, Tod. *Surviving Lamentations: Catastrophe, Lament, and Protest in the Afterlife of a Biblical Book*. Chicago: University of Chicago Press, 2000.
Lonergan, Bernard J. F. *Grace and Freedom: Operative Grace in the Thought of St. Thomas Aquinas*. Edited by J. Patout Burns. New York: Herder & Herder, 1971.
Long, D. Stephen. "Aquinas and God's Sovereignty." In *The Sovereignty of God Debate*, edited by D. Stephen Long and George Kalantzis, 42–60. Cambridge: James Clark & Co, 2009.
———. "D. Stephen Long's Response." In *The Sovereignty of God Debate*, edited by D. Stephen Long and George Kalantzis, 183–9. Cambridge: James Clark & Co, 2009.
———. *Speaking of God: Theology, Language and Truth*. Grand Rapids: Eerdmans, 2009.
Louvin, Ira, and Charles Louvin. "Great Atomic Power." MGM K 11277, 1952.
Lowry, Robert. "Shall We Gather at the River?" Online: http://www.cyberhymnal.org/htm/s/w/swgatriv.htm.
MacIntyre, Alastair. *After Virtue: A Study in Moral Theory*. Notre Dame: University of Notre Dame Press, 1984.
Mahmood, Saba. *Politics of Piety: The Islamic Revival and the Feminist Subject*. Princeton: Princeton University Press, 2005.
Mansini, Guy. "The Abiding Theological Significance of Henri de Lubac's Surnaturel." *The Thomist* 73/4 (2009) 593–619.
Margalit, Avishai. *The Ethics of Memory*. Cambridge, MA: Harvard University Press, 2002.
Maritain, Jacques. *God and the Permission of Evil*. Translated by Joseph W. Evans. Milwaukee: Bruce, 1966.

Marshall, Ellen Ott. *Though the Fig Tree Does Not Blossom: Toward a Responsible Theology of Christian Hope.* Nashville: Abingdon, 2006.

Massengale, Sanford J. "I Don't Want to Get Adjusted to This Life." Recorded by Iris Dement. *Lifeline.* Flariella, 1004, 2004.

Matustik, Martin Beck. *Radical Evil and the Scarcity of Hope: Postsecular Meditations.* Bloomington: Indiana University Press, 2008.

McIntosh, Mark A. *Mystical Theology: The Integrity of Spirituality and Theology.* Malden, MA: Blackwell, 1998.

Meeks, M. Douglas. "Foreword." In Jürgen Moltmann, *The Experiment Hope.* Translated by M. Douglas Meeks. London: SCM, 1975.

Metz, Johann B. *Faith in History and Society.* New York: Seabury, 1980.

Mitchell, Margaret M. *The Heavenly Trumpet: John Chrysostom and the Art of Pauline Interpretation.* Louisville: Westminster John Knox, 2002.

Molnar, Paul D. "The Function of the Trinity in Moltmann's Ecological Doctrine of Creation." *Theological Studies* 51 (1990) 673–697.

Moltmann, Jürgen. *The Coming of God: Christian Eschatology.* Translated by Margaret Kohl. Minneapolis: Fortress, 1996, 2004.

———. *The Crucified God: The Cross of Christ as the Foundation and Criticism of Christian Theology.* Translated by R. A. Wilson and John Bowden. London: SCM, 1974.

———. *Experiences in Theology: Ways and Forms of Christian Theology.* London: SCM, 2000.

———. *The Experiment Hope.* Translated by M. Douglas Meeks. London: SCM, 1975.

———. "The Final Judgment: Sunrise of Christ's Liberating Justice." *Anglican Theologial Review* 89/4 (2007) 565–75.

———. *The Future of Creation.* Translated by Margaret Kohl. London: SCM, 1979.

———. *God in Creation: An Ecological Doctrine of Creation. The Gifford Lectures, 1984-1985.* Translated by Margaret Kohl. London: SCM, 1985.

———. *History and the Triune God: Contributions to Trinitarian Theology.* New York: Crossroad, 1992.

———. *Hope and Planning.* Translated by Margaret Clarkson. London: SCM, 1971.

———. *In the End—The Beginning: The Life of Hope.* Translated by Margaret Kohl. Minneapolis: Fortress Press, 2004.

———. *Man: Christian Anthropology in the Conflicts of the Present.* Translated by John Sturdy. London: SPCK, 1974.

———. *On Human Dignity: Political Theology and Ethics.* Translated by M. Douglas Meeks. Minneapolis: Fortress, 1984.

———. "The Presence of God's Future: The Risen Christ." *Anglican Theological Review* 89/4 (2007) 577–88.

———. "The Presence of God's Future: The Risen Christ." Lecture. Trinity Institute Conference: *God's Unfinished Future: Why It Matters Now.* New York, January 23–24, 2007. New York: Trinity Television and New Media, 2007. 6 DVDs.

———. *Religion, Revolution, and the Future.* New York: Scribner, 1969.

———. "The Theological Basis of Human Rights." In *Semper Reformanda: World Alliance of Reformed Churches.* Online: http://www.warc.ch/where/21gc/study/09.html.

———. "Theology as Eschatology." In Moltmann et al., *The Future of Hope: Theology as Eschatology,* edited by Frederick Herzog, 1–50. New York: Herder & Herder, 1970.

Bibliography

——— . *Theology of Hope: On the Ground and the Implications of a Christian Eschatology.* Translated by James W. Leitch, 1965. New York: Harper & Row, 1967.

——— . *The Trinity and the Kingdom of God: The Doctrine of God.* Translated by Margaret Kohl. London: SCM, 1981.

Moltmann, Jürgen, editor. *How I Have Changed: Reflections on Thirty Years of Theology.* London: SCM, 1997.

Moltmann, Jürgen, et al. eds. *A Passion for God's Reign.* Grand Rapids: Eerdmans, 1998.

Morrill, Bruce T. *Anamnesis as Dangerous Memory.* Collegeville, MN: Liturgical, 2000.

Morris, Wayne. *Theology Without Words: Theology in the Deaf Community.* Aldershot: Ashgate, 2008.

Morrow, William S. *Protest Against God: The Eclipse of a Biblical Tradition.* Sheffield: Sheffield Phoenix, 2007.

Mote, Edward. "My Hope Is Built." In *Hymns of Praise.* 1836. Online: http://www.cyberhymnal.org/htm/m/y/myhopeis.htm.

Mullins, Ryan. "Some Difficulties for Amos Yong's Disability Theology of the Resurrection." Seminar Paper. *Theology, Aesthetics, and Culture: Conversations with the Work of David Brown,* University of St. Andrews, Sept 6–8, 2010.

Musser, Sarah. "Comfort in the Whirlwind? Job, Creation, and Environmental Degradation." *Word & World.* 32/3 (2012) 286–93.

Munztel, Philip Alan. "Hope and the Moral Life: A Study in Theological Ethics." PhD diss., Yale University, 1984.

Neal, Ryan A. *Theology as Hope: On the Ground and Implications of Jürgen Moltmann's Doctrine of Hope.* Eugene, OR: Pickwick, 2008.

Niebuhr, Reinhold. *Moral Man and Immoral Society: A Study of Ethics and Politics.* New York: Scribner's Sons, 1932. Reprint, Louisville: Westminster John Knox, 2002.

Ngien, Dennis. "The God Who Suffers." *The Christian Century* 41 (1997) 38.

Northcott, Michael S. "BP, the Blowout and the Bible Belt: Why Conservative Christianity Does Not Conserve Creation." *The Expository Times* 122/3 (2010) 117–26.

Oakes, Edward. "The Surnaturel Controversy: A Survey and a Response." *Nova et Vetera* 9/1 (2011) 625–56.

Oatman, Johnson, Jr. "Higher Ground." 1898. No Pages. Online: http://library.timelesstruths.org/music/Higher_Ground/.

Obama, Barack. *The Audacity of Hope: Thoughts on Reclaiming the American Dream.* New York: Crown Publishers, 2006.

O'Connor, Kathleen M. *Lamentations and the Tears of the World.* Maryknoll, NY: Orbis, 2003.

Osmer, Richard Robert. *The Teaching Ministry of Congregations.* Louisville: Westminster John Knox, 2005.

Paris, Peter. "When Feeling Like a Motherless Child." In *Lament: Reclaiming Practices in Pulpit, Pew, and Public Square,* edited by Sally A. Brown and Patrick D. Miller, 111–20. Louisville: Westminster John Knox, 2005.

Parker, Rebecca Ann. "This Holy Ground." In *A House for Hope: The Promise of Progressive Religion for the Twenty-First Century,* John A. Buehrens and Rebecca Ann Parker, 3–17. Boston, MA: Beacon, 2009.

Parsons, Susan Frank. "Accounting for Hope: Feminist Theology as Fundamental Theology." In *Challenging Women's Orthodoxies in the Context of Faith,* edited by Parsons, 1–20. Aldershot: Ashgate, 2000.

Bibliography

———. *The Ethics of Gender.* Malden: MA: Blackwell, 2002.
———. *Feminism and Christian Ethics.* Cambridge: Cambridge University Press, 1996.
Parsons, Susan Frank, ed. *Challenging Women's Orthodoxies in the Context of Faith.* Aldershot: Ashgate, 2000.
Pieper, Josef. *Faith, Hope, Love.* San Francisco: Ignatius, 1997.
Polkinghorne, John. *The God of Hope and the End of the World.* New Haven: Yale University Press, 2002.
Ralston, Richard. "Universal Freedom: The Only Hope For Health Care." *Americans for Free Choice in Medicine* (2005). Online: http://www.afcm.org/universalfreedom.html.
Ramsey, Kerry. "Losing One's Life for Others: Self-Sacrifice Revisited." In *Challenging Women's Orthodoxies in the Context of Faith,* edited by Susan Frank Parsons, 121–33. Aldershot: Ashgate, 2000.
Rasmusson, Arne. *The Church as Polis: From Political Theology to Theological Politics as exemplified by Jürgen Moltmann and Stanley Hauerwas.* Notre Dame: University of Notre Dame Press, 1995.
Responding to Domestic Abuse: Guidelines for Those with Pastoral Responsibilities. London: Church House Publishing, 2006.
Reynolds, Thomas E. *Vulnerable Communion: A Theology of Disability and Hospitality.* Grand Rapids: Brazos, 2008.
Richardson, Mark. "Introduction." Lecture. Trinity Institute Conference: *God's Unfinished Future: Why It Matters Now.* New York, January 23–24, 2007. New York: Trinity Television and New Media, 2007. 6 DVDs. Transcript provided in personal correspondence from Richardson.
Romero, Miguel. "Aquinas on the *corporis infirmitas*: Broken Flesh and the Grammar of Grace." In *Disability in the Christian Tradition: A Reader,* edited by Brian Brock and John Swinton, 105–51. Grand Rapids: Eerdmans, 2012.
Rossing, Barbara R. "Prophecy, End-Times, and American Apocalypse: Reclaiming Hope for Our World." *Anglican Theological Review* 89/4 (2007) 549–64.
———. "Prophecy, End-Times, and American Apocalypse: Reclaiming Hope for Our World." Lecture. Trinity Institute Conference: *God's Unfinished Future: Why It Matters Now.* New York, January 23–24, 2007. New York: Trinity Television and New Media, 2007. 6 DVDs.
———. *The Rapture Exposed: The Message of Hope in the Book of Revelation.* New York: Basic, 2005.
"Stop Emitting Co2 or Geoengineering Could Be Our Only Hope." The Royal Society. August 28, 2009. Online: http://royalsociety.org/news/stop-co2/.
Ryan, Thomas F., *Thomas Aquinas as Reader of the Psalms.* Notre Dame: University of Notre Dame Press, 2000.
Sands, Kathleen. "Tragedy, Theology, and Feminism in the Time after Time." In *Rethinking Tragedy,* edited by Rita Felski, 82–103. Baltimore: Johns Hopkins University Press, 2008.
———. *Escape from Paradise: Evil and Tragedy in Feminist Theology,* Minneapolis, MN: Fortress Press, 1994.
Sanders, John. *The God Who Risks: The Theology of Providence.* Downers Grove, IL: InterVarsity, 1998.
Sauter, Gerhard. *What Dare We Hope? Reconsidering Eschatology.* Harrisburg, PA: Trinity, 1999.

Bibliography

Scaer, David P. "Jürgen Moltmann and His Theology of Hope." *Journal of the Evangelical Theological Society* 13/2 (1970) 69–79.

Smith, James K. A. *Desiring the Kingdom: Worship, Worldview, and Cultural Formation.* Grand Rapids: Baker Academic, 2009.

———. *The Fall of Interpretation: Philosophical Foundations for a Creational Hermeneutic.* Downers Grove, IL: InterVarsity, 2002.

Sokolowski, Robert. *Christian Faith and Human Understanding: Studies on the Eucharist, Trinity, and the Human Person.* Washington, DC: Catholic University of America Press, 2006.

Stackhouse, Reginald. *The End of the World?: A New Look at an Old Belief.* New York: Paulist, 1997.

Stålsett, Sturla. *The Crucified and the Crucified: a Study in the Liberation Christology of Jon Sobrino.* New York: Lang, 2003.

Standaert, Michael. *Skipping Towards Armageddon: the Politics and Propaganda of the Left Behind Novels and the LaHaye Empire.* New York: Soft Skull, 2006.

Sturm, Douglas. "Praxis and Promise: On the Ethics of Political Theology." *Ethics* 92/4 (1982) 733–50.

Surin, Kenneth. *Freedom Not Yet: Liberation and the Next World Order.* Durham and London: Duke University Press, 2009.

———. *Theology and the Problem of Evil.* Oxford: Blackwell, 1986.

———. *The Turnings of Darkness and Light: Essays in Philosophical and Systematic Theology.* Cambridge: Cambridge University Press, 1989.

"The Symbol of Chalcedon." Online: http://m.ccel.org/ccel/schaff/creeds2.iv.i.iii.html.

Tanner, Kathryn. *Christ the Key.* Cambridge: Cambridge University Press, 2010.

———. *God and Creation in Christian Theology: Tyranny or Empowerment?* Minneapolis: Fortress, 2005.

———. *Jesus, Humanity and the Trinity.* Minneapolis: Fortress Press, 2001.

———. *The Politics of God: Christian Theologies and Social Justice.* Minneapolis: Fortress, 1992.

———. "Social Theory Concerning the 'New Social Movements' and the Practice of Feminist Theology." In *Horizons in Feminist Theology: Identity, Tradition, and Norms,* edited by Rebecca Chopp and Sheila Greeve Davaney, 179–97. Minneapolis: Fortress, 1997.

Taylor, Charles. *Sources of the Self: The Making of the Modern Identity.* Cambridge, MA: Harvard University Press, 1989.

Thomas, Sandra. "Spray-Tanning: The Only Hope for People Like Me." Online: http://ezinearticles.com/?Spray-Tanning---The-Only-Hope-For-People-Like-Me&id=3583769.

Tran, Jonathan. *The Vietnam War and Theologies of Memory: Time, Eternity, and Redemption in the Far Country.* Malden, MA: Blackwell, 2010.

Trinity Institute. *God's Unfinished Future: Why It Matters Now.* Conference, January 23–24, 2007. New York, NY: Trinity Television and New Media, 2007. 6 DVDs.

Trinity Wall Street. "Jürgen Moltmann: The Life-Power of Hope." Interview, November 8, 2006. Online: http://www.trinitywallstreet.org/news/articles/jrgen-moltmann-the-life-power-of-hope.

Van Nieuwenhove, Rik. "'Bearing the Marks of Christ's Passion': Aquinas's Soteriology." In *The Theology of Thomas Aquinas,* edited by Nieuwenhove and Joseph Wawrykow, 277–302. Notre Dame: University of Notre Dame Press, 2005.

Bibliography

Vanier, Jean. "The Spiritual Needs of the Handicapped." *Letters of L'Arche*, National Institute on Mental Retardation. Toronto: Summer (1974) 24–27.

Volf, Miroslav, and William Katerberg, editors. *The Future of Hope*. Grand Rapids, MI: Eerdmans Publishing, 2004.

von Balthasar, Hans Urs. *Dare We Hope "That all Men be saved?" with a short discourse on hell*. San Francisco: Ignatius, 1988.

Wadell, Paul J. *Becoming Friends: Worship, Justice, and the Practice of Christian Friendship*. Grand Rapids: Brazos, 2002.

———. "Growing Together in the Divine Love: The Role of Charity in the Moral Theology of Thomas Aquinas." In *Aquinas and Empowerment: Classical Ethics for Ordinary Lives*, edited by G. Simon Harak, 134–69. Georgetown: Georgetown University Press, 1997.

Ward, Graham. *Christ and Culture*. Malden, MA: Blackwell, 2005.

———. *The Politics of Discipleship: Becoming Postmaterial Citizens*. Grand Rapids: Baker Academic, 2009.

———. "Suffering and Incarnation." In *The Blackwell Companion to Postmodern Theology*, edited by Ward, 192–209. Oxford: Blackwell, 2001.

Wawrykow, Joseph. "Grace." In *The Theology of Thomas Aquinas*, edited by Rik van Nieuwenhove and Wawrykow, 192–221. Notre Dame: University of Notre Dame Press, 2005.

Weinandy, Thomas G.. *Does God Suffer?* Notre Dame: University of Notre Dame Press, 2000.

Weller, Shane. *A Taste of the Negative: Beckett and Nihilism*. London: Modern Humanities Research Association and Maney Publishing, 2005.

Williams, Rowan. *Tokens of Trust: An Introduction to Christian Belief*. London: Westminster John Knox, 2007.

Wright, N. T. *Surprised by Hope: Rethinking Heaven, the Resurrection, and the Mission of the Church*. New York: HarperOne, 2008.

Yoder, John H. *Body Politics*. Nashville: Discipleship Resources, 1989.

———. *For the Nations: Essays Public and Evangelical*. Grand Rapids: Eerdmans, 1997.

Yong, Amos. *Theology and Down Syndrome: Reimagining Disability in Late Modernity*. Waco: Baylor University Press, 2007.

Young, Frances M. *Brokenness and Blessing: Towards a Biblical Spirituality*. Grand Rapids: Baker Academic, 2007.

———. *Face to Face: A Narrative Essay in the Theology of Suffering*. London: T. & T. Clark, 1990.

Žižek, Slavoj. *The Sublime Object of Ideology*. London: Verso, 1989.

Scripture Index

Old Testament

Genesis
1:31 — 41
6:6b — 41

Job — 108–9

Psalms
— 128, 150
137 — 178

Isaiah — 179–80

Lamentations — 177–81

Ezekiel
18:23 — 154

New Testament

Matthew
16:5–12 — 176
24 — 86n21
25:31–46 — 83n14

Mark
— 12
8:4–21 — 176
9:9–10 — 176

Luke
22:24 — 176

John
3:16 — 43–44
13:1 — 144
16:22 — 139
19:30 — 144

Acts of the Apostles
17:28 — 123

Romans
1:24–28 — 52–53
3:21–25a — 96–97
4:25 — 52
6:10 — 54n215
8:24–25 — 35
15:4 — 30

1 Corinthians
1:9 — 137
15:28 — 39, 48

Scripture Index

2 Corinthians

1:20	30

Ephesians

2:12	144
3:10–13	97
3:20–21	1
4:15	187

Colossians

2:9	40

1 Timothy

1:1	128–29

2 Timothy

1:12	127

Hebrews

2:3	42
6:18–19	127, 149
10:19–22	97
10:23	149
10:36	144
11:1—12:2	160
11:1	35, 132–33
11:6	131
11:11	42
13:7–8	160
13:8	165

James

4:2–3	85n19

2 Peter

1:14	130

1 John

4:16	43–44

Revelation

	57, 62–65, 84
16:16	59
21	63
21:5	47n183
21:20	59

Subject and Name Index

abandonment by God. *See* godforsakenness
accountability, 74–75, 81, 86, 109–10, 181–82, 184, 197–200, 202, 207, 212–14, 216
Adam, A. K. M., 79n3
Adorno, Theodor, 168–71, 174–75
agency, 24–25, 65, 67–72, 76, 99–100, 101–2, 105–11, 127–28, 134–35, 143–44, 150–51, 156–57, 160–61, 167, 185–86, 198–200, 205–7, 210–14, 216
  divine, 92–93, 130–31, 156–57, 160–61, 185–86
Anselm of Canterbury, 121–22
apocalypse, 9–10, 23n62, 25, 27, 36, 48–50, 56–58, 77–78, 147–48, 169n4, 217n1, 220
  end-time, 27, 38, 57–68, 81, 97, 105–6
  eschaton, 20–21, 31–32, 39, 44, 100, 187, 209–10
  popapocalyptic, 217–22
  rapture, 10, 55–67, 76, 81, 84, 106–7
Aquinas, Thomas. *See* Thomas Aquinas
Arians, 19–20, 124
Aristotle, 69–70, 129–130
Arius. *See* Arians
Athanasius, 15–16
atheism, 5, 24–27, 36, 219–20

attributes, divine, 20–22, 89–91, 95–96, 118–19, 125, 146–47, 175. *See also* impassibility and immutability
Augustine, Saint, 45n174, 70–71, 139–40, 150, 158
authority, 23n61, 26–27, 38–39, 79, 81–82, 84, 101, 149n141, 168, 202, 205
  divine, 26–27, 38–39
  doctrinal, 202, 205
  ecclesial, 101–2
  of experience, 81–83
  of interpretation, 84–86
  of Moses, 23n62

Barnes, Rev. F. C., 131
Barton, John, 83–84n15
basileia tou theou, 67–76
Bauckham, Richard, 23n63, 31, 53, 92
Baxter, Stephen, 218–20
beatitude, 72–73, 127–33, 133–38, 139–45, 145–46, 150–51, 155–59, 161–64, 175, 223
Bedford, Nancy Elizabeth, 89, 123n26
Benedict XVI, 6, 109–10, 128–29, 139–40, 144–45, 46
Bloch, Ernst, 24–26, 29, 31–36, 39, 47–48, 49–50, 53n208, 75–76, 97–98
Blunt, Martin, 8

Subject and Name Index

body
   human, 46, 48–49, 50–51, 61, 65–66, 93n34, 98–99, 105, 122–23, 134–35, 138, 140–41, 146–47, 157–59, 162, 167, 177–79, 183–85, 187–91, 192–200, 204–8, 213–14, 222
   of Christ. *See* Christology
Borsch, Frederick Houk, 10n23
Brown, Sally A., 178–79
Buffum, Herbert, 139
Burns, L., 8
Butler, Judith, 167, 192, 196–201, 203

Carter, R. Kelso, 141
Castelo, Daniel, 6, 95–96, 108, 115–17, 120, 122–23, 124–25
catastrophe, 12, 27, 36, 41–42, 49–50, 81, 115, 217–23. *See also* devastation *and* disaster
certainty of hope, 24–25, 27, 30–31, 35, 38, 50–51, 75–76, 98–99, 129, 131–35, 141–46, 148–9, 152–53, 170–71, 195–96, 214, 216
Cessario, Romanus, O. P., 127, 134–35, 143–44
Chalcedon, Council of, 95–96, 117–18, 125–26
charity. *See* virtues, theological
Christology
   body of Christ, 51–52, 94–97, 98–99, 112–13, 136–37, 144–45, 151, 154, 158–59, 167, 176, 179, 183–84, 187–88, 196, 200, 204–6, 219–22
   incarnation, 20–21, 40, 87–91, 91–97, 120–21, 124–28, 132–33, 146–47, 158–59, 195, 215–16

   Moltmann's and Moltmannian, 12–24, 26–40, 45–49, 51–55, 58–61, 75–76, 80–82, 83n14, 86, 87–97, 106–11, 127–28, 151, 154–55, 215
   perfection of Jesus Christ, 5, 21, 94–95, 124–29, 133, 137–38, 144–45, 147–48, 158–59, 164, 217, 223
   suffering of Jesus Christ, 14–20, 23–24, 26–27, 31–45, 46, 51–55, 65–67, 75–76, 87–91, 91–97, 107–8, 117–23, 124–29, 133, 174, 205–10, 215–16 (*see also* Passion, of Christ)
Chrysostom, John, 161
Coakley, Sarah, 205–6, 208–10
companionship, 36, 70–71, 73–74, 107–8, 137, 153, 163–64, 176, 222
compassion
   divine, 7, 14–15, 24–25, 36, 74–76, 84, 87–91, 110–11, 115–23, 124, 129, 156–57, 164–66, 177–83, 215, 217, 221–23 (*see also* impassibility and immutability)
   human, 74–75, 101–2, 174, 208
constancy, 29, 42, 44, 90–91, 95, 97–98, 115–17, 120, 124–25, 137, 141, 144, 162–64, 177–78, 221–23
continuity
   cosmic, 106, 129, 132–33, 142, 144–45, 145–48, 167, 170–71
   doctrinal, 112–13, 115, 132, 214
   of hope, 28–29, 78–81, 86, 90–91, 97–100, 190–91, 196, 214, 221
Cousteau, Jacques-Yves, 8
covenant, 89, 115–16, 144–45, 177–78, 215–16, 219–20
Creamer, Deborah B., 185

Subject and Name Index

creation, 7, 13–24, 24–45, 45–55, 59–67, 70–76, 80–81, 84, 87, 89–94, 97–100, 101–3, 106–10, 115–17, 118–23, 124–25, 128–29, 129–31, 133–34, 135–37, 141–43, 145–48, 150–51, 152, 158–60, 165–66, 170–77, 182–83, 184–85, 191, 199–200, 215, 220–22

creatio ex nihilo, 41–42, 174–75

creeds, 80–81, 125

Crosby, Fanny, 148, 151–52

cross, 14–24, 26–27, 31–39, 46, 49, 51–53, 66–67, 76, 79–80, 84, 87, 89, 91–94, 108, 127, 151, 185, 205–10, 221–23. *See also* Passion, of Christ

crucifixion. *See* cross

Cunningham, Conor, 174–75

curiosity, divine, 60, 67–68

Cyril of Alexandria, 17–18, 125

de Lubac, Henri, 139, 149n141

dependence
  creaturely, 51–52, 70, 72–73, 100–5, 106–7, 124–25, 140–41, 148–51, 151–52, 160–61, 164, 167, 170–71, 183–86, 192, 198–200, 203–10, 212
  divine, 43, 70, 72–73, 95–96

depression, 1, 4, 163–64, 189, 216

Derrida, Jacques, 173–74, 181n27

desire, 7–8, 9, 59, 61, 68, 104–6, 108–10, 134, 146, 151, 153–54, 155–61, 163–64, 171, 172, 174, 177–78, 183, 187, 193–94, 203, 212

despair, 1, 23–24, 32, 52–54, 70–72, 74–75, 87, 91, 137–38, 153–55, 165, 167–68, 174, 177–79, 180–181, 183, 204, 216, 221

desperation. *See* despair

devastation, 48, 62, 76, 97–98, 100, 114–15n5, 163–65, 174, 177–83. *See also* catastrophe *and* disaster

disability, 4, 6, 138, 167, 183–91, 214–15

disaster, 4–5, 11, 90, 93–94, 144, 181–82, 217–23. *See also* catastrophe *and* devastation

discipleship, 4, 6, 167, 183–91, 214–15

docetism, 15–16, 92–93

ecology, 8, 49–50, 62–66, 68–69, 76–78, 81, 101, 109, 147–48, 160

economy, 11, 33–34, 49–50, 52, 68–69, 80–81, 102–4, 109–10, 127–28, 140–41, 153–54, 158n173, 162, 170, 173, 190, 195–96, 209

Eiesland, Nancy L., 185

empire, 62–66

end time. *See* apocalypse

environment. *See* ecology

eschaton. *See* apocalypse

eternity, divine. *See* attributes, divine

evil, 25, 29–30, 44, 46–48, 59–60, 63–67, 73–74, 97–98, 122–23, 152–53, 157–58, 168, 178–79

experience
  creaturely, 31, 37–38, 45–46, 50–55, 70, 72–76, 80–84, 87, 91, 93–96, 100, 108–9, 133, 139, 142, 146–47, 151, 165, 172–73, 179, 181–83, 185, 187–88, 204–8, 220
  divine, 7, 12–25, 31, 34–38, 40–42, 48, 52–55, 65–66, 68, 72–76, 79, 81–84, 87, 89–91,

Subject and Name Index

experience, divine (*cont.*)
    91–97, 100, 110–11, 115, 151, 165, 172–73, 179, 185 (*see also* authority of experience)

faith. *See* virtues, theological
Farley, Edward, 208
Farley, Wendy, 73–74, 208
feminist theology, 6, 67, 71–72, 167, 200–14, 215
feminist theory, 6, 167, 192–200, 203–4, 215
Fiddes, Paul S., 24
Fiorenza, Francis Schüssler, 20–21
forgiveness, 22–23, 34–35, 53, 154–55 162–63
freedom
    divine, 19–20, 26–27, 43–44, 47–48, 108, 179
    human, 20, 22–23, 26–27, 34–38, 43–44, 45–55, 58–60, 65–66, 68–76, 77–78, 93–94, 101–6, 142–43, 150, 151–54, 158–60, 162, 174, 176, 179, 184–85, 190–91, 192–93, 196–97, 200–12
friendship, 53, 58–59, 103–5, 106–10, 135–38, 140–41, 154, 155–61, 161–64, 178, 188–91, 199, 215–23
Fulkerson, Mary M., 187–88, 205, 212–14

Gaventa, William C., 186
Gavrilyuk, Paul L., 6, 88, 117–18, 124n29, 125
grace, 5, 22–23, 43–44, 46, 67–68, 70–71, 96–97, 99–100, 103, 120, 128, 129–138, 143, 146–47, 148–51, 151–55, 155–61, 161–66, 204
grammar, 62, 83–86, 89–91, 95–96, 110–11, 112–23, 124–26, 129, 139–40, 142, 156–57,
164–66, 170–71, 175, 180, 185–86, 194–97, 204–5, 208
Gillespie, Michael A., 171–72
godforsakenness, 7, 12–24, 26–27, 32–33, 36–37, 45, 52–55, 65–66, 75–76, 81–85, 87, 92–97, 110–11, 122, 178–79
Goetz, Ronald, 13n31
Grenz, Stanley J., 78
Grosz, Elizabeth, 173–75, 192–94

Hauerwas, Stanley, 107–8, 188–89
Havergal, Frances R., 135
healing, 4, 62–65, 108–9, 153–54, 185–86, 190–91, 206
Healy, Nicholas, 149n141
heaven, 3, 6, 9–10, 20, 24–25, 31–32, 40, 42, 46–47, 50–51, 52–53, 64–67, 75–76, 80–81, 86, 87, 93–96, 97–100, 106–10, 114, 129–30, 139–48, 157–58, 161–64, 170–71, 176, 179–80, 190–91, 215–16, 222. *See also* Kingdom of God
Hellenism, 20–21, 88–89, 92–93, 115–16, 124–25
Helms, Richard B., 8
hermeneutics. *See* interpretation
Heschel, Susannah, 23n63
Hofheinz, Marco, 23n63
Hollywood, Amy, 195n64
Holy Spirit, 13–14, 16–17, 24, 26–27, 29–32, 38–40, 42, 61, 91–93, 101–2, 113, 117, 119, 126, 135–36, 142, 145, 148, 152, 154–55, 159–60, 165, 176, 200, 204, 210, 216
hope
    certainty of. *See* certainty of hope
    continuity of. *See* continuity, of hope

Subject and Name Index

hope (*cont.*)
    passion of, 70–71, 129–31, 133–34, 142, 148–51, 151–55, 158–60
    theological virtue of. *See* virtues, theological
Horton, Michael Scott, 175–76
humility, 18, 103, 108–9, 136–37, 152, 156–57, 162, 167, 212–14
Hütter, Reinhard, 149n141

identity, 22, 28, 56n220, 76, 81–82, 90–91, 92, 95–97, 104, 106, 108–9, 128–29, 133–34, 140–41, 163, 170, 175–76, 189, 192–200, 203–14, 220. *See also* subjectivity
Ignatius, 124–25
immutability. *See* impassibility and immutability
impassability and immutability
    divine, 12–24, 41–44, 76, 83–91, 96–97, 114–29, 155–57, 164, 183, 215–16, 220–23. *See also* attributes, divine; compassion, divine *and* suffering of God
incarnation. *See* Christology
independence. *See* dependence
indeterminacy, 82, 167–77, 214
infinity, divine. *See* attributes, divine
injustice. *See* justice
interdependence. *See* dependence
interpretation
    biblical, 19, 39, 40–41, 52–53, 60, 62–67, 68, 78–81, 83–86, 108, 110–11, 115–17, 121–22, 132–33, 177–79
    theological, 28–29, 31–32, 39, 78–80, 103–4, 120–22, 129–30, 181n27, 204, 205, 211–12 (*see also* authority of interpretation)
Irigaray, Luce, 167, 192–96, 199–201, 203

Johnson, Blind Willie, 115
Johnson, Elizabeth, 11n26, 106
Jordan, Mark, 131n64
justice, 3–4, 23–24, 29–30, 39, 45–55, 58–60, 66–67, 67–76, 77–78, 98–99, 100–102, 128–29, 142–45, 147, 150–51, 159–61, 163–64, 177–79, 183, 207n92, 208–10, 220–23
Justin Martyr, 124–5
Jervey, Ben, 8
judgment, 22–23, 45–47, 58–60, 62n252, 65–66, 83, 86n21, 88, 96–97, 99, 113, 122, 128–29, 153, 155, 177

Keller, Catherine, 11n26
Keshgegian, Flora A., 182–83
King, Martin Luther, Jr., 9, 14
King, Richard, 5n2
Kingdom of God, 7, 18–26, 29–42, 46–48, 53–55, 61, 65, 68–69, 95–96, 97–100, 102, 145, 157–58, 160–61, 184n35. *See also* heaven
Krašovec, Jože, 177–78

language. *See* grammar
L'Arche, 188–91
Left Behind, 57, 62–65, 112n1
liberation. *See* freedom
Linafelt, Tod, 181–82
literalism, 64–65, 84–86
Long, D. Stephen, 6, 120–22
Lord's Prayer. *See* prayer
Louvin Brothers, 141
love. *See* virtues, theological
Lowry, Robert, 164

Subject and Name Index

Luther, Martin, 17–18, 160n176

Mahmood, Saba, 210–12, 214
Mansini, Guy, 149n141
Marshall, Ellen Ott, 56, 67–76, 105–6
Massengale, Sanford J., 133
Meeks, M. Douglas, 39
memory, 86, 182–83, 208–9
Metz, Johann Baptist, 182
mission, 2, 5–6, 22, 30–32, 126
modernity, 30–32, 58–59, 78–111, 112–14, 116–17, 164–66
Molnar, Paul D., 81–82, 91
Morris, Wayne, 185
Mote, Edward, 124
Mullins, Ryan, 191
Munztel, Philip Alan, 70
Musser, Sarah, 108–9
mutability. See impassibility and immutability

Neal, Ryan A., 13, 24, 26–28, 34, 36–37, 40–44, 51n202, 79–80
Nicea, Council of, 117–18, 125
Niebuhr, Reinhold, 159n175
nihilism, 6, 167–77, 214, 215
Northcott, Michael S., 109n70

Oakes, Edward, 149n141
Oatman, Johnson, Jr., 129
Obama, Barack, 8–9
obedience, 18–19, 50–53, 164, 205–6, 209, 213
O'Connor, Kathleen M., 179–80
Olson, Roger E., 78
Open Theism, 83–86
Osmer, Richard Robert, 11

panentheism, 60n242, 101, 175–76
Paris, Peter, 179
Parker, Rebecca Ann, 10n22
Parsons, Susan Frank, 201–4, 214

passibility. See impassibility and immutability.
Passion
of Christ, 14–15, 18, 34, 53–55, 87, 89, 92–93, 117–18, 124–25, 127–28, 140–41, 209–10. See also Christology and cross
peace, 10, 17–28, 29–30, 49–50, 53, 59, 6871–72, 102–4, 108, 145, 146, 160, 170–71, 182, 207n92, 221
perfection
divine. See attributes, divine
of Jesus Christ. See Christology
perseverance, 6, 98n45, 109–10, 114, 139–41, 141–45, 153, 155, 177, 180, 214, 221–23
Pieper, Josef, 127, 130–31, 131–34, 148–9, 152–55
Pinches, Charles, 107
Polkinghorne, John, 11n26
popapocalyptic. See apocalypse
poverty, 3, 11, 50–51, 59–60, 64–65, 104, 108–9, 122–23, 137, 146, 160–61, 187–88, 204, 219–21
power, relational, 70–73, 105–6
prayer, 85, 87, 101–3, 139–40, 198–99, 151, 155–60, 161–64, 209, 217
Lord's Prayer, 40, 54
predestination, 148–50
promise, 24–42, 48–49, 51–52, 56–57, 61, 65, 70, 75–76, 81–82, 91–94, 97–98, 127–28, 141–45, 146–47, 148–50, 155–56, 173–77, 182–83
providence, 148–51, 156–57, 161n179

Ralston, Richard, 8
Ramsey, Kerry, 202, 205–10
rapture. See apocalypse

Rasmusson, Arne, 103–4
reconciliation, 3–4, 33–34, 39, 46–47, 54–55, 60, 68–69, 75–76, 98–99, 108, 162–64, 170–71, 177, 183, 189, 191–92, 199, 208
redemption. *See* salvation
relational power. *See* power, relational
repentance, 51–52, 62–63, 98–99, 108–9, 154–55, 177–78, 180
  divine, 41–42, 91
responsibility, 1, 3, 9–10, 27, 48, 49–50, 65, 67–76, 101–2, 105–10, 138, 140–41, 151, 160, 164, 170–71, 174, 177, 180, 189, 195, 198–99, 211–12, 214, 215, 218
resurrection, 4, 7, 13, 18–24, 26–42, 46–55, 58, 61, 65–67, 75–76, 77–78, 81, 87, 91–97, 97–100, 101, 104–5, 117–18, 124–25, 127–29, 133–35, 139–41, 145–48, 154–55, 158–59, 167, 169n4, 174–77, 181–83, 183–91, 195, 199–200, 209–10, 213–14, 215–16, 218–19
  bodily, 61, 98–99, 134–35, 146–47, 176–77, 183–91, 195, 200, 213
revelation, 12–15, 25–29, 32–33, 27–42, 75–76, 82, 130–31, 138–39, 201–2
Reynolds, Thomas E., 184–85
Richardson, Mark, 27, 56–58
righteousness, 14, 27–28, 44, 46–48, 58–60, 96–97, 98–99, 108–9, 115–16, 124, 129–30, 159–60
Romero, Miguel, 138
Rossing, Barbara R., 56, 58, 60n242, 62–65, 81, 84

sacraments, 51n202, 101–2, 134–35, 137, 142, 145, 149n141, 157–58, 200, 210
  baptism, 51–2, 137–38, 145
  eucharist, 2, 81, 137, 145, 158–59
salvation, 9–10, 15–16, 18–19, 22, 23–24, 29–30, 31, 33–34, 43–50, 58–59, 61, 65, 74, 89, 93–98, 101–2, 122–23, 125–29, 134–36, 141–45, 147–48, 148–51, 151–55, 157, 161, 169n4, 170–71, 181–82, 195, 199–200, 207–9, 217–18
Sands, Kathleen, 73–74, 208–9
Sanders, John, 85–86
Scaer, David P., 33
secular, 3, 12, 20, 55–56, 77–80, 88–89, 94, 102–5, 112–13, 201–4, 210–12
simplicity, divine. *See* attributes, divine
Smith, James K. A., 187
Sokolowski, Robert, 121–22
soul, 29–30, 48, 61, 125–27, 130–31, 138–40, 189–91
Stålsett, Sturla, 13n31
Standaert, Michael, 10
Sturm, Douglas, 29–30
subjectivity, 82–83, 167, 186–91, 192–200, 200–214
suffering, of God, 13–20, 23–24, 26–27, 32–34, 36–38, 40–45, 46, 51–55, 60n242, 65–67, 73–76, 81–86, 87–91, 91–97, 101n50, 110–11, 115–17, 119–23, 124–29, 151, 213. *See also* impassibility and immutability
  of Jesus Christ. *See* Christology

Tanner, Kathryn, 6, 27, 94–96, 99–100, 113–14, 127–28, 140–41, 146–48, 156–57, 165–66, 172–73, 200–202

Subject and Name Index

Taylor, Charles, 102–3, 104–5
Teresa of Avila, 208
theological virtues. *See* virtues, theological
Thomas Aquinas, 6, 17n46, 67n261, 69–71, 89–90, 112–66, 170–71, 186–87, 215
tragedy, 67, 73–5, 208–10, 214, 218
transcendence, 15–16, 21–22, 79–80, 81–83, 89–91, 96–97, 101–5, 110–11, 115–17, 117–18, 124–29, 165, 172–73, 176–76, 179, 183, 192–94, 213, 215
Trinity, 16–20, 38–39, 44, 81–83, 89–91, 91–100, 103–4, 110–11, 117–23, 125–29, 165, 174–76
Trinity Institute, 56–58, 67, 101
Trinity Wall Street, 101
trust, 11, 54–55, 57, 65–67, 71–72, 74, 86, 124, 131–32, 143, 163–64, 178–89, 207–8, 221–22

unity, divine. *See* attributes, divine

van Nieuwenhove, Rik, 127–28
Vanier, Jean, 188–89

virtues, theological, 67–75, 112n1, 113, 127, 129–45, 148–55, 159, 161, 164–66, 215–16
  faith, 67–69, 129–45, 150, 153, 155–56, 158–61, 162–64, 175, 216, 221
  hope, 67–71, 75, 112n1, 113, 127–38, 142–45, 150–51, 151–52, 158–60, 161–66, 216 (*see also* certainty of hope *and* continuity of hope)
  love, 69, 70n271, 129–45, 150, 151–61, 163, 175, 220
Volf, Miroslav, 98

Wadell, Paul J., 137, 163
Ward, Graham, 176–77
Wawrykow, Joseph, 129n54
Weinandy, Thomas G., 6, 93n34, 101n50, 124
Weller, Shane, 173–75
Williams, Rowan, 160
Woodhead, Linda, 202
Wright, N. T., 98n45

Yoder, John H., 158n173
Yong, Amos, 190–91
Young, Frances M., 190–91

www.ingramcontent.com/pod-product-compliance
Lightning Source LLC
Chambersburg PA
CBHW070246230426
43664CB00014B/2417